The Ratification
of the Fourteenth Amendment

The
Ratification of the
Fourteenth Amendment

Joseph B. James

Mercer
University Press

ISBN 0-86554-098-5

All books published by Mercer University Press are produced
on acid-free paper that exceeds the minimum standards set by the
National Historical Publications and Records Commission.

Library of Congress Cataloging in Publication Data
James, Joseph B. (Joseph Bliss), 1912-
The ratification of the Fourteenth Amendment.
Bibliography: p. 307.
Includes index.
1. United States—Constitutional law—Amendments—14th.
2. Civil rights—United States.
3. Due process of law—United States.
4. United States—Constitutional history.
I. Title.
√ KF4757.J34   1984   342.73'085   83-26481
ISBN 0-86554-098-5 (alk. paper)   347.30285

90563

Table of Contents

Preface vii

Chapter One
    The Launching 1

Chapter Two
    Setting Sail.. 11

Chapter Three
    Choppy Seas.. 25

Chapter Four
    Cross Currents 39

Chapter Five
    The Growing Storm.. 51

Chapter Six
    Gusty Gales.. 67

Chapter Seven
    Thunder Rumbling from the South 79

Chapter Eight
    Murky Southern Skies 97

Chapter Nine
    Troubled Southern Waters....................................... 115

Chapter Ten
    Another Tack 133

Chapter Eleven
      Still on Course... 147

Chapter Twelve
      Shifting Winds 157

Chapter Thirteen
      Uncertain Currents.. 181

Chapter Fourteen
      Changing Course 201

Chapter Fifteen
      Which Channel?.. 217

Chapter Sixteen
      Full Speed Ahead 231

Chapter Seventeen
      Running before the Wind 247

Chapter Eighteen
      Dangerous Passage.. 261

Chapter Nineteen
      Making for Port.. 277

Chapter Twenty
      An Uncertain Anchorage 289

Appendix
      The Fourteenth Amendment.................................. 305

Bibliography.. 307

Index 325

Preface

Even while preparing my earlier study on *The Framing of the Fourteenth Amendment*, it seemed obvious that there would need to be a sequel that would trace the steps taken by each state on the proposal to the final proclamation as a part of the Constitution. That study would need to take note of what both supporters and opponents of the amendment understood it to mean for them and for future generations. It would need to include public arguments voiced in political campaigns and private sentiments stated in correspondence and diaries.

Such an examination of the ratification process would necessarily have to be kept in perspective as only one factor of that unsettled period—the aftermath of the war known as Reconstruction. The broad background of the national scene in all of its many facets would need to be constantly kept in mind as well as events affecting the amending process in individual states.

These things I have attempted to do. I have tried to understand the motives of those who led efforts to bring about a restored Union. Those efforts involved various approaches to the problem in both theory and practice. Idealism and pragmatism are to be found in both North and South, and sectional interests are to be detected within the victorious states. Even in the South, a variety of responses to the problems of the vanquished can be seen.

Ratification has been perceived by me as not only a part of Reconstruction, but as a step in the continuing evolution of the American Constitution. It incorporated a highly significant portion of that document in a process marked by uniquely irregular procedures and dramatic events. Perhaps this process was a natural result of the unusual conditions that produced it.

In my efforts to understand and to present the story of ratification, I have been aided by the growing list of scholars who have taken a fresh look at the history of Reconstruction. They have illuminated many previously obscure topics and have caused many views to be altered. My own work has been influenced by these contributions and by the availability of the new source material.

My thanks are extended to all those who have helped me in any way during the preparation of this present study. Such people are too numerous to acknowledge individually, but I am deeply grateful.

—*Joseph B. James*

Chapter One

The Launching

For more than a hundred years, the courts have applied the Fourteenth Amendment to the United States Constitution to pertinent cases that came before them. Although questions have been raised about both its meaning and the correctness of its adoption process, the latter has never had legal effect due to its long usage and the indirect pronouncements of the Supreme Court concerning its acceptance as law.[1]

Nevertheless, the story of its ratification is indeed a strange and fascinating chapter in constitutional history. It goes well beyond the natural confusion that would be expected on the heels of a great civil war and the political upheavals accompanying party realignments that resulted from national disruption of power relationships. The nature of these unique conditions and the emerging attitudes of in-

---

[1]*Coleman v. Miller*, 307 U.S. 433 (1939).

dividuals and of different regional and interest groups furnish the backdrop for the ratification struggle and have influenced the course of history in the United States, even to the present. Actions and statements of participants reveal a great deal about what people thought they were endorsing, to say nothing of contemporary analysis of the procedures used in ratification.

After much discussion and political maneuvering, the sessions of the Thirty-ninth Congress in 1866, from which the eleven states of the defeated South were excluded, finally approved a compromised version of the amendment that had been worked out in a Senate Republican caucus. It was known to be a victory for no particular faction of the dominant party.[2] Faced by the practical reality of a political struggle for survival in the congressional elections of 1866, the Republicans had closed ranks and agreed on what they considered to be a platform on which they could all stand in that test of political strength; it included their interpretation of the amendment. Pennsylvania's Thaddeus Stevens, for example, had approved the proposal as the best plan then obtainable and a necessary one to prevent demoralization of the party.[3]

The official report of the Reconstruction Committee was carefully written as a campaign document after Congress had already passed the Fourteenth Amendment, for the Committee wanted to present it as the minimum statement of conditions on which the Union might be restored.[4] In seeking ratification, the Republicans always presented the proposal as an essential and reasonable guarantee for the future. In their support of this concept, Republicans

---

[2]See detailed discussion of these events in Joseph B. James, *The Framing of the Fourteenth Amendment* (Urbana IL: University of Illinois Press, 1956), especially chs. 10 and 11.

[3]*Congressional Globe*, 39th Cong., 1st sess., 311. *New York Times*, 15 June 1866; Salmon P. Chase to his daughter, 15 June 1866, Salmon P. Chase Papers, Library of Congress.

[4]"Report of the Joint Committee on Reconstruction," *Reports of the Committees of the House of Representatives*, 39th Congress, 1st session (1866), 2, no. 30 pt. 1; *New York Herald*, 15 June 1866, is a typical recognition of the amendment as a political platform. Also see Francis Fessenden, *Life and Public Services of William Pitt Fessenden* (Boston: Houghton Mifflin Co., 1907) 2:293.

carried their political battle to the country in various speeches and arguments.

The amendment, however, was not a singular, burning issue; other topics figured in the campaign, and many speakers did not even refer to the amendment. In different places, purely local or state issues seemed more important, and the proposal was emphasized or deemphasized according to the needs of the moment. It was not presented as a radical document; rather, its moderate tone was repeatedly proclaimed by speaker after speaker as well as by writers of editorial comment. The *Chicago Tribune* stated that "the conscience of the North yielded four-fifths of its demands to the perverseness of the President and the obstinacy of circumstances."[5]

The most critical point of contention—the promise to readmit a Southern state to congressional representation if it approved the amendment—never received an official statement. There was no claim that such admission would take place even when all states had approved. Senator John Sherman of Ohio claimed that the proposed amendment was moderate but should include such a pledge of readmission.[6] From time to time a commitment was implied, and perhaps public opinion might have forced such a pledge if the states of the former Confederacy had quickly ratified the amendment through action of their legislatures, which had been authorized under the presidential plan.

No pledge was ever made by Congress, and motions to that effect were dropped. A resolution of the Reconstruction Committee stating the intention to readmit the Confederate states upon adoption of the amendment was tabled on 20 July 1866.[7] Obviously, a sizable group of those in Congress opposed a formal commitment, preferring the speedy readmission of the first state, Tennessee, as a subtle indication that restoration would follow the amendment's approval by each excluded state.

---

[5]*Chicago Tribune*, 25 June 1866.

[6]*The Sherman Letters: Correspondence Between General and Senator Sherman from 1837 to 1891*, ed., Rachel Sherman Thorndike (New York: Charles Scribner's Sons, 1894) 277.

[7]*Congressional Globe*, 39th Cong., 1st sess., 3981.

The Report of the Committee of Fifteen was a political document that played no part in the passage of the amendment in Congress. Only when action had been completed was it presented, being printed and made available to Congress and the public much later.[8] The lengthy committee report was carefully phrased by the chronically ill chairman of the Joint Committee, Senator William P. Fessenden of Maine, to serve as a campaign document.[9] Senator James W. Grimes of Iowa, also a member of the Committee of Fifteen that was responsible for the amendment, concurred in this evaluation by writing, "I am happy to be able to say that they [the individual parts] meet with general approval, and we feel much more confident, and stronger since their passage than before."[10] (The individual parts of the proposed Fourteenth Amendment were often referred to as if they constituted separate proposals.)

The political value of the report was generally recognized. *The Nation* pronounced it "an able state paper drawn up with the consciousness that upon it a great party must take its stand, and upon its reasoning Congress must depend to maintain its position before the country."[11]

A minority report, representing the opinion of the three Democrats on the Joint Committee, was written by Senator Reverdy Johnson of Maryland. It, too, was aimed at possible influence in the approaching elections and was not even introduced until two weeks after the majority report had been filed.[12] In explanation of this tardiness, Senator Johnson testified that he had been notified of the majority's intention to submit its report only minutes before the fact.

Senator Lyman Trumbull of Illinois objected strongly to accepting the minority report at all because of its lateness, contending that such a move would set a bad precedent. In reply, Reverdy Johnson

---

[8]Ibid., 3038.

[9]Fessenden, *Life of Fessenden*, 2:62.

[10]William Salter, *The Life of James W. Grimes* (New York: D. Appleton Co., 1876) 299.

[11]*The Nation* (1866) 2:744.

[12]*Congressional Globe*, 39th Cong., 1st sess., 3646.

pointed out that the majority had not submitted its report in time to be considered by Congress before it approved the amendment. The majority report had neither been read nor made available in print until later, when fifty thousand copies were printed. The order was doubled to one hundred thousand by 12 July.[13] Did not the public, for whom the majority report had been prepared, have a right to both sides of the question?[14] Thus spurred, Chairman Fessenden smoothed things out by expressing a willingness to receive the report.[15]

On another front, a running battle had developed over procedure. On 15 June, Congressman John Bingham of Ohio, who as a member of the amendment's framing committee had contributed much to its most important section, asked the House of Representatives for unanimous consent to introduce a concurrent resolution: "That the President of the United States be requested to transmit forthwith to the Executives of the several states of the United States copies of the article of amendment proposed by Congress to the State Legislatures...to the end that the said States may proceed to act upon the said amendment. . . ." When discussion arose concerning whether or not the President needed time for consideration and approval, the Speaker of the House ruled that the signature of the President was not required and that the action of the secretary of state's office was purely a ministerial one.[16] Three days later, Bingham was again asking consent to introduce such a concurrent resolution. When objection was made, his motion for suspension of the rules was passed by a vote of ninety-two to twenty-five. The previous question on the passage of the resolution as posed by Bingham was approved.[17]

In reply to such pressure from the Congress, President Johnson sent an official communication on 22 June stating that copies of the

---

[13]Ibid., 3767.

[14]Ibid., 3646.

[15]Ibid., 3649.

[16]Ibid., 3197-98.

[17]Ibid., 3241.

amendment had been forwarded to state governors two days before Bingham's resolution had cleared the House. The President failed to say that the copies had been sent only the day following the submission of the resolution.

He did raise a serious question concerning the passage of a proposal to amend the Constitution by a Congress representing only twenty-five of the thirty-six states. He emphasized that his forwarding of the proposal for official ratification represented no personal approval but only the performance of a ministerial duty.[18] The *Chicago Tribune* regarded the message as an open declaration of war on the amendment by the chief executive.[19]

Questions raised by Johnson had already been considered in Congress during the preceding days. On 18 June, Congressman Henry J. Raymond of New York had insisted that ratification would necessitate the approval of three-fourths, or twenty-seven, of the thirty-six states.[20] This same issue had already been thoroughly aired without conclusion in 1865 in relation to the Thirteenth Amendment. Not only the propriety of submission by part of the Congress, but ratification by states still unrepresented had been questioned. As early as January of that year, a good deal of discussion about the validity of these procedures was seen in various magazines and newspapers. One viewpoint was Charles Sumner's theory that reconstruction left no place for consideration by other than "loyal" states. These made up a "quorum of the states" having legislatures and actually participating in government, and only these could be counted in ratifying the amendment.[21] According to this reasoning, nineteen states outside the South would be sufficient to ratify.

---

[18]James D. Richardson, *A Compilation of the Messages and Papers of the Presidents, 1789-1897* (Washington DC: Bureau of National Literature and Art, 1898) 6:391-92.

[19]*Chicago Tribune*, 25 June 1866.

[20]*Congressional Globe*, 39th Cong., 1st sess., 3242.

[21]*New York Evening Post*, 28 September 1865, and comments in various newspapers. Sumner's statement goes back to 4 February 1865 when he introduced a declaratory resolution to that effect. See Charles Sumner, *Works of Charles Sumner* (Boston: Lee and Shephard, 1820-1883) 9:233; also Charles Sumner Papers, Harvard University Library and Library of Congress.

As early as December 1865, Thaddeus Stevens of Pennsylvania was using the same kind of analysis in the House of Representatives. Vindictively, he expressed the hope that "none of the rebel states shall be counted in any of the amendments of the Constitution until they are duly admitted to the family of States by the law-making power of their conquerer."[22] In January, Robert C. Schenck of Ohio expressed his belief that the amendments must be approved by three-fourths of the loyal states before requiring such action by Southern states as a condition of their defeat. Any other approach, he believed, would lead to sure defeat of the Republican party.[23] By February of 1866, while the Joint Committee was laboring to frame a plan of reconstruction in the form of amendments to the Constitution, others like John M. Broomall of Pennsylvania were ready to turn such ideas on procedure into formal resolutions.[24]

Others, however, not convinced by such debators as Stevens and Schenck, were not so sure that a change in the Constitution by less than three-fourths of the total number of states would endure. They wished to avoid any possible difficulties on this count by exacting ratification as the price of representation in Congress. Lincoln's address to the Congress in 1862 was quoted to support the idea that an amendment could not be made a permanent part of the Constitution without two-thirds of the Congress concurring with three-fourths of the states, which necessarily would include the slave states.[25]

To require ratification as a condition of representation would, in the opinion of a correspondent of Senator Lyman Trumbull of Illinois, "secure Tennessee and other southern states at once for the amendment and thus secure their adoption."[26] It will be remembered that the same idea had been presented to the same states by the executives in connection with the Thirteenth Amendment. Before

---

[22]*Congressional Globe*, 39th Cong., lst sess., 74.

[23]*New York Herald*, 5 January 1866.

[24]*Congressional Globe*, 39th Cong., lst sess., 919.

[25]Ibid., 1167.

[26]W. B. Thomas to Lyman Trumbull, 22 May 1866, Lyman B. Trumbull Papers, Library of Congress.

reconstruction was complete, it would also be used in regard to the Fifteenth Amendment's ratification by seceded states.

Although such a pledge of readmission on condition of ratification was endorsed by many, a formal resolution to that effect was never passed by Congress. The Joint Committee had made the recommendation of a formal congressional resolution stating that any state that ratified the proposal would be admitted to representation in Congress when the amendment had been proclaimed law. This plan was deliberately put aside for a variety of reasons including the desire of some to exact additional and more drastic terms.[27]

The formal opinion of the Joint Committee on Reconstruction, as expressed in its report, was "That Congress would not be justified in admitting such communities to a participation in the government of the country without first providing such constitutional or other guarantees as will tend to secure the *civil rights* to all citizens of the republic; a just *equality of representation*; protection against claims founded in rebellion and crime; a temporary restoration of the right of suffrage to those who have not actively participated in the efforts to destroy the Union and overthrow the government, and the exclusion from positions of public trust of, at least a portion of those whose crimes have proved them to be enemies to the Union, and unworthy of public confidence."[28]

The amendment was a compromise, according to the *New York Times*: "it is believed to be the most favorable compromise to which the North would accede."[29] Years later, George E. Boutwell, one of the framers, declared that "it was impossible in 1866 to get farther than the provisions of the Fourteenth Amendment."[30] From some uncommitted height above the coming fray, *The Nation* made this pronouncement: "God does not wholly commit the work of regenerating the human race either to antislavery associations or Congres-

---

[27]George S. Boutwell to Charles Sumner, 17 June 1866, Sumner Papers; *Congressional Globe*, 39th Cong., lst sess., 3981.

[28]"Report of the Joint Committee on Reconstruction."

[29]*New York Times*, 15 June 1866.

[30]George S. Boutwell, *Reminiscences of Sixty Years in Public Affairs*, 2 vols. (New York: McClure, Phillips Col, 1902) 1:41.

sional majorities and we may be sure witnesses their failures and disappointments with perfect equanimity."[31]

On a more practical plane, *Harper's Weekly* saw in the proposed amendment a means of averting a party split. "It is to secure the gains already made," the periodical asserted. In order to avoid allowing restoration to be entrusted to traitors, it was necessary to "Maintain the ascendency of the Union Party until its work is accomplished."[32] Many felt that presidential support was necessary: "Because there is nothing in the amendment which is not strictly in consonance with the views which the President has often expressed, we hope that for the sake of harmony he will not oppose it."[33] Such hopes of presidential support were often expressed either because of a real possibility of his support or because of a desire to show how reasonable the amendment really was.

Comments appearing in papers of the South indicated little regard for the Fourteenth Amendment; the general belief was that it would fail. However, some saw in this failure the probable cause for drastic action by Congress, especially in regard to suffrage for blacks. Evidence fails to confirm that there was no fear of what radicals would do if it was rejected.[34] The opinion of former vice-president of the Confederacy, Alexander H. Stephens, as expressed in testimony before the Joint Committee on Reconstruction, was "that these terms ought not to be offered as conditions precedent." A restricted suffrage including more qualified blacks would not be nearly so objectionable as a general or universal voting right. It was a matter for the individual states to decide and any change should come from that source.[35] The minority report of the Joint Committee, presented by

---

[31]*The Nation*, 15 June 1866.

[32]*Harper's Weekly*, 16 June 1861.

[33]Ibid., 23 June 1866.

[34]Southern reaction appeared in the *Memphis Avalanche, Baltimore Sun, New Orleans Picayune* and the *Richmond Examiner*; also see Michael Perman, *Reunion Without Compromise*: The South and Reconstruction 1865-1868 (London: Cambridge University Press, 1973) 169, and Joseph B. James, "Southern Reaction to the Proposal of the Fourteenth Amendment," *Journal of Southern History* 22 (November 1956): 479-97.

[35]"Report of the Joint Committee of Reconstruction."

Senator Reverdy Johnson of Maryland, expressed much the same opinion.[36]

Jonathan Worth in North Carolina thought that "No Southern State, where the people are free to vote, will adopt it."[37] In Mississippi, the *Jackson Clarion* voiced a common view when it declared that Southern people "should not cooperate in [their] own humiliation."[38] Before any state in the South had acted, the *Chicago Tribune* summarized opinion from Southern newspapers as almost unanimously opposed to the amendment.[39] As will be seen, the disqualification measure in the amendment was the most unacceptable part to many in the South. It was widely recognized that rejection might give Radicals the excuse to impose black suffrage, but the general attitude was that of the *Jackson Clarion*—noncooperation in their own humiliation.

All states in the North would promptly ratify the amendment, predicted the *Chicago Tribune*. It warned, however, that if President Johnson did not apply pressure, the South would reject it. With presidential opposition to the amendment that paper felt certain that only congressional reorganization of states in the South would enable it to pass.[40] How accurate this was, time and events would demonstrate.

---

[36]Ibid., 39th Cong., 1st sess., 2, no. 30, pt.2.

[37]Jonathan Worth to Benjamin S. Hedrick, 1 July 1866, Benjamin S. Hedrick Papers, Duke University Library.

[38]*Jackson Clarion*, 20 June 1866.

[39]*Chicago Tribune*, 21 June 1866.

[40]Ibid., 15 June 1866.

Chapter Two

Setting Sail

Scarcely had the proposed amendment been received by state executives when the legislature of Connecticut, under great pressure to ratify, held an overtime session and stamped its formal approval.[1] Republican control in the legislature had been maintained in the elections by 13 to 8 in the Senate and 141 to 95 in the House.[2] A new Republican governor, Joseph H. Hawley, had won over his Democratic opponent in a close race by only 541 votes.

The issues had already been closely drawn in the national arena by the contest between President and Congress. The Civil Rights Bill had been vetoed to emphasize the clash of strength on the basic issues of 1866. While the nation watched, Democrats in convention in early

---

[1] *American Annual Cyclopedia and Register of Important Events of the Year* (New York: D. Appleton, 1866) 255.

[2] Ibid.

February at Hartford had passed resolutions commending President Johnson, claiming the right of representation in Congress for states of the South, and criticizing Congress for attempting to determine illegally the franchise in excluded states.

O. S. Seymour, the Democratic nominee as Connecticut's governor, reflected the prevailing attitude when he declared, "We are all, I take it, for preserving the Constitution as it is; for healing the wounds of the Union...."[3] Later that February, Republicans, also in convention in Hartford, endorsed the position of Congress and at the same time assured the President of support. Johnson's veto message consequently caused much confusion among Republican political councils in Connecticut.[4]

Before retiring from office on 2 May 1866, Republican Governor William A. Buckingham of Connecticut commented on what he considered proper requirements for the excluded Southern states: in addition to other conditions, "we may justly demand such action as will secure the people from taxation to pay for an unsuccessful attempt to destroy their liberties, and a proper guarantee against the repudiation of pecuniary obligations made necessary in preserving the national Government." The party must insist that leaders in the rebellion be excluded from any voice in reconstruction or the administration of the restored governments. In his opinion, Congress should also demand that the reorganized states guarantee equal rights and equal protection before the law to all citizens.[5] In several respects, these ideas ran parallel to the points then being written into the Fourteenth Amendment by Congress.

In his inaugural address that same day, Governor Hawley initiated the black vote as an issue by claiming that the entire white population of the South must not be considered as the sole basis for representation while four million blacks were excluded from the ballot. (That would be the result of the passage of the Thirteenth Amendment, which in effect had repealed the three-fifths compro-

---

[3] Ibid.

[4] Ibid., 252-53.

[5] *New York Herald*, 8 May 1866; *Connecticut Senate Journal* (1866) 28; *Connecticut House Journal* (1866) 15.

mise in the original Constitution.) Slavery, said Governor Hawley, must be abolished in fact, and secession as a doctrine must be abandoned. There must be security against taxation to pay for treason and "full protection, safety and honor everywhere for the rights of all loyal citizens without distinction of race or color." In endorsement of the amendments still to be formally proposed, Governor Hawley said "they [the amendments] look to the security for the future and are not a part of any idle claim to indemnity for the past; they are not selfishly sought for a class or party, but demanded for all mankind, and they are essential to the success and glory of a Christian Democratic Government."[6]

On 19 June, only three days after the official copies of the proposed Fourteenth Amendment had been sent from Washington, Governor Hawley sent the proposal to the Connecticut legislature with his recommendation to ratify. A resolution to that effect was introduced immediately in the Senate. When a motion to postpone consideration until the next session was made, the Senate defeated it 10 to 6. After debate, the resolution of ratification was approved on 25 June by a vote of 11 to 6.[7] The very next day, the resolution was officially received in the House where it was considered on 27 June. A motion for postponement similar to that lost in the Senate was also defeated in the House 107 to 84. Debate ensued and the ratification resolution was approved on 29 June 1866 by a vote of 131 to 92.[8] These votes appear to have been along strict party lines with some members not voting.

In congratulating Connecticut on being the first to ratify, the *Cincinnati Commercial* commented that "the amendment was not ratified ... without quite a contest, wherein the Copperheads had a chance to spit venom and do considerable wriggling."[9] Connecticut action took place against the background of a proposed state constitutional amendment to grant equal suffrage to blacks. In fact, the earlier re-

---

[6]*Connecticut Senate Journal*, 43; *New York Herald*, 3 May 1866.

[7]*Connecticut Senate Journal*, 355-57.

[8]*Connecticut House Journal*, 384-410.

[9]*Cincinnati Commercial*, 7 July 1866.

jection of suffrage for blacks by the Connecticut voters, coming as it did before the Fourteenth Amendment had been finalized, undoubtedly constituted one of the influences on the Congressional decision to avoid a direct position on that topic.[10]

Both the national press and individuals throughout the country had been speculating on the fate of the proposal for a fourteenth amendment, engaging in much analysis of its contents. Even before the congressional work was complete, the Washington correspondent of the *Philadelphia Press* had predicted that twenty-two of the necessary twenty-eight ratifications (assuming the admission of Colorado as a new state) would come from Illinois, Rhode Island, Michigan, New York, Maryland, Massachusetts, Pennsylvania, West Virginia, Maine, Ohio, Kansas, Minnesota, Colorado, Indiana, Nevada, Wisconsin, Missouri, Vermont, Connecticut, New Hampshire, Oregon, and California. The other six would necessarily have to come from the remaining fifteen, including not only the defeated South but New Jersey, Delaware, and Kentucky.[11] This tabulation would indicate some general doubt concerning a predictable outcome.

Much of the friendly press, like the *Chicago Tribune*, emphasized the compromise nature of the amendment and tried to identify it with Johnson's ideas. In rejecting the "violent and obnoxious ideas and propositions of Thaddeus Stevens and in adopting the policy of President Johnson," declared the *New York Herald*, Congress "has saved the republican party from dissolution and has given it a powerful platform for the approaching elections."[12]

Many had indeed hoped that the amendment itself might furnish a common ground for all factions of the Republican party including that led by the President. In early July, Chief Justice Salmon P. Chase had expressed his disappointment that this had not happened.[13] As

---

[10]Referred to in message of Governor Joseph K. Hawley, 2 May 1866, in *Connecticut Senate Journal*, 43.

[11]Quoted in *New York Herald*, 15 June 1866.

[12]*New York Herald*, 8 May 1866.

[13]S. P. Chase to his daughter, 2 July 1866, Salmon P. Chase Papers, Library of Congress.

strife between president and Congress went on, some developed a strong opinion in favor of hasty ratification, believing that Johnson would thus be discredited or would have to make his peace. They did not wish to await new elections to pass on the amendment in the various states. *Harper's Weekly* summed up this attitude on 7 July: "As it is desirable that all possible delays should be avoided and as there is no doubt whatever that the legislatures of the States faithfully represent the sentiment of the people, we hope that at the earliest possible moment they will be convened to pass upon the Amendment."[14]

Senator John Sherman expressed similar ideas as well as a growing mistrust of Johnson in a letter to his brother, General W. T. Sherman. The Senator claimed that many in Congress had been led by Johnson to believe that he favored the "Amendments" and would aid in their adoption. Now it was obvious that nothing was further from the truth. "I almost fear he contemplates civil war,"[15] confessed Sherman. He later elaborated on this theme, saying that Johnson had promised to approve the amendment if Radicals would do away with efforts for black suffrage and the state suicide theory.[16]

The Nation publicly expressed what Sherman had written privately. In summary, there seemed to be suspicion that the President would take advantage of the national desire to obtain a restored Union in order to form a contingent of those in Congress who favored readmission of Southern states and the representatives from those states now awaiting an opportunity to be duly seated. If he could in this way get enough to constitute a majority, the combination would elect a speaker and ask recognition by the President as the legal Congress. This he would give and aid the new body in expelling those who would not accept such a state of affairs. In this way and in the name of the United States, opposition in a divided North could be crushed. *The Nation* concluded that "The proceedings of the Union Caucus at Washington show that our apprehensions are shared by

---

[14]*Harper's Weekly*, 7 July 1866.

[15]John Sherman to W. T. Sherman, 8 July 1866, W. T. Sherman Papers, Library of Congress.

[16]See speech reported in *Cincinnati Commercial*, 29 September 1866.

many of the oldest and coolest politicians there."[17] Indeed as early as March, Senator Garrett Davis of Kentucky openly expressed an outline of the possibility. If the President should tell Southerners, "Get together with the Democrats and Conservatives of the Senate, and if you constitute a majority, I will recognize you as the Senate of the United States. What then will become of you gentlemen? You will quietly come in and form a part of that Senate."[18] Montgomery Blair regularly referred to this idea in speeches during July.[19]

The *New York Times* on 17 July summarized the possibilities much the same as *The Nation*. It was presented in connection with the apparent fear of radicals that a compromise with Johnson could be obtained.[20] It appeared that enough radical Republicans took this talk seriously as to discuss such possibilities and desirable precautions in a secret caucus.[21]

With the background of such rumblings, the haste to admit Tennessee assumes increased meaning. Much of the support for the plan outlined above would inevitably be dispersed with the beginning of actual restoration in Tennessee. An indication of the undercurrents that were feared as being able to turn opinion against congressional reconstruction was the report of a statement by General Ulyses Grant, a man of considerable prestige. Although he opposed some of the main features of the amendment, he believed "that the Southern loyal representatives should have been admitted to their seats and an opportunity should have been given them to vote upon the joint resolution to amend the constitution before the same was submitted to the several State legislatures."[22]

While these things were discussed nationally, the spotlight turned briefly to New Hampshire, which had taken up the matter of

---

[17]*The Nation*, 19 July 1866.

[18]*Congressional Globe*, 39th Cong., 1st sess., appendix, 304.

[19]*New York World*, 19 July 1866; *Boston Daily Advertiser*, 28 August 1866.

[20]*New York Times*, 17 July 1866.

[21]Sumner to John Bright, 3 September 1866 in Charles Sumner, *Memoir and Letters of Charles Summer*, ed., Edward L. Pierce, 4 vols. (Boston: Roberts Brothers, 1877-1893) 4:298.

[22]*New York Times*, 9 July 1866.

ratification soon after the Fourteenth Amendment had been officially proposed. While Connecticut was still in the process of ratification, the New Hampshire legislature, dominated by Republicans in both houses,[23] began consideration of the report by its select committee on the amendment in the House of Representatives. The minority of the committee filed a full statement of its objections at the same time, 26 June 1866.[24]

Hastily, the second reading took place; the third reading was made the special order of business in the House for that same day. More sober judgment finally caused a postponement to the next morning at eleven. Continued difficulties caused a new hour to be set, this time at three o'clock. Again, it was postponed until an evening session and finally was made the special order for the next morning, 28 June. The question was not called until that afternoon when the motion to ratify was approved 207 to 112.[25] Apparently the vote was along party lines.

The following day, the New Hampshire Senate received formal notification of the House action. Immediately it caused the resolution to be read twice and referred to a special committee.[26] On 2 July, as was to be expected, a favorable report was forthcoming. Again the minority submitted a full statement of its objections. These may be summarized in thirteen points:

1. The states most deeply interested were not permitted to be represented in the Congress that proposed the amendment.

2. "There is nothing in the present condition of any section of the country which renders any amendment to the constitution necessary."

3. The amendment would pave the way for the destruction of the entire constitutional pattern as it had been.

4. The inclusion of several separate subjects in one omnibus proposal was not proper.

---

[23]Senate Majority was 9-3; House, 208-118; See *Annual Cyclopedia* (1866) 537.

[24]*New Hampshire House Journal* (1866) 176.

[25]Ibid., 190-231.

[26]*New Hampshire Senate Journal* (1866) 63.

5. "The proposed amendment is ambiguous or contradictory in its provisions."

6. The amendment was to be regarded as "a dangerous infringement upon the rights and independence of all the States . . ." due to its assuming control over their legislation in "matters purely local in their character."

7. The second section divided taxation from representation to which it had always been attached.

8. It would be unfair to discriminate in representation on the basis of those barred (such as paupers in many states), and it would be difficult to apply due to lack of adequate statistics.

9. Such an extension of the suffrage as proposed in the amendments would lower the quality of voting.

10. The disqualification section was unjust in that it would punish presently loyal people without trial.

11. It would usurp the power of the President to pardon.

12. The debt provision insulted the people by suggesting repudiation when its real purpose was to protect the United States bondholders from taxation by throwing up barriers that would the exempt the wealthy from their share in tax burdens.

13. "The only occasion and real design of the proposed amendment is to accomplish indirectly what the general government has and should have no power to do directly, namely, to interfere with the regulation of the elective franchise in the States, and thereby force negro suffrage upon an unwilling people."[27]

Again delays developed. The amendment was made the special order of business, laid on the table, and taken up until it finally passed on 6 July 1866 by a party vote of nine to three.[28]

It seems remarkable that so much resistance as has been noted existed in New England. The arguments used were those that would, with variations, become the core of opposition arguments everywhere. In fact, they may be said to reflect arguments that had already been made in Congress before formal acceptance of the proposed amendment by the necessary two-thirds.

---

[27] Ibid., 70-73.

[28] Ibid., 73-94.

However before Connecticut had completed its ratification and before New Hampshire had begun its debate on the proposal, major public attention shifted to the border state of Tennessee. Even if no commitments had been made concerning any connection between ratification and readmission of representatives to Congress, there was considerable sentiment in favor of readmission, especially for a state that had shown a clear division of opinion and action during the war. This attitude was reported to have produced a letter to Governor W. G. Brownlow of Tennessee signed by some forty members of Congress asking him to convene the legislature in special session so as to ratify the Fourteenth Amendment. Although nothing was promised, it was emphasized that once this was accomplished, Tennessee would quite possibly have representatives seated in Congress before it adjourned for the summer.[29] That an uneasy relationship existed between the President and Congress and that Andrew Johnson was a Tennessean were naturally assumed to be factors in such developments.

Small wonder that the people of the nation watched attentively when a special session was summoned by the violently radical "Parson" Brownlow. In his call, the governor frankly informed the Tennessee legislators that Congress wanted their ratification of the Fourteenth Amendment as a guarantee of their future loyalty. He deemed the equal protection of all citizens as perfectly proper and the disqualification of leading Confederates as exceedingly mild.[30] To the assembled legislators on 6 July 1866, Brownlow again pointed out that the purpose of the session was to consider ratification of the proposed amendment. He hastily summarized its provisions and observed that it showed magnanimity on the part of Congress to demand such easy terms for restoration.[31]

When Governor Brownlow wrote Chief Justice Chase on 20 June concerning the prospects for passage of the amendment, he was plainly doubtful. He anticipated no difficulty in the Senate but looked for considerable opposition in the House. He complained of

---

[29]*Cincinnati Commercial*, 15 June 1866.

[30]*Tennessee Senate Journal* (1866) 3-4.

[31]Ibid., 7-9.

Johnson's use of the patronage against him and testified that of the nine newspapers in thirty-one counties where the Union party was strong, seven were for the President in his opposition to Congress.[32]

In the Tennessee Senate, Trimble immediately moved to take up the resolution of ratification. Under suspended rules, this was accomplished. The opposition, represented by Senator Carrigan, then moved for a substitute of the entire resolution, which would refuse ratification because of the absence of one-third of the members. On a test motion to adjourn, the opposition was defeated fourteen to five, and the substitute resolution was voted down thirteen to six. After a sharp debate concerning which committee should consider the ratification resolution, it was referred to the judiciary committee.[33]

The following Monday, while the Tennessee House was still vainly trying to assemble a quorum, the Senate considered the advisability of referring the question of ratification to the voters. The motion to accomplish this was withdrawn, and the resolution to ratify was laid on the table. Two days later, 11 July, it was taken up again. By a vote of thirteen to five, the majority defeated a motion to refuse to construe the amendment as conferring on blacks any right of suffrage, jury duty, holding office, or intermarrying with whites. Further, the resolution would refuse to recognize in the proposed amendment the granting of any power to the federal government to interfere with the conduct of the state's affairs under its existing Constitution. Although not defeated outright, the motion was placed on the table. The previous question was demanded by a vote of eleven to seven, and the ratification resolution was approved fourteen to six.[34] Thus did the Senate of the war-torn border state of Tennessee perform its task with relative dispatch amid many doubts and much pressure from outside forces. Governor Brownlow's prediction was proven accurate for the Senate and would be even more so for the House.

---

[32] W. G. Brownlow to S. P. Chase, 20 June 1866, Chase Papers.

[33] *Tennessee Senate Journal*, 13-18.

[34] Ibid., 23-25.

On 5 July the Tennessee House of Representatives called the roll and found only forty-four present. The next day fifty-one answered roll call; the quorum of fifty-six still could not be found. Telegrams were sent and the request by an absent member, M. F. W. Dunaway, to resign was refused.[35] On 7 July there were still only fifty-one present, but two days later fifty-five were in their seats, lacking only one to complete the quorum. The next day, however, the number had dropped to fifty-one. July 11 found only fifty-two in attendance.[36]

The controversy over such delaying tactics became sharper when attempts to present correspondence from members explaining their absence failed. Instead, warrants for arrest specifying absentees by name were voted. The next day with only fifty-two present, the sergeant-at-arms reported that he had been unable to find the absent members. On 13 July only fifty-three were present, and new warrants were issued.[37]

A new tactic was tried on 14 July when an attempt was made to declare that a quorum would consist of two-thirds of the body "holding seats" if this constituted a majority of those entitled to seats. Instead, new warrants were voted. With only fifty present on 16 July, the House issued a summons to absent members to be present or to show cause. On that day the House was informed of the arrest of one of its members after a wild night-chase by mule and on foot through the hills from Carter Station. The next day details of further attempts to catch fugitive members reached the House where a quorum was still lacking.

The official records indicate what was obviously the case: there was much local opposition to the arrests, resulting in considerable aid to members who wished to keep out of the hands of the officers.[38] A correspondent of Illinois congressman, Elihu B. Washburne, reported that a quorum had been in town several days but that they had avoided attendance and had "eluded detectives." The correspon-

---

[35]*Annual Cyclopedia* (1866) 729.

[36]*Tennessee House Journal* (1866) 5-12.

[37]Ibid.

[38]Ibid., 13-16.

dent claimed that feeling was running high, and threats had been made against the life of the high-handed "Parson" Brownlow as well as against other radical leaders.[39]

On 17 July, a member named Williams, who had been previously arrested, was joined by another representative, Martin. The legislature then refused to recognize the jurisdiction of a criminal court that issued a writ of habeas corpus for these two. In such a tense situation with the legislative and judicial branches in dispute—the executive actively siding with the legislative and two members in custody by force—there is nothing surprising in the roll call on the next day when only thirty-five responded.

Finally on 19 July, fifty-four members were in their seats, and the imprisoned two were invited to take theirs. Refusing to do so, Martin and Williams remained under custody in a nearby committee room with the door opened to the chamber, but they would not answer roll call. Under such conditions the resolution of ratification of the Fourteen Amendment was passed by a vote of forty-three to eleven with the unbending duo marked "present, not voting." When the speaker ruled that there was not a quorum, he was overruled, with the record showing both the speaker and the two under arrest as not voting.[40] It is interesting to note that the official certificate of ratification that was finally forwarded to Washington bore the signature of the speaker pro tempore instead of the overruled speaker.[41]

Not waiting to report his exploit by slower means, Brownlow sent telegrams to Washington. One to the secretary of the Senate stated: "Battle fought and won. Constitutional Amendment carried in the House—forty-three against eleven."[42] Secretary of War Stanton received another from his radical supporter in Tennessee: "My com-

---

[39]Incomplete letter to E. B. Washburne, 14 July 1866, Elihu B. Washburne Papers, Library of Congress.

[40]*Tennessee House Journal*, 16-25; *Cincinnati Commercial*, 23 July 1866, quoting *Nashville Press and Times*.

[41]E. M. Coulter, *William G. Brownlow: Fighting Parson of the Southern Highlands* (Chapel Hill: University of North Carolina Press, 1937); Gideon Welles's Diary, 23 July 1866, Welles Papers, Library of Congress; *Cincinnati Commercial*, 23 July 1866; *The Nation*, 26 July 1866; *Knoxville Whig*, 1 August 1866.

[42]*New York Herald*, 20 July 1866.

pliments to the President, we have carried the Constitutional Amendment in the House, Vote 43 to 11, two of his tools refusing to vote."[43] Another wire from the obviously jubilant Brownlow to Bingham of Ohio, who stood ready to lead the fight to admit Tennessee, read "Battle fought and won. The Amendment was ratified in the House today by 43 to 11. Two of Johnson's tools refused to vote. Give my compliments to the dead dog in the White House."[44] A different version was quoted in the *New York Times*: "Give my compliments to the dirty dog in the White House."[45]

Once the voting was over in Nashville, the two members, having sought release from custody by means of a writ of habeas corpus issued by Judge Frazier, were released. The sergeant-at-arms of the House was held in contempt, but was assessed only the cost of court.[46] The verdict of the historian, Ellis P. Oberholtzer, seems no overstatement. He declared that the legislature of Tennessee "promptly ratified the new Fourteenth Amendment amid some of the most violent and irregular scenes in the history of parliamentary government in America."[47]

In an effort to gain an early momentum as well as to convince the doubtful, including President Johnson, that the amendment would be ratified, three states had moved rapidly to approve it. Two New England states, Connecticut and New Hampshire, were followed by the border state of Tennessee. Like other Confederate states, Tennessee was unrepresented in Congress. Because the President was a Tennessean, it was hoped that prompt admission of that state would help to persuade him to aid ratification.

Republicans continued to make a very real effort to demonstrate to Andrew Johnson that his purposes and interests were not in conflict with those of the amendment. Its passage would remove all

[43]*New York Times*, 20 July 1866.

[44]*Cincinnati Commercial*, 20 July 1866.

[45]*New York Times*, 20 July 1866.

[46]*Annual Cyclopedia* (1866) 729. Whole story appears in *Knoxville Whig*, 20 July-1 August 1866.

[47]Ellis P. Oberholtzer, *A History of the United States Since the Civil War*, 5 vols. (New York: MacMillan and Co., 1917-1937) 1:187.

doubts as to the constitutionality of the Civil Rights Act that he had vetoed. Direct action on suffrage for blacks, which was being considered in several states, was carefully omitted from the amendment. Among the reasons for taking such positions was the fear of offending advocates of states' rights in many areas of the country, including New England.

Chapter Three

Choppy Seas

The issue of Tennessee's readmission became the focus of national attention at once. In a personal clash with Thaddeus Stevens, John Bingham fought to prevent the recommital of a resolution to seat Tennessee's representatives who had been in Washington waiting for such a favorable opportunity. Stevens was ready to approve their being seated but disagreed with Congress's methods. However, when the final vote came, Stevens actually supported Tennessee's admission to Congress after trying to delay or block it earlier to permit other procedures.[1]

In the debate, questions concerning irregularities in Governor Brownlow's ratification procedures were raised but put aside by House leaders. Boutwell of Massachusetts summed up this attitude well when he remarked that he was not "troubled by the informalities

---

[1]*Congressional Globe*, 39th Cong., 1st sess., 3981; *New York Herald*, 25 July 1866; *New York Times*, 20, 21 July 1866.

apparent in the proceedings of the Tennessee Legislature upon the question of ratifying the Constitutional Amendment." "It received the votes of a majority of the members of a full House," he continued, "and when the proper officers shall have made the customary certificate and filed it in the Department of State, it is not easy to see how any legal objection can be raised, even if two-thirds of the members were not present, although that proportion is a quorum according to the Constitution of the State."[2]

During the day that the House of Representatives in Washington approved the readmission of representatives of Tennessee, senators were receiving messages urging similar action. Horace White and Joseph Medill of the Chicago *Tribune* had wired Speaker Colfax urging favorable action and instructing him to "show this to Judge Trumbull and such members as you choose."[3] Medill had already directly urged that some official statement be issued about restoration on the basis of ratification when that process was complete.[4]

For seven hours on 21 July, a tedious debate on the readmission of Tennessee dragged on in the Senate.[5] Eventually the resolution that it approved differed little from that passed by the House. On 23 July the House approved the Senate version without change or debate.[6] On that same day, President Johnson read to Secretary Welles a dispatch from Speaker Heiskell of the Tennessee House of Representatives informing him that Heiskell could not sign a certificate of ratification due to the lack of a quorum.[7] According to the *New York Times*, the message had arrived the night before.[8]

---

[2]*Congresssional Globe*, 39th Cong., 1st sess., 3976.

[3]Horace White and Joseph Medill to Schuyler Colfax, 20 July 1866. It is significant that this message now reposes in the Lyman B. Trumbull Papers, Library of Congress.

[4]Joseph Medill to E. B. Washburne, 17 July 1866, Elihu B. Washburne Papers, Library of Congress; Joseph Medill to Lyman Trumbull, 17 July 1866, Trumbull Papers.

[5]*Cincinnati Commercial*, 22 July 1866; *New York Times*, 22 July 1866.

[6]Ibid., 24 July 1866.

[7]Gideon Welles Diary, 23 July 1866, Welles Papers, Library of Congress.

[8]*New York Times*, 23 July 1866.

Regardless of whether the amendment had been ratified, President Johnson received the joint resolution and sent a message before two o'clock on 24 July saying that he approved the congressional action to admit Tennessee's representatives.[9] The message was received in the House at approximately three o'clock, producing considerable excitement. Members gathered around the secretary who had brought the message and scanned its contents before it was officially read. Everything was silent during the reading until the President's approval was announced. Loud applause then erupted.

Upon the reading of the next sentence, which indicated Johnson's unwillingness to recognize the power of Congress to set up additional qualifications for duly elected representatives of the states, laughter broke out. Immediately after the reading, credentials of Tennessee congressmen were turned over to the committee on elections. Within thirty minutes this committee recommended seating all Tennessee members. There was no opposition, and the members were sworn in amid much applause. Not long after, one hundred guns boomed at the city hall to celebrate the restoration of the first of the seceded states.[10]

Loyal Tennessee unionists had remained in Congress to represent the state until 1863, longer than any other Southern state. Tennessee had a military governor, Andrew Johnson, who was appointed by Lincoln in 1862. He served until presidential reconstruction had developed, and he approved a constitution under irregular circumstances. An election authorized by that document placed W. G. Brownlow in the executive mansion in Nashville in February 1865. With such a government and with this volatile background, the history of Tennessee and the ratification of the Fourteenth Amendment was not typical of ex-Confederate states.

Brownlow himself, a mountain preacher and journalist, had delivered thundering tirades against all traitors and secessionists and had worked closely with congressional Radicals to achieve a revolutionized order in the state. Despite these actions, he had more in common with the President than the fact that they both came from the

---

[9]Ibid., 25 July 1866.

[10]*Cincinnati Commercial*, 25 July 1866.

mountains of East Tennessee. As military governor, Johnson used irregular and crudely direct methods of control that also served as punishment for ex-Confederates. His words, "treason is a crime and must be made odious," were much in the same vein as Brownlow's threats to hang and exterminate disloyal elements.[11]

Nevertheless, the two men had taken different directions, and by July 1866, they were hostile to each other, especially in regard to the congressional policy of reconstruction and to the Fourteenth Amendment. Johnson, like the Radicals, believed that the South should be contrite, confess its sins, and declare its loyalty to the Union. His approach, however, was more personal and expressed itself in executive pardons based on individual professions of guilt and applications for reinstatement as loyal citizens.

These pardons were available to leaders while amnesty was proclaimed for others who renounced rebellion and pledged their loyalty.[12] It was against pardons such as these that section three of the Fourteenth Amendment was directed. It became the most objectionable feature of the proposal to the South and undercut executive pardoning power.

In spite of such developments concerning the amendment and in spite of the appparent changes in Johnson as perceived by associates, he remained much the same in many ways. He had always been a Democrat and his position attracted Democrats. His election as vice-president on the Union party ticket with Lincoln had not made him a Republican but did help attract conservative Republicans.

It was this coalition, or this appearance of a coalition, with which the President and Congress approached the next ratification debates held in New Jersey. Before action could be taken, however, much happened on the national scene that would affect the states' recep-

---

[11]For details see E. M. Coulter, *W. G. Brownlow: Fighting Parson of the Southern Highlands* (Chapel Hill: University of North Carolina Press, 1937); and T. B. Heard, *Political Reconstruction in Tennessee* (Nashville TN: Vanderbilt University Press, 1950).

[12]For Tennessee reconstruction and Johnson's attitude, see Eric L. McKitrick, *Andrew Johnson and Reconstruction* (Chicago, 1960) especially 137-52. Also see J. G. Randall and David Donald, *The Civil War and Reconstruction* (Lexington MA: D. C. Heath and Co., 1969) 585-86.

tion of the proposal. With the admission of Tennessee, many felt that
the conservatives had surrendered altogether to the President, in
substance if not in form.[13] The Radical press showed discourage-
ment.[14] Thaddeus Stevens was neither jubilant nor noticeably discouraged by Tennessee's admission to Congress, and summed up his
policy of expediency in a speech to the House 28 July:

> I do not pretend that she is loyal. I believe this day that two-thirds of her
> people are rank and cruel rebels. But her statesmen have been wise and dil-
> igent enough to form a constitution which bridles licentious traitors and se-
> cures the State government to the true men. And she has an executive fit to
> ride the whirlwind.[15]

Johnson's adherents sought to capitalize on this feeling in the National Union Convention, which had been called in June to assemble
in Philadelphia during August. The uniting of Democrats, conservative Republicans, and Southern leaders under Johnson-recon-
struction was to dramatize the prospect of a restored Union.

To be sure, Congress had proposed the Fourteenth Amendment, which the President and the Philadelphia convention opposed. It had been promoted and justified as the security required if
the country was to be reunited. The campaigns of Congressmen running for reelection, and of many candidates for state government in
the North, centered on this proposal as the opposition to Johnson's
efforts to form a coalition against congressional reconstruction.
Johnson's uncompromising and violent attack on Radicals had
caused many to abandon him even though there existed the possibility of reconciling the two groups on the basis of his approval of the
amendment (which many thought demonstrated an attempt to work
with him). To do this, Johnson would have sacrificed Democratic
support, leaving Southern supporters in a position of opposition
which he had stimulated.

The President refused to budge from his determined opposition
to the congressional program suggested by the Fourteenth Amend-

---

[13]*New York Herald*, 23 July 1866.

[14]*New York Independent*, 2 August 1866.

[15]*Congressional Globe*, 39th Cong., 1st sess., 3488.

ment. A meeting of Southern Loyalists was called in September partly to cancel the influence of the Union convention of August. But even here, the Northern Republicans were a restraining influence.

Many of its supporters considered the purpose of the Fourteenth Amendment to be a compromise not only among congressional Republicans but one that could in good conscience be acceptable to the President. As has already been noted, he authorized its reference to state governments only as a ministerial act, indicating his personal disapproval. In fact, plans for a National Union Convention were being made as early as 18 June when Senator Doolittle of Wisconsin prepared and discussed with the President a call for a convention to be held 14 August.

Discussion developed concerning whether or not to include in the call a strong statement against the amendment. Doolittle reasoned that such wording should be omitted in order to secure the signatures of Henry J. Raymond and others on the national committee. There was hesitation about forwarding the amendment to the states without the President's opposition being known, but Seward had already dispatched it.[16]

Cabinet discussion reached no consensus about the amendment despite opposition from Hugh McCulloch and Gideon Welles. William H. Seward's strong position against it played a large part in Johnson's disapproval.[17] William Dennison had talked with Bingham and favored it. Johnson read a proposed message before Cabinet members, but it did not meet with general approval.[18] It was more strongly stated than the one sent on 22 June.[19]

The first presidential draft expressed a reasoned objection to a change in organic law that would reduce the rights of states in the

---

[16]Welles Diary, 18-20 June 1866, Welles Papers.

[17]Glyndon G. Van Deusen, *William Henry Seward* (New York: Oxford University Press, 1967) 451; William E. Smith, *The Francis Preston Blair Family in Politics*, 2 vols. (New York: Macmillan Co., 1969) 364-65.

[18]Welles Diary, 22 June 1866, Welles Papers.

[19]See James D. Richardson, *A Compilation of the Messages and Papers of the Presidents 1789-1897*, 20 vols. (Washington DC: Bureau of National Literature and Art, 1896-1899) 6:391.

Union. The President considered it dangerous to upset the balance that had worked so well and objected to its origin in a Congress not truly representative of the whole—eleven of the states most affected had not been consulted. If they should ratify, "it can in no way be imputed to them as their voluntary act." "For this reason I have been, and am still of the opinion that this Amendment, thus irregularly presented and at a time unfavorable to calm and careful consideration, ought not to be ratified."[20]

The official call for a National Union Convention in Philadelphia on 14 August was issued 25 June and signed by an executive committee that included some Democrats and some Johnson-conservatives. A. W. Randall, O. H. Browning, James R. Doolittle, Edgar Cowan, Charles Knapp, and Samuel Fowler affixed their signatures. It was endorsed as part of the call by David S. Norton, J. W. Nesmith, James Dixon, and T. A. Hendricks. It was directed to thirty-six states, nine territories, and the District of Columbia. In order to be seated, delegates must subscribe to the principles of no secession, no slavery, and no right to keep states unrepresented.[21] Opposition to the amendment, as has been seen, was carefully omitted.[22]

On 26 June, O. H. Browning divulged that he, along with Seward, McCulloch, Randall, Cowan, and Doolittle, had met with the President the previous Saturday night. After discussing the call paragraph by paragraph, all had approved the final wording. Browning communicated this to Thomas Ewing of Ohio and asked him to publicly endorse the convention. He did so on 30 June. Similar procedures were undoubtedly used with many influential people.[23] At the President's wish, Senator Doolittle sent requests for endorsements of the convention to all members of the Cabinet. This action not only helped bring about the resignation of Attorney General James Speed, Secretary of Interior James Harlan, and Postmaster-General

---

[20]Undated draft in Andrew Johnson Papers, Library of Congress.

[21]Call by A. W. Randall et al., Thomas Ewing Papers, Library of Congress.

[22]Michael Les Benedict, *A Compromise of Principle: Congressional Republicans and Reconstruction 1863-1869* (New York: W. W. Norton and Co., 1974) 193.

[23]O. H. Browning to Thomas Ewing, 26 June 1866, Ewing Papers; also letter in Hamilton Fish Papers, Library of Congress.

William Dennison but created a delicate problem for Secretary of War Edwin M. Stanton. Stanton supported the Fourteenth Amendment, though its measures were not strong enough to suit him, and thus did not want to endorse a convention that opposed the amendment.[24] The secretary of war went so far as to compose a careful statement of his position, but after reflection, never released it. His words were very specific as to the Fourteenth Amendment:

> I am in favor of securing the civil rights of all citizens of the United States in the States lately in rebellion, am in favor of equalizing the representation in Congress so as to give the loyal States their due weight in the legislative branch of the Government, and am also in favor of repudiating the rebel debt, and of guaranteeing as sacred the national debt incurred to suppress the rebellion, and especially the obligations of the nation to its soldiers and their widows and orphans. These being the objects of the proposed amendments to the Federal Constitution adopted by Congress, I am in favor of those Amendments.[25]

Despite partial reorganization of the Cabinet arising out of events surrounding the Philadelphia convention and out of President Johnson's stand against the amendment, Secretary Stanton remained at his post as an opposition leader within the official household of the chief executive. In early September, Representative John A. Bingham of Ohio, leader in the framing and the ratification fight, wrote Stanton urging him to stay on despite the pressures to resign. The people were relying on the secretary, wrote Bingham, for Stanton alone of all those in the administration was on the side of the amendment and of restoration on that basis. "The Amendment is directly in issue," he wrote, "and will be I have no doubt carried by the popular vote from Maine to California and ratified by the legislature of every Northern State except it be New Jersey."[26]

In July, events were coming to an impass because of differing beliefs between the President and the congressional majority about reconstruction and the Fourteenth Amendment (about which the

---

[24]Edwin M. Stanton to Doolittle, 16 July 1866, Edwin M. Stanton Papers, Library of Congress.

[25]Unsigned draft in Stanton's handwriting. Notation indicates it was prepared in connection with the Philadelphia convention but was never used. Stanton papers.

[26]John A. Bingham to Stanton, 3 September 1866, Stanton Papers.

President was taking an even stronger position). Henry J. Raymond, editor of the *New York Times* and national chairman of the Republican party, was discouraged by the patent disunity produced by plans for the National Union meeting in Philadelphia. "It allows the opposition to charge that the convention was designed to throw everything into Democratic hands."[27] Many Republicans did recoil as Democrats became prominently involved.[28]

It is worth emphasizing that no mention was made of the pending amendment in the call or in Browning's letter, which accompanied a copy of it. Browning did express the compelling stimulus in this way: "After having waited almost seven months for Congress to act in the great work of reconciliation and reconstruction and nothing having been done which had not better have been left undone, we have come to the conclusion that it was high time for the people to act."[29] This oblique reference to the Fourteenth Amendment and perhaps other unnamed acts is all that might be recognized as an allusion to the proposed change in the Constitution.

The emphasis in both Browning's letter and the call for the convention was on readmission of nonrepresented states. There was a great deal of pressure brought on congressmen to do something about restoration whether on the basis of the Fourteenth Amendment or not. An example is a letter to Senator Lyman Trumbull of Illinois from a Quincy constituent suggesting immediate admission upon ratification of the amendment. Such a promise would, in the writer's opinion, "secure Tennessee and other Southern states at once for the amendments and thus secure their adoption." It would have "a most happy effect upon the country."[30]

Later in the summer with no promise of readmission apparent, Joseph Medill of the *Chicago Tribune* wrote Senator Trumbull that "the Amendment amounts to nothing as a plan unless you pass an

---

[27]Henry J. Raymond to Thurlow Weed, 12 July 1866, quoted in T. W. Barnes, *Memoirs of Thurlow Weed* (Boston: Houghton Mifflin Co., 1884).

[28]Michael Les Benedict, *A Compromise of Principle*, 194; *New York Evening Post*, 19 July 1866.

[29]O. H. Browning to Thomas Ewing, 26 July 1866, Ewing Papers.

[30]W. B. Thomas to Trumbull, 26 May 1866, Trumbull Papers.

enabling act declaring that upon its ratification the outside States may come in." "We can't stand on nothing," he declared. "If Congress should adjourn," he added with vehemence, "without giving us some plan of reconstruction and offering some terms of admission to the South, you will be beaten to death and your party will suffer a worse defeat in Illinois than in 1862."[31]

Medill also sent a letter in the same vein to Representative E. B. Washburne of Illinois. A plan of restoration was needed, he claimed. The amendment might be said to be such a plan but "Congress *has not said so.*" No official statement in any binding form had been made that representatives of excluded states would be admitted upon ratification. "The great mass of our party and of the democrats suppose that those are the terms of reconstruction adopted by Congress and the Republican party is endorsing the Amendment en masse with that understanding." What if they are deceived and "it is the intention of Congress to exclude the South permanently or so long as the Republicans have control of Congress?" How could he go before the people on such an issue? "We must offer some perfected plan else our party will surely suffer defeat."[32] Others were asking the same thing.[33]

It is true that no pledge of admission on the basis of the adoption of the Fourteenth Amendment was made. Speakers did contribute to the assumption, it was certainly implied in many public and private statements, and it was occasionally stated outright that the admission of Tennessee demonstrated congressional policy. Columbus Delano did so in Coshocton, Ohio, when he pointed to Tennessee as a "guarantee that when a State ratifies this amendment, she will come in."[34]

Senator Trumbull, slow to break with Johnson and one of the more moderate spokesmen among the advocates of the amendment, did definitely promise at Evanston, Illinois, that when ratification should be complete, all states ratifying would be restored.[35] *Harper's*

---

[31] Joseph Medill to Trumbull, 17 July 1866, Trumbull Papers.

[32] Joseph Medill to E. B. Washburne, 17 July 1866, Washburne Papers.

[33] Henry Asbury to Trumbull, 21 July 1866, Trumbull Papers.

[34] *Cincinnati Commercial*, 31 August 1866.

[35] Ibid., 3 September 1866.

Weekly recognized that if there was a commitment by the party to restoration, it had emerged from congressional action, resolutions of state conventions, and the "general tone of the Union press." That journal's conclusion was that "virtually, therefore, Congress said that, in the present condition of public feeling, it was satisfied to admit a state which should do as Tennessee had done."[36]

Although it is true that the Southern attitude, intensified at least by Johnson, drove moderates into the Radicals' camp, it is not clear that ratification would have brought about readmission, at least in any swift manner and with no further conditions. As one of Senator Charles Sumner's correspondents put it, the amendment "is only an installment, not a finality."[37] Privately, Congressman John M. Broomall of Pennsylvania expressed his regret "that the public press persisted in putting forth the Amendment as the terms of reconstruction." Radicals had no such purpose.[38] Others were thinking about this same question of no pledge as the fall elections approached. Thaddeus Stevens, himself, was pointedly asked if he had ever "publicly by speech or letter declared that, if the Southern states ratified the Constitutional Amendment, [he would be] willing to admit them to representation in Congress?"[39] Unfortunately, no available record contains his possible reply. We do know that Stevens had no intention of early readmission if he could prevent it.

The *New York Herald* raised the question directly: "Shall the excluded States be restored, or shall they still be excluded?"[40] This question was said to be the real issue, but it was clouded, perhaps by intent. Speakers using familiar emotional tactics deliberately perpetuated war hatreds instead of working for a unified nation and decisions concerning the attainment of peace. Professor Howard K. Beale has termed the arguments about the Constitution "pure sham" although

---

[36]*Harper's Weekly*, 13 October 1866.

[37]Charles Sumner, *Memoir and Letters of Charles Sumner*, ed., Edward L. Pierce, 4 vols. (Boston: Roberts Brothers, 1877-1893) 4:311.

[38]J. M. Broomall to Stevens, 27 October 1866, Stevens Papers, Library of Congress.

[39]D. D. Thompson to Stevens, 22 October 1866, Stevens Papers.

[40]*New York Herald*, 21 August 1866.

they carried some weight due to widespread ignorance about the South. He is certainly correct in asserting that "Nobody understood" the exact relation of the Fourteenth Amendment to the fall campaign.[41]

Successful, though highly controversial, methods used in the unusual events surrounding the Tennessee ratification, were not allowed to delay for even a day the installation of that state's congressional delegation. (Congress's habit of avoiding critical evaluation of any certified official act of a state has long been a part of American history.) Even President Johnson, fully cognizant of the entire situation, quickly approved. As military governor of his native state during part of the late war, he was completely aware of conditions there and had acted on occasion in a manner reminiscent of "Parson" Brownlow. He had spoken out bitterly against all "rebels" in words that had been nationally quoted.

Despite the election of Andrew Johnson with Abraham Lincoln on the Union party ticket, he remained essentially a Democrat. There were, however, many points of agreement between him and Republicans who wished to restore the Union. His personal approach to the reconstruction problem was different from that of less conservative Republicans, but he had not repudiated the Fourteenth Amendment. He had used his powers to help secure Southern support for the Thirteenth Amendment, as Republicans now wished him to do for the Fourteenth.

By means of the National Union Convention, called through his influence to meet in Philadelphia in August, the President joined with conservative Republicans, Democrats, and Southern supporters. Restoration of the Union without further delay was the stated objective, but no mention of the Fourteenth Amendment as an obstacle to reconciliation was mentioned in the official call for the convention.

It seemed that this was the critical time when all efforts could be brought together for the purpose of peaceful restoration. The entire history of the next few years might well have been different if such a development had taken place. No specific "sticking points" existed,

---

[41]Howard K. Beale, *The Critical Year: A Study of Andrew Johnson and Reconstruction* (New York: Harcourt Brace, 1930) 147.

but a mutual attitude of distrust of political motives prevented the joining of forces. By the time the National Union Convention had assembled, the President and others had declared themselves opposed to the amendment and the opportunity was lost.

Chapter Four

Cross
Currents

The *Chicago Tribune*, which had earlier declared the amendment to be a compromise "by which the conscience of the North yielded four-fifths of its demands to the perverseness of the President and the obstinacy of circumstances," declared 25 June 1866 that the purpose of the North was to establish "impartial suffrage all over the land," and that this objective could best be served by the adamant refusal of the South to approve the Fourteenth Amendment.[1]

Ample evidence exists that the radical's purpose went much further. Thaddeus Stevens had said it was all that could be obtained at that time.[2] George S. Boutwell later summed up the opinion he rep-

---

[1]*Chicago Tribune*, 25 June 1866.

[2]*Congressional Globe*, 39th Cong., 1st sess., 3148.

resented by saying, "It was impossible in 1866 to go farther than the provisions of the Fourteenth Amendment."[3]

At the same time in late June, the *New York Herald* was also praising the amendment as a rejection of "the violent and obnoxious ideas and propositions of Thaddeus Stevens" and the adoption of the policy of the President. By so doing, Congress had "saved the Republican party from dissolution and had given it a powerful platform for the approaching fall elections."[4]

As for the South, the terms "may not be altogether palatable," said the *New York Times*, "but after all they are not unreasonable."[5] Chief Justice Salmon P. Chase was of the opinion that Congress would "now admit Senators and Representatives from such States lately in rebellion as may ratify this Amendment." No plan of admission had yet been approved but it would probably be on the condition of ratification and conformity of state laws to the amendment.[6] Old-line Democrats like Congressman Benjamin G. Harris of Maryland scorned the amendment and looked forward to the Southern states' rejection of it. "Thank Heaven," he said, "there are Southern States enough to make Southern contempt for it effectual."[7]

There were many of different political persuasions who believed that unrepresented states would be admitted if they ratified the amendment despite the deliberate failure of Congress to promise to admit them . Popular opinion might well have forced it.[8] Even after the election was over and advocates of the amendment had won in the North, General Ulysses S. Grant expressed the desire "to see the course that would be pursued" if Southern states began to ratify.[9]

---

[3]George S. Boutwell, *Reminiscences of Sixty Years in Public Affairs* (New York: McClure, Phillips Co, 1902) 1:41.

[4]*New York Herald*, 15 June 1866.

[5]*New York Times*, 15 June 1866.

[6]Chase to his daughter, 15 June 1866, Salmon P. Chase Papers, Library of Congress.

[7]*Congressional Globe*, 39th Cong., 1st sess., 3179.

[8]*Reminiscences of Carl Schurz* (New York: Doubleday, Page and Co., 1908-1909) 3:236-37.

[9]William B. Hesseltine, *U. S. Grant, Politician* (New York: Dodd, Mead & Co., 1935) 80.

It is possible, as Whitelaw Reid reported, that the South would have approved anything in the early days after the war.[10] However, beaten and baffled though Southern leaders were, they soon learned that they were faced not with absolute requirements but with options that they could accept or reject. They recalled that on the advice of the President they had accepted the Thirteenth Amendment. By the time the Fourteenth Amendment was referred to the states, the President and organized groups in the North were again applying pressure; this time for the South to resist ratification.[11] Without presidential pressure on the South to ratify the amendment, observed the *Chicago Tribune*, that section would undoubtedly reject the proposal.[12]

These pressures plus other contributing factors made unclear the proper course for Southerners to pursue. They were not certain that they should actively participate in the National Union Convention in August, but on the other hand, if they did not, their actions could be interpreted as evidence of disloyalty to the Union.[13] In addition, some acute observers believed that Johnson could not possibly be reelected, and that possibility posed a problem in following his advice.[14] Such doubts entered into the general belief that a strategy of "masterly inactivity" was the correct policy. The overall situation was pervaded by the ever-present maneuvering for positions of power in whatever political structure might evolve. While Radicals appeared to be testing how far they could go, some leaders in the South were testing what favorable agreement might be possible.[15] An

[10]Whitelaw Reid, *After the War; A Southern Tour, May 1, 1865 to May 1, 1866* (Cincinnati: Moore, Wilstark and Baldwin, 1866) 206-207.

[11]Avery Craven, *Reconstruction: The Ending of the Civil War* (New York: Holt, Rinehart and Winston, 1969) 72-91.

[12]*Chicago Tribune*, 15 June 1866.

[13]A. R. Wright to A. H. Stephens, 30 June 1866, A. H. Stephens Papers, Library of Congress.

[14]Herschel V. Johnson to A. H. Stephens, 5 July 1866, Herschel V. Johnson Papers, Duke University Library.

[15]Michael Perman, *Reunion Without Compromise: The South and Reconstruction, 1865-1869* (London: Cambridge University Press, 1973) 208-41.

element in all of this was the continuation of the Johnson policy of pardoning leading ex-Confederates.[16]

As to his politics in the North, the President was moving toward a new party to represent a realignment of old ones. He was cutting his ties with the Republicans who did not favor his policies, leaning closer to that part of the Democratic party that had cooperated in winning the war. It is possible to see how he could arrive at such a strategy in the dislocated politics of 1866, but it realistically left him without a stable base from which to operate within any existing party organization.[17]

In the days before 14 August and before the National Union Convention in Philadelphia which focused widespread publicity, much discussion of the amendment was reported in the press. These aspects of the mammoth congressional campaigns throw considerable light on our understanding of the Fourteenth Amendment and its relation to other issues both national and local.

Governor Oliver P. Morton of Indiana supported the proposed amendment in a 18 July speech, saying that the amendment was a necessary tool for preventing the South from taking the political power it had been offered by the Thirteenth Amendment (which had repealed the three-fifths compromise). Morton saw the defeated slave states gaining new seats in the House of Representatives with no assurance that blacks would be represented.[18]

In explanation of the first section, Morton declared:

> By this it is intended to throw the equal protection of the law around every person who may be within the jurisdiction of any state, whether citizen or alien, and without regard to condition or residence, not only as to life and liberty, but also as to property. It has happened in times past that several of the Southern States discriminated against the citizens of other States, by withholding the protection of the laws for life and liberty, and denying to them the ordinary remedies in the courts for the vindication of their civil rights, and hence the adoption of this provision.

---

[16]Jonathan T. Dorris, *Pardon and Amnesty Under Lincoln and Johnson: The Restoration of the Confederates to Their Rights and Privileges* (Chapel Hill: University of North Carolina Press, 1953) 324.

[17]David Donald, "Why They Impeached Andrew Johnson," *American Heritage* 8 (December, 1950) 25.

[18]*Cincinnati Commercial*, 19 July 1866.

This widely-quoted statement is significant in that it faithfully reflects the prevailing thought; it would be repeated by those familiar with the purposes of the amendment's framers. It shows what the understanding of ordinary citizens was as obtained from public discussion during the ratification process. It should be noted that Morton's emphasis was not on protecting blacks. In discussing other parts of the amendment, he was equally careful to emphasize that no suffrage for blacks was conferred, acknowledging that the states still had exclusive power to regulate the franchise. At the time, Northern states would not have favored it any other way. This was a very sensitive subject in many areas.

Senator Lyman Trumbull in a Chicago speech of 2 August specified that the Civil Rights Bill had been in accord with President Johnson's views, for Trumbull had introduced it after many personal conferences with the chief executive. The first section of the amendment, therefore, he had reason to think, was what Johnson had originally endorsed because it was "a reiteration of the rights set forth in the Civil Rights Bill" that had been passed over the executive veto. Perhaps it had been unnecessary to place it in a constitutional amendment, "but it had been thought proper to put in the fundamental law the declaration that all good citizens were entitled to equal rights in this Republic, and that all who were born here, or who came here from foreign lands and were naturalized, were to be deemed citizens of the United States in every State where they might happen to dwell."[19]

Trumbull explained that the second section based representation on voters, knowing full well that it did not. This topic had been thoroughly debated and although such a proposal had been made, it was defeated due to the larger percentage of those ineligible to vote, principally women and children in certain sections of the country, especially the East.[20] The third section merely disfranchized high Confederate officials, and the fourth guaranteed bounties and pen-

[19]*Chicago Tribune*, 2 August 1966.

[20]See Joseph B. James, *The Framing of the Fourteenth Amendment* (Urbana: University of Illinois Press, 1956) 56.

sions and specifically repudiated any obligations or payments to the South for emancipated slaves. In a final flourish, Trumbull asserted that all Democrats opposed these simple measures. This entire presentation is very much like many made in the campaign; it made the amendment seem only simple justice to which nobody had any rational reason to object.

Senator James H. Lane of Oregon spoke at Indianapolis while news of the National Union Convention was still reverberating throughout the land. He confirmed Trumbull's statement that the first section was "simply a re-affirmation of the first clause of the Civil Rights Bill." He would accept the section on representation, but as a Westerner whose state would benefit by it, he preferred representation of actual voters. In regard to suffrage, he reassured Indianans by saying that Congress had nothing to do with voting in Indiana.[21]

That same day, Representative Robert C. Schenck of Ohio spoke in Dayton. He also claimed that the amendment guaranteed what was already in the Civil Rights Bill; it put everybody on the same legal footing. Who could say that this was not just?[22] In this as in many statements made in the campaign, one gets the definite impression that those who justified the amendment before the voters were, in the words of Senator Fessenden of Maine, "terribly afraid of their constituents."[23]

A week later Senator Thomas A. Hendricks of Indiana gave a Democratic version of the situation in regard to the amendment.[24] While in Indianapolis, he asserted that 1866 was no time to amend the Constitution. Eleven states were unrepresented in Congress and the passions of war were still strong, with regional and partisan strife rampant.

In criticism of the second section, Hendricks claimed that it had been framed so that alien representation in the North might be continued and that Maryland, West Virginia, Tennessee, and Missiouri

---

[21]*Cincinnati Commercial*, 10 August 1866.

[22]Ibid.

[23]Francis Fessenden, *Life and Public Services of William Pitt Fessenden* (Boston: Houghton Mifflin Co., 1907) 2:118.

[24]*Cincinnati Commercial*, 9 August 1866.

might have full representation while half their voters were disfranchised. He emphasized that voting had always been considered a privilege, not a right. According to the amendment, he charged, blacks would now be eligible to hold office, serve on juries, and otherwise participate equally in all states including Indiana. Again a sensitive nerve was deliberately touched. In Hendricks' opinion, the third section seemed an unjust treatment of many who had held office under the Confederacy. As for the fourth section, Hendricks labeled it "the bondholders section." Many worthy men held bonds, "but this section is to quiet the fears of the contractors and public officers who have grown suddenly rich during the war, whose drawers are full of bonds and coupons." This was the main thrust of the amendment, claimed the Indiana Democrat. It was intended to be carried into law by its appeal to the masses on other points that had been artificially thrown together in one document. The conspiracy was to bind Congress so it could not pay the public debt in greenbacks or even to tax the bonds. Repudiation of the Confederate debt had been inserted merely to cover up this purpose.

Letters to other congressmen gave some basis for such claims. One from a banker to Justin Morrill claimed that payment in currency was really "a partial repudiation of the public debt."[25] Another fear voiced in speeches and letters was that if some combination of conservatives and Southerners could gain control, Confederate debts would be assumed and compensation for slaves would be undertaken.[26] As in a number of speeches, that of James A. Garfield of Ohio in late August emphasized the debt section. He apparently was concerned that a Democratic-election victory would bring Confederates to power with repudiation a principal objective.[27]

At the same time that Hendricks attacked the amendment, John A. Bingham made a rousing speech in favor of it. He was the principal author of the significant first section of the amendment and would be the leader in the House of an unsuccessful effort in the next session

---

[25]E. G. Spalding to Morrill, 23 July 1866, Morrill Papers, Library of Congress.

[26]See speech of Baker of Illinois, 9 July 1866 in *Congressional Globe*, 39th Cong., 1st sess., appendix p. 251.

[27]*Cincinnati Commercial*, 25 August 1866.

to pass an enabling act to admit representatives of seceded states to Congress upon ratification of the amendment.[28] Unlike some of his more statesmanlike efforts in Congress, this speech was full of election abandon in which he waved the "bloody shirt" with gusto. As one of its principal authors, however, his explanation of the first section is worth special attention. It gave the power to "any citizen" to correct wrongs done by a state; it would "protect alike the high and the low;" it embodied the golden rule and would prevent men in Georgia from being imprisoned, as in the past, for teaching the Bible. What Hendricks had termed the "bondholders section," protected pensions and other just claims. "We cannot desert the widows and orphans of loyal Union soldiers!" he shouted.[29]

The speech that Bingham delivered on 22 August in Bowerstown, Ohio, had much greater import.[30] Headlines in the *Cincinnati Commercial* read: "The Constitutional Amendment Discussed by Its Author." Yet a good part of the address ran like this:

> The issue, and the whole issue, to be decided in the coming election is, whether loyal men—men who kept unbroken through these years of conflict their obligations of fealty to the Constitution and government—shall rule it by just laws, or whether those who conspired through these years of conflict to overthrow that Government by arms, shall rule it by unjust laws and such legislation as must ultimately end in anarchy and the ruin of the Republic.

Nevertheless, he did comment directly on the meaning of the first section that he had done much to frame:

> It is the spirit of Christianity embodied in your legislation. It is a simple, strong, plain, declaration that equal laws and equal and exact justice shall hereafter be secured within every state of this Union by the combined power of all the people of every State. It takes from no State any right which hitherto pertained to the several States of the Union, but it imposes a limitation upon the States to correct their abuses of power, which hitherto did not exist within the letter of the Constitution, and which is essential to the nation's life.

One of the chief objects, he declared, was to give equal protection of law to all human beings.

---

[28]*Congressional Globe*, 39th Cong., 2d sess., 1080.

[29]*Cincinnati Commercial*, 10 August 1866.

[30]Ibid., 27 August 1866.

Hereafter, the American people can not have peace, if as in the past, States are permitted to take away freedom of speech, and to condemn men, as felons, to the penitentiary for teaching their fellow men that there is a hereafter, and a reward for those who learn to do well.

Another purpose of the second section was to make certain that a South Carolina voter should have no greater representation in Congress than a voter in Ohio. Furthermore, the fourth section would guarantee that no state could tax loyal people to pay for disloyalty. Bingham denounced moves to tax war bonds in the states as being Democratic talk aimed at reducing the value of the national obligation. "The Nation that won't keep faith with its defenders, living and dead, is not fit to have defenders, and cannot have them long." Disqualification of Confederate leaders he praised as the lightest kind of punishment. "They ought to thank God they are permitted to live anywhere on this side of the deepest hell."

After reading this speech one might well wonder what other presentations were like if editorial comment had any validity in praising him for a statesmanlike speech "without the verbiage of the stump orator, or the claptrap of the mere partisan."[31]

Another voice, *Frank Leslie's Illustrated Newspaper*, had gone so far as to assert that "the feelings of the different parties of the country are more embittered now than they were while the conflict was raging."[32] The *New York Times* called attention to Speaker Schuyler Colfax's speech in Indianapolis.[33] Obviously hoarse from daily speaking, he reached a peak of oratory by claiming that he loved the amendment because it rehearsed the contents of the Declaration of Independence. Refusal of the South to adopt the proposal would be something that the South would long regret. Suffrage for blacks, however, he asserted to be unessential to citizenship.[34] This last was directed toward allaying the concern of people in the Midwest, In-

---

[31] Ibid.

[32] *Frank Leslie's Illustrated Newspaper*, 4 August 1866.

[33] *New York Times*, 7 August 1866.

[34] *Cincinnati Commercial*, 9 August 1866.

diana in particular, about giving the vote to blacks in their states or to interfere by national law with the state control of the franchise.

In a Cleveland address on 3 September, President Johnson threw the challenge of suffrage for blacks into the teeth of those who advocated it by indirection in the Fourteenth Amendment. "You complain of the disfranchisement of the negroes in the Southern States, while you would not give them the right to suffrage in Ohio today. Let your negroes vote in Ohio before you talk about negroes voting."[35]

Concern about suffrage for blacks in the North spread far beyond those in the Midwest. Hamilton Fish of New York expressed his lack of support for "that part of the proposed Amendment which restricts the control of each State over the laws regulating suffrage within its limits by making the exercise of that control the price of representation in the Federal Congress."[36]

Statistical analysis of the practical effect of the Fourteenth Amendment should blacks not be permitted to vote in Northern states had already been published in the *Chicago Tribune*. According to this presentation, several states in the North owed a member in Congress to the presence of sizable numbers of black people. Even in Illinois, it was asserted that the eight thousand blacks who resided there almost made the difference between the fraction of a unit (seventy-three thousand) on which that state received a fourteenth representative. Ohio, Pennsylvania, New York, and Indiana would have to choose between allowing the black vote under the Fourteenth Amendment or losing a representative in Congress. New Jersey and Connecticut might lose one should they deny blacks the vote.[37] With such publicity, small wonder that in a state like Indiana, politicians seeking votes had to soft-pedal the importance of the suffrage provisions in the amendment.

---

[35]Walter L. Fleming, *Documentary History of Reconstruction* (Cleveland: Arthur H. Clark Co., 1906-1907) 1:226.

[36]Hamilton Fish to Charles Dana, F. A. Conkling, et al., 12 October 1866, quoted in Allen Nevins, *Hamilton Fish: The Inner History of the Grant Administration* (New York: Dodd, Mead & Co., 1936) 101.

[37]*Chicago Tribune*, 19 June 1866.

The *Atlantic Monthly* printed one of several analyses of the constitutional proposal, claiming: "There is not a distinctly 'radical' idea in the whole amendment." The article elaborated:

> It simply ordains that the national debt shall be paid and the Rebel debt repudiated; that the civil rights of all persons shall be maintained; that Rebels who have added perjury to treason shall be disqualified for office; and that the Rebel States shall not have their political power in the Union increased by the presence on their soil of persons to whom they deny political rights, but that representation shall be based throughout the Republic on voters, and not on population. The pith of the amendment is in the last clause.

The amendment, in conclusion, was described as being "conciliatory, moderate, lenient, almost timid." The saviors of the country were arrayed for it, with Johnson heading the opposition that included all rebels.[38] Thus was the war feeling deliberately injected into the debate.

In a more calmly worded statement, *Harper's Weekly* stated what it deemed to be the issue:

> The question is whether the Democratic party with its tendency and policy clearly understood, shall determine the conditions upon which the late rebel States shall resume their full relations in the Union. Is the Democratic view of the situation truer, is the Democratic interpretation of the Constitution more just, is the spirit of the Democratic party move favorable to justice, equal liberty, and reverence for law, than those of the Union party. These are the questions which must determine our votes in the coming elections.[39]

In such a manner was the fate of the Fourteenth Amendment wrapped up in the decision at the polls.

Extremists were not pleased with what advocates of the Fourteenth Amendment called a just and reasonable basis for settling the most pressing problem of the country—disunity. Moderates, although sometimes critical, felt that peace could be achieved on the basis of ratification. Southern states would then be readmitted, pledge or no pledge. Popular opinion would demand their restoration. Even those who were most doubtful about the Fourteenth

---

[38]"The Johnson Party," *Atlantic Monthly* (July 1866): 18:378-79.

[39]*Harper's Weekly*, 28 July 1866.

Amendment felt it to be the best plan obtainable under the circumstances.

As time went on, however, those representing special viewpoints began to organize to increase their influence, tending to fragment public opinion. President Johnson, with the help of Northern supporters, encouraged Southern delay. In the disarray of the traditional parties, a new alignment might emerge. Conservative Republicans, Southern supporters of presidential reconstruction, and some Democrats moved to unite their efforts under the leadership of Andrew Johnson. Other groups sought to combine in various ways to gain approval for the amendment.

Using emotional tactics to continue war feelings, Radicals provided solid support of the amendment, construing it as the only way to guarantee the important results of the war and to prevent the South from resuming power in the national government. When local sentiment permitted, they urged suffrage for blacks as a support for war gains. The Thirteenth Amendment had erased the three-fifths compromise and blacks were now to be counted as whole persons for the purpose of figuring representation. They believed that civil liberties would be endangered without the amendment.

Some feared that this piece of legislation would endanger the balance of power between the states and federal government. Others proclaimed that bondholders would be the principal beneficiaries from the debt-guarantee section. Still others held that widows and orphans needed its protection to be sure of their pensions. Many argued that state rights, including the right to regulate suffrage, might be lost. They were not necessarily opposed to suffrage for blacks, but, by taking this position, presented a common front with those who opposed votes for blacks.

Amid all these views, a strong body of opinion still regarded the Fourteenth Amendment as a reasonable and generous document that was needed to pave the way for peace and prosperity. As in most modern elections, there were so many varied and complicated issues, some not even related to the amendment, that a clear mandate on any one of them would be impossible to determine.

Chapter Five

The
Growing Storm

Riots in Memphis in May and in New Orleans at the end of July were not good omens for the National Union Convention that assembled in Philadelphia on 14 August. As interpreted in the North, they were patent proofs of the failure of Johnson's Southern policy. Democrats actually accused Radicals of instigating bloodshed in the South.[1] Efforts at reconciliation between president and Congress largely ceased with the August convention.[2]

---

[1] W. E. Smith, *The Francis Preston Blair Family in Politics* (New York: MacMillan Co., 1933) 2:375; "Is the South Ready for Reconstruction?" Campaign pamphlet, Library of Congress, 14.

[2] Leon Burr Richardson, *William E. Chandler, Republican* (New York: Dodd, Mead & Co., 1910) 71.

Democrats and Conservatives of the North urged Southern representatives to come to the three-day meeting in Philadelphia.[3] Despite many misgivings, a goodly number did respond. After the meeting concluded, people like Herschel V. Johnson of Georgia and Governor William L. Sharkey of Mississippi claimed that it had been a success.[4]

Usually, antisecessionists of some prominence and others less notable were selected as delegates from the South; leading exconfederates were generally omitted or refused to participate.[5] The appearance of being ultraconservative or being associated with Northern antiwar policies was carefully avoided. C. L. Vallandigham and Fernando Wood had to be sidetracked tactfully.[6] Most newspapers in the South reacted favorably, but there was some criticism.[7] Governor James L. Orr and B. F. Perry of South Carolina attended as did Alexander H. Stephens after much hesitation. General Richard Taylor claimed that Johnson insisted on his being present to "promote good feelings and an early restoration of the Union, and give aid to the President in his struggle with the extremists."[8] Henry J. Raymond of the *New York Times* supported the convention, though with some doubts.[9] Opponents of the President thought the assembly would have the effect of tempering the demands of Radicals.[10]

When the convention convened, James R. Doolittle of Wisconsin, John A. Dix of New York, John A. Andrew of Massachusetts, and

---

[3]Michael Perman, *Reunion Without Compromise: The South and Reconstruction, 1865-1869* (London: Cambridge University Press, 1973) 212-18.

[4]*Richmond Times*, 17 August 1866; *Jackson Clarion*, 8 September 1866.

[5]Perman, *Reunion Without Compromise*, 220.

[6]Van Deusen, *William H. Seward* (New York: Oxford University Press, 1967) 459; James G. Randall and David Donald, *Civil War and Reconstruction* (Lexington MA: C. C. Heath and Co., 1969) 599.

[7]*Lynchburg Republican*, 21 August 1866.

[8]Richard Taylor, *Destruction and Reconstruction: Personal Experiences of the Late War* (New York: Appleton Co., 1879) 253.

[9]*New York Times*, 1 September 1866; Eric L. McKitrick, *Andrew Johnson and Reconstruction* (Chicago: University of Chicago Press, 1960) 395.

[10]*New York Times*, 25 August 1866.

James Dixon of Connecticut were leading figures from the North. All states and all territories were represented, except Utah, Arizona, and Montana. Doolittle was made chairman. The theme of unity was dramatized by the delegates of Massachusetts and South Carolina entering arm in arm to tumultuous applause. Raymond read the opening address that had previously been approved by a convention committee.[11] A platform or statement of principles was adopted opposing the Fourteenth Amendment and supporting Johnson. This resolution insisted that in amending the Constitution according to its provisions, "all states of the Union have an equal and indefeasable right to a voice and a vote thereon."[12] It went on record that control of the franchise was a reserved right of the individual states with which Congress would not interfere.[13]

In other parts of the resolution, there was recognition of the "sacred and inviolable" nature of the national debt and the invalid character of "any obligation incurred in making war against the United States."[14] Other principles adopted included the immediate return to Congress of Southern representatives, the constitutional right of each state to determine its voters, and federal aid to Union soldiers and their families.[15]

As if in reply to the National Union Convention, a Southern Unionist assembly was held in Philadelphia on 13 September. It represented discontent with presidential policies and called for protection of its rights by the Fourteenth Amendment.[16] Frederick Douglass was a delegate from New York and although the assembly did not endorse suffrage for blacks, his presence caused some em-

---

[11]*New York Herald*, 15 August 1866; *Harper's Weekly*, 1 September 1866; *Annual Cyclopedia* (1866) 757.

[12]Edward McPherson, *The Political History of the United States of America during the Period of Reconstruction* (Washington DC: Philip and Solomons, 1871) 214.

[13]Ibid., 241; Walter L. Fleming, *Documentary History of Reconstruction* (Cleveland: Arthur H. Clark Co., 1906) 1:213-15.

[14]Ibid.

[15]Smith, *The Blair Family*, 2:370; *Proceedings of the National Union Convention* (1866) 16-17.

[16]*Annual Cyclopedia* (1866) 816, 758.

barrassment to those already trying to hold back such tendencies.[17] Although it endorsed the Fourteenth Amendment, the statement was mild. The meeting was promptly dubbed "The Black and Tan Convention."[18]

Still later in September a Soldiers and Sailors Convention met in Cleveland, Ohio[19] in support of Johnson's program. Later, another military group assembled in Pittsburgh, Pennsylvania. It was a meeting sponsored by the President's opponents. Benjamin F. Butler launched an attack on Johnson and set the mood for this meeting.[20]

While all these conventions were creating national excitement, President Johnson issued a proclamation on 20 August declaring the end of the insurrection in all states. (Texas alone had not been included in a previous proclamation in April.) In the President's words, "peace, order, tranquility and civil authority now exist in and throughout the whole of the United States of America."[21] The proclamation would have special implications later as Congress moved into its program of military reconstruction.

In the courts, the Milligan case had already been argued in the spring and a decision by the Supreme Court had been reached, though it was not to be announced with its full opinion until December.[22] The usual indiscreet comments by justices had caused the thinking of the court to be known by a good many.[23] The issue of the

---

[17]Thaddeus Stevens to William D. Kelley, Stevens Papers, Library of Congress; Michael Les Benedict, *A Compromise of Principle: Congressional Republicans and Reconstruction, 1863-1869* (New York: W. W. Norton and Co., 1974) 200.

[18]John Hope Franklin, *Reconstruction: After the Civil War* (Chicago: University of Chicago Press, 1961) 66; Benedict, *A Compromise of Principle*, 200.

[19]*Annual Cyclopedia* (1866) 759.

[20]Robert S. Holtzman, *Stormy Ben Butler* (New York: MacMillan Co., 1954) 163.

[21]Richardson, *A Compilation of the Messages and Papers of the Presidents, 1789-1897* (Washington DC: Bureau of National Literature and Arts, 1898) 6:434-38.

[22]Charles Fairman, *Reconstruction and Reunion: 1864-1888*, vol. 6 in *History of the Supreme Court* ed., Paul A. Freund (New York: MacMillan Co., 1971).

[23]Orville Hickman Browning, *The Diary of Orville Hickman Browning*, ed., Theodore C. Pease and J. G. Randall (Springfield IL: Collections of the Illinois State Historical Library, 1933, 1938) 2:67, 69-70; Charles Fairman, *Mr. Justice Miller and the Supreme Court* (Cambridge: Harvard University Press, 1939) 130-31.

power of a military tribunal in an area where civil authority was in control had arisen in Indiana during the war and had been argued before the highest court by the esteemed advocate, Jeremiah Black, assisted by no less an emerging Republican than Congressman James A. Garfield,[24] arguing for civil supremacy against a team that included B. F. Butler of Massachusetts.

The case was little noted at the time but was to assume immense importance in 1867 during the later stages of the ratification of the Fourteenth Amendment. Before the proclamation of the end of all insurrection, Justice Samuel Nelson decided in chambers *In re Egan* that "the moment the rebellion was suppressed, the ancient laws resumed their accustomed sway."[25]

Although much had been said in the early summer about special sessions of legislatures being called to pass on the proposal to amend the Constitution, New Jersey was the first. The governor's proclamation of an extra session was issued 30 August; it assembled 10 September. Governor Marcus Ward's message recommended ratification as "the most lenient amnesty ever offered to treason, while every provision is wisely adapted to the welfare of the whole country."[26] Immediately the next day, 11 September, the measure passed the House thirty-four to twenty-four.

Even in the more sedate Senate, the ratification vote was not long delayed. Scovill, addressing this body, expressed the usual points: fear of renewed power of the South in national government and the need of guarantees for the future. Mincing no words he asserted that Congress should make impartial suffrage the basis of recognizing the state governments in the South once the presidentially recognized governments had been overturned. Such action seemed necessary to Scovill in order to give permanence to institutions, the character of which had been settled by the long and bloody struggle. All this he believed to be closely related to faith in true democracy and the

---

[24]Fairman, *Reconstruction and Reunion*, 143.

[25]Ibid.

[26]Ibid., 148.

expressions concerning the equality of man in the Declaration of Independence.[27]

Winfield, an opposition spokesman, proclaimed what he saw as being increasingly apparent—there was no known end to the conditions demanded by Radicals in Congress. No sooner had one set of conditions, said to be necessary as guarantees for the future, been complied with by Southern states than new conditions were put forward. Unless Congress laid down this Fourteenth Amendment as the sole and complete basis for accepting the South back into a normal relationship to the Union, nothing would be accomplished by ratification.[28] This analysis gradually came to be the accepted argument against the amendment despite implied conclusion to the contrary in 1866.

Scovill replied with added explanations in a running debate that expended the afternoon until the vote was taken at half past four. The close vote of eleven to ten was announced while numerous spectators in the galleries clapped their hands and cheered until by order of the chair, they were quieted. That same day the articles of ratification were signed by Governor Marcus L. Ward.[29] In September, New Jersey thus became the fourth state to approve officially the omnibus amendment submitted in June as a platform for the November elections. It is important to note the closeness of the vote in this very strategic state legislature, for a shift in party strength as a result of legislative elections would bring unusual results in the fight for ratification.

On the very same day that New Jersey went on record in favor of the Fourteenth Amendment, the legislature of the state of Oregon heard Governor A. C. Gibbs recommend ratification.[30] That Oregon body was made up of Republican majorities of fourteen to eight in the Senate and twenty-four to twenty-three in the House.[31] The po-

---

[27]*New York Herald*, 12 September 1866.

[28]Ibid.; *Annual Cyclopedia* (1866) 339.

[29]Ibid.

[30]*Oregon House Journal* (1866), appendix, 427.

[31]*Annual Cyclopedia* (1866) 605.

litical situation was so close in the House that later events were to upset this majority and create another special problem concerning the ratification of the amendment.

In his inaugural address on 12 September, the new Governor of Oregon, George L. Woods, emphasized that the South must accept congressional terms in order to be readmitted into active partnership in the Union. These terms were, in the opinion of the new governor, both lenient and proper. Failure to ratify the proposed amendment "is a tacit admission of their part that they will not yield obedience, and insist on dictating their own terms." In urging the amendment's approval by the Oregon legislature, Governor Woods declared that "Upon its incorporation into the supreme law depends the safety, prosperity and permanence of the republic."[32]

That same day, the Senate Committee on Federal Relations received the proposed ratification resolution. Early the next day, 13 September, this committee reported favorably. The challenge of a tabling motion was successfully withstood by a vote of fourteen to eight, and the measure was made the special order of business for the following day.[33]

A second challenge in the form of a motion to refer the question to the voters was rejected on 14 September by the same vote, fourteen to eight. Only on the final vote did the solid Republican phalanx waver. On this test, the division was thirteen to nine in favor of ratification. This came at the end of an afternoon of sharp parliamentary battle during which a motion to adjourn had to be defeated before voting on the amendment was possible.[34]

After passage in the Senate, the resolution of ratification was referred to the judiciary committee of the lower house on 17 September. After two days, it was favorably reported, meeting a barrage of parliamentary obstacles such as countermotions to table and refer. On into the evening the debate continued. A climactic moment came when two members of the judiciary committee that had reported in favor of the resolution entered a formal protest that they "were not

---

[32]*Oregon House Journal* 29-30.

[33]*Oregon Senate Journal* (1866) 25ff.

[34]Ibid., 36.

notified of any meeting of the committee at any time, nor were they at any time consulted with reference to said report."

Finally, however, the previous question was called and the motion adopted by a vote of twenty-five to twenty-one.[35] The closeness of this vote in the House in approving the Senate resolution to ratify is especially important in view of two things: first, the later surrender to Democrats of two disputed seats held by Republicans at the opening of the session;[36] and second, the later attempts of the Oregon legislature to rescind its ratification of the Fourteenth Amendment.

As the party battle thundered toward its climax in the North, the first of the states operating under the presidential plan in the South took up the matter of ratification. The state was Texas. In August, Governor J. W. Throckmorton had recommended the rejection of the proposal as "impolitic, unwise, and unjust." The loyalty of Texas to the Federal government was strongly asserted "notwithstanding the . . . untoward direction given to measures proposed for the settlement of the grave questions growing out of the late unhappy contest between the Government and the Southern States, and notwithstanding the measures so proposed have received the sanction of the National Legislature, yet . . . with proper conduct on our part, I do not despair of receiving liberal and generous treatment from our Northern countrymen." Johnson's policy was praised as an indication of the fairness already beginning to be apparent in public sentiment, replacing the "wild hurricane of passion, engendered by fanaticism and misguided philanthropy."[37]

No action was forthcoming from the Texas legislature for two months while its members watched and listened to the events transpiring in the North. As the House Committee was preparing its report to be presented in October, Rutherford B. Hayes, congressman from Ohio, wrote to Guy M. Bryan of Texas that "this plan contains the best terms you will ever get—and they should be promptly ac-

---

[35]*Oregon House Journal* 76-77.

[36]*Annual Cyclopedia* (1866) 605.

[37]*Texas House Journal* (1866) 19-20.

cepted." As an additional warning, he added, "Don't let Andy Johnson deceive you. He don't know the Northern people."[38]

On 13 October, Ashbell Smith made the report for the Federal Relations Committee of the House of Representatives. Although it based its unfavorable recommendation primarily on the substance of the proposals rather than procedure, its arguments were prefaced by a statement that "the proposing of these Amendments to States which were excluded from all participation in their initiation in Congress, is a nullity." Constitutional requirements, reported the House Committee, had been "violated in letter and in spirit."[39]

Point by point the Texas legislative committee analyzed the amendment. The first section, in the opinion of the representatives, "proposes to deprive the States of the right which they have possessed since the revolution of 1776 to determine what shall constitute citizenship of a State." It was not desirable to abandon the broad constitutional principles previously adhered to and to transfer to Congress almost unlimited power.[40] The most violent attack was reserved for the second and third sections. These sections constituted a "nefarious conspiracy to transfer, as far as crafty and iniquitous legislation can effect the object, the government, the civilization of these States from the white race to the negroes." Justice for the black man was a transparent pretence, for many states in the North had always denied the vote to free blacks. Because the black population of the South was a large proportion of the whole, such an enfranchisement would destroy the political and social institutions in these states.

The third section would mean the virtual disqualification of all people who might be considered truly eligible to hold office. It would be both wicked and weak "to barter our birthright for the empty shadow of representation offered in these Amendments." The proposal asked them "to be the instruments of the degradation of their

[38]Rutherford B. Hayes to Guy M. Bryan, 1 October 1866 quoted in Rutherford B. Hayes, *Diary and Letters of Rutherford B. Hayes*, ed., Charles Richard Williams (Columbus OH: Ohio State Archaeological Society, 1924) 3:32-33.

[39]*Texas House Journal*, 577; Charles W. Ramsdell, *Reconstruction in Texas* (New York: Columbia University Studies in History, Economics, and Public Law, 1910) 120.

[40]*Texas House Journal*, 578.

own people."[41] In this argument one glimpses a substantial objection that is not merely a reaction against unpleasant terms. It is a realization that if enforced, the disqualification of leaders and the simultaneous enfranchisement of those who heretofore had exercised no part in government would leave the representation in Washington of no value to those called upon to ratify—they would not be represented.

The principle of the fourth section was not objected to, but was of no importance in Texas since it was already provided for in their state constitution. The fifth section, however, was seen by the committee as leaving the control of the state legislative, judicial, and executive functions to the mercy of a congressional majority.[42]

In conclusion, the committee claimed that the proposed amendment was a virtual repeal of the Tenth Amendment—in short, a complete constitutional revolution in the relationship of states to the central government. In spite of the Radicals' dire threats as to what would happen should the amendment be rejected, the recommendation of the committee was based on principle. The state of Texas would obey in good faith the Constitution as amended should the proposal be ratified. This was pledged despite expressed disapproval of constitutional procedures used in its proposal. The resolution to "not ratify" was approved by a vote of seventy to five.[43]

An adverse report of a Senate committee was likewise sustained in that body.[44] This report, presented on 22 October, placed emphasis on two things: false premises of the proposed amendment and the interference with citizenship and franchise requirements of the states. In the first instance, it was pointed out that, contrary to most Northern opinion, the Southern people were not hostile and that their representation in Congress would not be in any way dangerous to the country. Similarly, there was no hostility toward blacks that

---

[41]Ibid., 578-80; *New York Herald*, 31 October 1866.

[42]*Texas House Journal*, 580.

[43]Ibid., 580-82. This rather concrete picture of what might be in store for Texas as the result of rejection shows a more realistic analysis by Southerners than is generally supposed.

[44]*Texas Senate Journal* (1866) 415; Ramsdell, *Reconstruction in Texas*, 120.

would "spend its fury upon the head of the devoted African, unless the federal government interposes in his behalf." The loyalty of Texas and the South was wrongly questioned. Any foreign foe of the United States would unhesitatingly be fought by those who had openly and honestly withdrawn from Congress, accepted the issue of war, and frankly acknowledged defeat.[45]

There was no hatred of blacks, the committee reported. They had not sought these freedoms, nor the rights of citizenship. Texas was willing to grant citizenship but not the power to vote, because, as they saw it, the moral and intellectual status of blacks was not considered to be good enough to make their voting safe or wise. As to the disqualification of Texas leaders, it would be ex post facto to punish in this manner for treason.[46]

In summary, the committee considered the proposed amendment as "unnecessary, and dangerous to the future peace of the Republic" because it not only was based on false assumptions but sought to "alter the form and fashion of our Government, centralize all power in the Federal Congress, making the States mere appendages to a vast oligarchy at the National Capital." It would force Texas to disfranchise and call traitors its noblest men, and give blacks the suffrage. The committee considered that adoption of the proposal involved the "loss of honor as a people, and our self-respect as individual men." Believing these things and that adoption would not hasten harmony or give representation in Congress, the committee of the Senate recommended concurrence in the House resolution to reject the amendment "respectfully, but firmly." This was done by a vote of twenty-seven to one on 27 October.[47]

While Texas debated and acted on the Fourteenth Amendment, the political campaign moved toward its conclusion in the North. Carl Schurz delivered a strong radical speech, typical of many others, in Philadelphia on 8 September.[48] Thaddeaus Stevens spoke very sim-

---

[45]*Texas Senate Journal*, 418-23.

[46]Ibid., 420.

[47]Ibid., 423.

[48]Carl Schurz, *Speeches, Correspondences, and Political Papers of Carl Schurz*, ed., Frederick Bancroft (New York: G. P. Putnam, 1913) 379-416.

ilarly in Bedford a few days earlier[49] and was likewise widely quoted in the press. Schurz began his address by blaming the administration for not carrying out the North's common resolve at war's end to reinstate seceded states only after imposing "irreversible stipulations" that would keep intact the results of the war. It will be remembered that Schurz had made an extended tour of the South in the summer of 1865 at the invitation of the President and under the persuasion of Stanton, Chase, and Sumner. The purpose of the trip was to gather information about conditions in the South. His report had been regarded as ammunition for a radical program and had been published under pressure from Congress.[50]

Now a year later, Schurz declared that the situation posed great danger if no firm guarantees were required. "You admit the late rebel States to representation and power in the National Government such as they are, unconditionally; you remove the brakes from the reactionary movement without having first secured and fortified the results of the war by amendments to the Federal Constitution; and I predict the reaction will go so far as to call in question all legislation that was had during the absence from Congress of the eleven rebel States."

According to Schurz, Southerners and Johnsonites would together gain majority control of Congress and repeal all obstacles to the admission of rebel leaders. Representation of the South would be increased, thus adding to the dangers. Of course all laws aimed at protecting the newly freed black man would be repealed. The new majority would then demand compensation for slaves and damage done by the armies. Pensions would be cancelled, thus causing much suffering to the widows and orphans of the war. The majority that Schurz feared might even authorize pensions to Confederate soldiers. It might go so far as to thwart all worthwhile legislation until the rebel debt be assumed. Northern support might be bought by the

---

[49]*Cincinnati Commercial*, 11 September 1866.

[50]Joseph B. James, *Framing of the Fourteenth Amendment* (Urbana IL: University of Illinois Press, 1956) 11, 51, 107-17; Schurz Report is in *Senate Documents*, 39th Cong., 1st sess., no. 2, p. 14ff.

issuance of bonds in such quantities that the credit of the nation would be ruined.

Schurz summarized the Fourteenth Amendment in these words: "It declares citizens all persons born or naturalized in the United States, and provides that such citizens shall be protected in the enjoyment of equal rights in whatever State they may reside." It would provide for equality of representation and for the disqualification of leaders of the rebellion. "Finally," he stated, "it provides that the validity of the National debt of the United States, including debt incurred by the payment of pensions, or bounties, shall not be questioned." The current political campaign he described as "the final battle of the war."

Such a speech indicates the appeal to special interests and war passions. As stated by Benjamin F. Wade at Ottowa, Ohio, four days later, "It is a continuation of the controversy through which you have gone. There is no change in the issues and the very men today that supported the policy of Jefferson Davis and were advocates of his system of government, are the same who now support Mr. Johnson."[51] Benjamin F. Butler, as presiding officer of the Republican state convention in Massachusetts, presented the issue in a similar fashion. "Shall those who have betrayed the country and tried to destroy it by force or by fraud control its destiny in the otherwise glorious future?"[52] Schurz privately estimated that "public sentiment is quite as it was in 1860."[53] Rutherford B. Hayes closed his remarks in Ohio by saying that some might say certain provisions, especially about the debt, were unnecessary, but one could not trust "rebels and Democrats."[54]

Faced in many areas by a possible handicap due to the drastic oratory of Sumner, Stevens, and other extremists, some Republican campaigners in the fall of 1866 were glad to read the soothing analysis of the *New York Herald* on 13 September.

---

[51]*Cincinnati Commercial*, 13 September 1866.

[52]*New York Herald*, 14 September 1866.

[53]Carl Schurz to his wife, 5 September 1866 in Carl Schurz, *Intimate Letters of Carl Schurz* (Madison WI: State Historical Society of Wisconsin, 1928) 368.

[54]*Cincinnati Commercial*, 8 September 1866.

There is nothing, after all, so very objectionable about this amendment—nothing which President Johnson himself has not, at one time or another, recommended to some Southern State or to Congress, and nothing upon which there should have been a disagreement between the President and Congress.

It is not the platform of Thaddeus Stevens, Sumner, or any of the noisy radicals of Congress. They can do nothing. It was adopted against their remonstrances and in spite of their threats. It embodies substantially, in fact, the President's original programs.

Harper's Weekly joined in, denouncing Thaddeus Stevens and Charles Sumner as persons without power in Congress. "Not a single important measure, sponsored by Stevens except the appointment of the committee had been adopted by the House." Sumner's proposals for impartial suffrage as a condition had received practically no support in Congress.[55]

These arguments fitted nicely with those given in a Cincinatti speech by Senator John Sherman of Ohio near the end of September. It, like speeches by less moderate speakers, was widely quoted. No radical measures came out of the committee that framed the Fourteenth Amendment, asserted Sherman. "That committee that has been the most conservative committee that ever sat in the Congress of the United States, although they are trying to prove to you that is so grossly Radical." As to the amendment, he declared, "we defeated every Radical proposition in it."[56]

That the arguments of the Republican campaign were inconsistent is frankly admitted in a most interesting bit of correspondence from B. R. Cowan, the chairman of the Ohio State Central Committee. In a letter to Chase in October, this campaign leader commented that "In the reserve counties some of our Speakers have openly advocated impartial suffrage, while in other places it was thought necessary, not only to repudiate it, but to oppose it."[57] Senator Henry Wilson of Massachusetts, when the elections were over, admitted the same sort of thing in an exchange with Senator Willard Saulsbury of Delaware

---

[55]*Harper's Weekly*, 6 October 1866.

[56]*Cincinnati Commercial*, 29 September 1866.

[57]B. R. Cowan to S. P. Case, 12 October 1866, Case Manuscripts, Library of Congress.

who was chiding him for avoiding suffrage for blacks as an issue in his state. "Knowing very well that I was in a state in which little progress had been made," replied Wilson. "I acted somewhat on the scriptural principle of giving 'milk to babes.'" He added that he had not hesitated to give "strong meat" in other sections.[58] These tactics of saying one thing in one place and another in a different locale have become more difficult with modern means of communication, but they apparently were effective in 1866.

Though the National Union Convention that met 16 August in Philadelphia passed a resolution opposing the Fourteenth Amendment, it exerted every effort to make it known that its sentiments and purposes were peaceful and its members men dedicated to the cause of unity. Its resolutions and speeches agreed with all parts of the amendment except those particularly singled out as not acceptable. These were concerned with the disqualification of leading ex-Confederates and the enfranchising of blacks. It offered a dramatic exhibition of North-South unity.

Other national meetings took place in Philadelphia, Cleveland, and Pittsburgh; the latter two conventions composed of those who had served in the military services. Publicity was given to them all in the press. Also in August, President Johnson had officially proclaimed the end of all war in the United States and peace throughout its borders.

Ratification of the Fourteenth Amendment had not been forgotten in the state legislatures. Connecticut, New Hampshire, and Tennessee had been followed by New Jersey and Oregon. There were lengthy arguments on both sides of the issue in both states. As in New Hampshire, there was considerable opposition, but resolutions of ratification passed. The Oregon struggle led to later issues about rescinding its action.

Texas also took up the proposed change in the Constitution but delayed action until October. The second and third sections bore the brunt of its criticism. One point of particular significance emerged: with the black vote and the disqualification of the ablest leadership in the state, representation in Congress, Texans declared, would be of

---

[58]*Congressional Globe*, 39th Cong., 2d sess., 42.

no value. This Southern state was the first to refuse ratification. Debate in the North varied in tone and substance from place to place, depending on the attitude of leading speakers. Even leading Radicals spoke calmly and moderately in some areas and emotionally in others. In that day of slow communication, it was possible to project several images in the same election.

Chapter Six

Gusty
Gales

Critical personal decisions necessarily were being made by many in public life. Politicians were having to choose among various courses that might decisively affect their future political careers. An example is Senator W. P. Fessenden of Maine, chairman of the Joint Committee on Reconstruction, which had framed the Fourteenth Amendment and recommended it to the Congress and to the country. He was not an extremely radical Republican, but he was not yet prepared to follow the lead of the President. Johnson had not made it easy to do so. In September, Fessenden received a letter from Hugh McCulloch, able member of the cabinet, which sought to make the choice harder. "I fear," wrote the secretary of the treasury, "that in severing yourself from the administration, you missed a grand opportunity of making yourself the foremost man in the nation."[1] The

[1]McCulloch to W. P. Fessenden, 11 September 1866, W. P. Fessenden Papers, Library of Congress.

moderate Fessenden was one of the Republicans who again made the hard choice in 1868 by voting against Johnson's conviction when he (Johnson) was impeached. This time he broke with the congressional majority. Others were making equally agonizing decisions about their proper course. John Sherman, Ohio senator, carefully was feeling his way through the political quicksands.[2] He survived and remained an extremely prominent figure on the political scene for many years.

Democrats repeatedly referred to the issue of restoration versus continued disunion. In New York, John T. Hoffman, Democratic gubernatorial candidate, presented the issue in this manner:

> What is the issue? It is whether secession, having been put down in theory and in practice—whether slavery, having been abolished—whether the South, having submitted to the authority of the government, the Southern States shall be represented in the Congress of the United States by loyal men.[3]

Some practical considerations such as representation and the effect of the Thirteenth Amendment in obliterating the three-fifths compromise were considered. *Harper's Weekly* commented that the North would be extremely foolish to permit admission of Southern representatives to Congress prior to some adjustment of the means of representation. Such adjustments to prevent actual gains in political influence by the South as a result of the war could never be made after restoration of representation.[4]

Graphically, the *New York Herald* illustrated the undesirable effect the Thirteenth Amendment would have if the basis of representation were not changed. A table of quotas showed that all the states of the South would gain at least one representative over the number alloted in 1860 as the direct result of the Thirteenth Amendment. In contrast, if suffrage for blacks should not be granted after adoption of the Fourteenth Amendment, each of these same states would lose two of the representatives permitted under the three-fifths compro-

---

[2] Roger D. Bridges, "The Constitutional World of John Sherman, 1861-1869" (Ph.D. diss., University of Illinois, 1970) 185-95.

[3] *New York Herald*, 13 September 1866.

[4] *Harper's Weekly*, 15 September 1866.

mise in the 1860 apportionment. Even with the reduction provided for in the Fourteenth Amendment, Southern states would be able to muster a minimum of forty votes in the House, a number sufficient to break the Radicals' ability to override a presidential veto. If, however, blacks were allowed to vote freely in the South, representation would be increased by eight over the 1860 apportionment and by twenty-one over the number it would have with only white suffrage.[5]

Guarantees of the national debt seem to have had more influence than many have assumed. This section was used to stir up support for the amendment, for the section, and hence the entire amendment, was said to be necessary if pensions for widows and orphans were to be guaranteed. The debt section, asserted the *New York Herald*, "embodies the great secret of the strength of this constitutional amendment in the Northern States." "It is the power of three thousand millions of dollars diffused in the national currency and securities broadcast over the land."[6] The *Cincinnati Commercial* went so far as to point to a rise in the price of Confederate bonds in London when the Philadelphia convention of the National Union Party made its dramatic appeal for renewed fraternity of North and South.[7]

Democrats like George H. Pendleton of Ohio stressed the revolutionary character of the proposed amendment. In Cincinnati, Pendleton asked former soldiers whether or not they had been fighting to change the government or to preserve it. The amendment, he asserted, could be stretched to cover all domestic regulation by a consolidated, not a federal government in Washington.[8] Almost at the same time, a soldiers and sailors convention in Pittsburgh was endorsing the congressional proposal.[9]

Radicals all along had blamed Johnson for not using his influence to win support for the amendment in the South. Now, as the contest

---

[5]*New York Herald*, 18 September 1866.

[6]Ibid., 20 September 1866.

[7]*Cincinnati Commercial*, 14 September 1866.

[8]Ibid., 21 September 1866.

[9]Walter L. Fleming, *Documentary History of Reconstruction* (Cleveland: Arthur H. Clark Co., 1906) 1:216-18.

was reaching its height, it was suggested to the President that he do precisely that in order to prevent Congress from writing even harsher terms after a radical victory if the South did not ratify. R. P. Allee wrote Johnson in this vein, urging that by quick ratification enough Southern votes could be had in the short session of Congress that would convene in December to erase the most obnoxious measures from the statutes. However, Allee counseled, this was a last resort and must be executed quietly—if at all."[10]

Such arguments gained strength from the growing conviction that extremists, who wanted black suffrage among other things, would not be pleased by the quick ratification. They implied, and sometimes stated outright, that they wished the amendment to fail in order that a more drastic program might be justified. It was hopefully predicted that when the election should show a congressional victory for his foes, Johnson would accept the decision and recommend ratification to the Southern states.

On one point, the real purpose of Radicals, both Democrats and extreme Radicals were in agreement. John T. Hoffman, Democratic candidate for governor of New York, claimed that Congress never wanted the amendment adopted and had put in the disqualification section to guarantee that result in the South. Thus rebuffed, Republicans could postpone admission of representation of Southern states until after 1868, the presidential election year.[11]

Following the general campaign line, the *Atlantic Monthly* and the *North American Review* blamed Johnson for failing to restore union and for fostering a continuing hope in the South for a dominant place in the federal government against the Republican party in a divided North.[12] Charles Sumner, who represented a very radical position and who had written articles for leading journals to popularize his views, addressed a Boston Music Hall audience on 2 October, going over much of the same ground. In support of the amendment he

---

[10]R. R. Allee to Andrew Johnson, 25 September 1866, Andrew Johnson Papers, Library of Congress.

[11]*New York Herald*, 29 September 1866.

[12]*Atlantic Monthly*, 18:506-13; *North American Review*, 103:520-49.

pointed out its necessity to "obtain security for the future." The only fault in the proposal was its inadequacy, he claimed.

Sumner favored what he termed the four E's: Emancipation, Enfranchisement, Equality, and Education. The most important of these was, at the moment, enfranchisement. "Their ballots will be needed in time to come and more than their muskets were needed in time past," stated the Massachusetts senator. He was in no hurry to admit representatives from the South and said so. He would like to demand all his objectives as conditions precedent to admission.[13] Obviously if his influence should become decisive, there would be small hope of readmission on the basis of the Fourteenth Amendment alone. It is equally true that there is little evidence that a majority supported his position at this time.

The *Independent* came out boldly on this subject and was widely quoted.

> We know personally every prominent member of Congress, and we know that the leaders do not mean to admit the unadmitted States on the mere adoption of the amendment. Moreover, we know personally the leading radicals of the republican party outside of Congress, and we know that they have no intention of making the amendment the final measure of admission.[14]

What seems to be a rather accurate analysis was voiced in a letter by Joseph Bailey of Pennsylvania to Secretary Edwin M. Stanton. "They demand other and far greater guarantees than are embodied in the proposed amendment to the constitution, but if they are ratified in a reasonable time I have no doubt public sentiment will settle down in a desire to have them religiously observed."[15]

The *Nation* elaborated on this theme and declared that, although there was no formal pledge of Congress to admit on the basis of the amendment, enough candidates were bound by commitments to guarantee restoration when it was ratified. Nevertheless, haste was

---

[13]Charles Sumner, *Works of Charles Sumner* (Boston: Lee and Shephard, 1870-1883) 11:5-26.

[14]*New York Herald*, 2 October 1866.

[15]Joseph Bailey to E. M. Stanton, 3 October 1866. E. M. Stanton Papers, Library of Congress.

essential, for the term of the existing Congress would expire the following March. Specifically the position of *The Nation* was this:

> If enough Southern States ratify the Amendment before next January to
> make its final passage secure, and to this in a spirit manifesting good faith, we
> believe that they will certainly be restored to their places in Congress. We be-
> lieve that the same result would probably attend such a ratification at any time
> before next February, but if the South should remain obstinate up to that
> time, we judge its subsequent submission would not avail it.[16]

As the *New York Herald* put it, "The issue, then, is this amendment or
something worse for the excluded states."[17] In retrospect there
seems to have been a good deal of real basis for such an analysis.

In Vermont where the legislature took up the question of ratification in October, the Republican party had complete power. The
address of the governor was received by a one hundred percent Republican Senate and a House with a working majority of 224 to 30.[18]
Nevertheless, the resolutions of the state Republican convention
that had met in June at Montpelier had sounded anything but
radical:

> That while approving the constitutional amendment lately proposed by
> Congress as a present practical measure toward securing just ends, we yet in-
> sist that every scheme of restoration is imperfect that is not based upon equal
> and exact justice to all.[19]

This position is a long way from the one taken by Governor Oliver P.
Morton of Indiana in a campaign speech during the heat of election.
Paraphrasing Chief Justice Roger B. Taney's words in his opinion accompanying the Dred Scott decision, he asked the rhetorical question, "I ask you what rights these rebels have that a loyal Government
is bound to respect and protect?"[20] Vermont Republicans had demanded restoration at the earliest possible moment, but insisted that

---

[16]*The Nation*, 4 October 1866.

[17]*New York Herald*, 4 October 1866.

[18]*Annual Cyclopedia* (1866) 762.

[19]Ibid., 761.

[20]*Cincinnati Commercial*, 9 October 1866.

representatives sent to Congress from the South should have loyal constituencies.[21]

Vermont Democrats had gone on record in their convention in late June with a direct accusation that Republicans, in a moment of accidental power, were seeking to perpetuate themselves in office "by depriving eleven States of their places in the Union contrary to their constitutional rights, and against the efforts of the President. . . ."[22] From the minority elected to the legislature in Vermont, it would seem that most of that state's citizens took little stock in the Democratic charge.

In recommending the ratification of the Fourteenth Amendment, the governor claimed that the issue had been between the congressional and executive policies. He expressed the wish that Southern states might be as well organized as was Vermont.[23] That same evening, 12 October, four senators and representatives spoke to a joint session of the legislature on the proposed amendment. Luke Poland, G. F. Edmunds, Justin S. Morrill, and Frederick E. Woodbridge spoke exhaustively on the contents and purposes of the Fourteenth Amendment as a program of congressional reconstruction.[24]

After some delay due to discussion on the appointment of a joint committee to consider the proposed amendment, a resolution of ratification was introduced and ordered printed on 15 October.[25] The next day the joint committee was appointed to consider it. One week later a favorable report was brought in by the committee. The resolution of ratification was then approved unanimously in the Senate.[26]

After preliminaries comparable to those in the Senate, the House heard the report of the committee on the same day it was received in the Senate, 23 October. Due possibly to the active minority opposi-

---

[21]*Annual Cyclopedia* (1866) 762.

[22]Ibid.

[23]*Vermont Senate Journal* (1866) 28-29.

[24]*Vermont House Journal* (1866) 114.

[25]*Vermont Senate Journal*, 41-46.

[26]Ibid., 75.

tion in the House, the vote was not taken quickly. The preamble to the ratification resolution was discussed and amended. Then the resolution itself was made the special order of business for 26 October.[27] Before the vote was called for, debate established the opinion that the South should be admitted if it adopted the amendment.[28] Later the resolution was amended by inserting a demand that Southern representatives to be seated in Congress should represent loyal constituencies and be loyal themselves.[29] These actions merely indicated the attitudes and forces at work in the House, for the Senate resolution was finally adopted 196 to 11,[30] while the House resolution was tabled.

Before another state could pass on the proposal, an event calculated to influence the result took place. This event was the publication of a political letter written by Secretary O. H. Browning and addressed to Colonel W. H. Benneson and Major H. V. Sullivan of Quincy, Illinois. It was in the form of a reply to their invitation to address the people of that city on the issues of the day. The letter was composed most carefully and was intended for publication. For three mornings, Browning rose early and labored on the letter. With a draft completed, he met on the night of 20 October with President Johnson, Henry Stanberry, Edgar Cowan, Thomas Ewing, and William Sharkey to discuss it. According to Browning, they all fully endorsed his wording and the idea of sending it for political use. "The President was especially solicitous that it be done."[31] It was indeed a strong argument against the pending amendment.

There was certainly some truth in Browning's analysis of the elections then being held in the North. He claimed that they were not truly "indicative of the judgment of the people of the Northern States upon the Constitutional Amendments." The proposal was not the

---

[27]*Vermont House Journal*, 61-78.

[28]Ibid., 117.

[29]Ibid., 150.

[30]Ibid., 139.

[31]Orville Hickman Browning, *The Diary of Orville Hickman Browning, 1865-1881*, ed., Theodore C. Pease and J. G. Randall (Springfield IL: Collections of the Illinois State Historical Library, 1933, 1938) 2:101.

main issue presented and considered by the voter, according to Browning.[32] "The people have had their fears alarmed and their passions and prejudices aroused," and naturally had "delusive ideas as to the character of the issues before the country." Suffrage for blacks, wrote Browning, had been the only cause of conflict between Congress and the President. If Johnson had agreed to this at first and forced it on the South, all would now be harmony in Washington.[33]

Browning opposed the proscription of the most intelligent leaders of the South. In regard to representation, he outlined the interesting idea that when the census of 1870 was taken, the black population of the South would be found to total no more than three-fifths of those enumerated in 1860, thus causing no change in apportionment in comparison with the North. Regardless of this, he thought it unfair to give representatation to nonvoting immigrants in the North and refuse it to blacks in the South.[34]

If the amendment should be adopted, wrote Browning, powers claimed under it "certainly will be used substantially to annihilate the State Judiciaries." Why had the due process clause been inserted when it was already to be found in all state constitutions?

> It is to subordinate the State judiciaries to Federal supervision and control; to totally annihilate the independence and sovereignty of State judiciaries in the administration of State laws, and the authority and control of the States over matters of purely domestic and local concern. If the State judiciaries are subordinate, all the departments of the State Governments will be equally subordinated, for all State laws, let them relate to whatever department of Government they may, or to what domestic and local interest, will be equally open to criticism, interpretation and adjudication by the Federal tribunals, whose judgments and decrees will be supreme and will override the decisions of the State Courts and leave them utterly powerless.

Although in this unusual and penetrating analysis of what the future might hold under the amended Constitution, Browning mentioned the many detailed difficulties and grievances that he thought

---

[32]*Cincinnati Commercial*, 26 October 1866; *Harper's Weekly*, 24 November 1866, differed with Browning and the President by declaring: "From Maine to Iowa this was the one issue."

[33]*Cincinnati Commercial*, 26 October 1866.

[34]Ibid.

would develop, not once did he suggest using the Fourteenth Amendment as a means of protecting corporations under its due process clause.[35] In many respects he foresaw much of the impact of the proposal, but not this latter implication.

In summing up the results of the fall elections, *The Nation* made the following analysis:

> The first point which has unquestionably been passed upon is, that the people will not trust the South, or its ally, the Democratic party of the North, to rule in our government. The second is, that the South shall not be restored unconditionally to its privileges in the Union. The third is, that Congress, and not the Executive, is to name the conditions of restoration. The fourth, that the conditions already proposed are abundantly liberal to the South.[36]

The comment by Carl Schurz, looking back on this campaign in which he was a participant, is particularly revealing. "In canvasses carried on for the purpose of electing a President," he wrote, "I had seen more enthusiasm but in none so much animosity and bad blood as in this."[37]

Political waters in 1866 were dangerous to all candidates; many did not survive. It was very difficult to read correctly the swirling currents of public opinion in a particular constituency. In general, however, the Democrats' theme was restoration versus disunion and the Republicans' theme was guarantees for the future.

Several issues involved in the race have not received sufficient attention. The Thirteenth Amendment would change the congressional strength of many states, not merely of those in the South. Elaborate analyses were presented to depict the results of added strength to the South and of altered representation of individual Northern states relative to each other.

The President was criticized for not urging adoption of the Fourteenth Amendment on the South, and radicals were charged with wishing to defeat the amendment in order that they demand more

---

[35]Complete letter published widely. Quotations from *Cincinnati Commercial*, 26 October 1866.

[36]*The Nation*, 15 November 1866.

[37]Carl Schurz, *Reminiscences of Carl Schurz* (New York: Doubleday, Page and Co., 1908-1909) 238.

stringent terms at a later date from an unrepentant South. Evidence indicates that radical leaders like Charles Sumner and Thaddeus Stevens actually had very little influence. Strongly Republican Vermont ratified the amendment in October with radical voices having little or no effect.

Secretary of the Interior Orville H. Browning issued a public letter meant to influence the election. It is especially significant because it had the specific approval of President Johnson and his chief advisers from both North and South. Browning's statement that black suffrage was the sole cause of differences between the President and Congress assumes added importance in view of the known approval of the statement by Johnson. Browning also predicted that later Supreme Court interpretations, should it be adopted, would reduce the power of states and their courts to insignificance. In view of modern developments, his words were almost prophetic.

Chapter Seven

Thunder Rumbling from the South

With the election campaign in the North about to end in a sweeping victory for the opponents of President Johnson, Southern states began to consider the amendment in their legislatures established by the presidential program for reconstruction. If the special case of Tennessee is omitted, until November, only Texas had considered the amendment. In the Lone Star State the first direct rejection was filed on 1 November. Now the spotlight of national attention turned with sharp focus upon the action of Georgia.

No state can be characterized as typical of the nation nor typical even of a single section. There were, however, certain factors in the Georgia situation, certain forces at work, certain events, and the reaction to them had much in common with most states of the deep

South. Of course, there were also certain unusual and even unique circumstances that prevent its being considered exactly comparable to any other state. It is nevertheless instructive to examine Georgia's reaction to the proposed Fourteenth Amendment and the issues raised in connection with its ratification in 1866.

As in most states of the South, there was a recognition of defeat, a desire for reconciliation and a natural desire not only to survive physically and economically, but to salvage whatever was possible of power and self-respect after the war. An example of the early desire for reconciliation is seen in the actions and words of General John B. Gordon when he spoke at the surrender at Appomattox, urging peace and the obeying of civil laws. His words caused Elihu B. Washburne of Illinois, one of the framers of the Fourteenth Amendment, to seek him out to congratulate him for his spirit of cooperation as seen in his final words to his troops.[1]

A general willingness to accept the inevitable entered into the desire of most Georgians to support President Johnson's efforts for restoration. Pardons were sought and granted by the President to those who were willing and able to help lead the people to make effective the Johnson policy. Joseph E. Brown, governor of Georgia during the war, was one who had been arrested, paroled, and later granted a pardon before he returned to the state to work for the President's program.[2]

None of this meant that there was no desire for the best possible terms or that there was no bickering over some of Johnson's "musts." A new constitution was dutifully drafted repealing secession, and the new government established under it duly ratified the Thirteenth Amendment.[3] Blocking payment for slaves was not pleasing to

----

[1] A. P. Tankersley, *John B. Gordon: A Study in Gallantry* (Atlanta: Whitehall Press, 1955) 221.

[2] E. S. Nathans, *A Constitutional History of Georgia, 1732-1945* (Athens: University of Georgia Press, 1948) 252.

[3] L. B. Hill, *Joseph E. Brown and the Confederacy* (Chapel Hill: University of North Carolina Press, 1939) 266.

many, nor was the repudiation of Georgia's war debt, something not easily distinguishable from a normal state debt.[4]

Alexander H. Stephens had testified before the Joint Committee on Reconstruction that a limited suffrage for blacks was not so objectionable as the universal right to vote. He had offered his opinion that these matters should be left to individual states.[5] Joseph E. Brown had published a letter in which he claimed that "madness alone could dream of political equality" between the races.[6]

While the work of framing the Fourteenth Amendment was drawing to a close, newspapers were arguing the merits of expediency versus continued resistance to what many regarded as tyranny and dishonor. A belief that there remained some rights capable of being defended was expressed.[7] With interest, Southerners watched the final break developing between President and Congress.[8] Those who set editorial policy feared and detested the possible effects of Congress's promotion of the amendment; still, some papers urged avoidance of any active part in events and national debates.[9] Events surrounding the final steps of the framing process were reported fully, especially those arising from discussions concerning the implications of suffrage for blacks and disqualification of whites.[10] Space in newspapers was shared with reports of the Southern tours of Generals J. B. Steedman and J. H. Fullerton, who had been sent by Johnson to report on the activities of the Freedmen's Bureau.[11] Early attempts to secure Tennessee's ratification includ-

---

[1]Albert B. Saye, *A Constitutional History of Georgia, 1732-1945* (Athens: University of Georgia Press, 1948) 254.

[5]"Report of the Joint Committee on Reconstruction," *Reports of the Committees of the House of Representatives* (1866) 39th Cong., 1st sess., pt. 3, 163.

[6]*Atlanta Intelligencer* 19 February 1866.

[7]*Tri-Weekly Constitutionalist* (Augusta), 6 May 1866. Other papers such as the *Memphis Avalanche* took the same position.

[8]*Tri-Weekly Constitutionalist*, 3 June 1866.

[9]*Georgia Weekly Telegraph* (Macon), 28 May 1866.

[10]*Georgia Journal and Messenger* (Macon), 6 June 1866.

[11]*Georgia Telegraph*, 4 June 1866.

ing the extended-quorum struggle in that state's House of Representatives were given full publicity.[12] Reports of opposition to the amendment in the North encouraged a willingness to oppose it in the South.[13]

In the manner of the times, editorial comments in newspapers on national events were quoted in all parts of the country. There was a tendency to play up any statement that would give comfort or hope about Northern attitudes on restoration. Equally quoted were extreme statements by Stevens, Sumner, and others whose remarks could be condemned or ridiculed. The official reports of both majority and minority opinions of the Joint Committee on Reconstruction were made available, the minority naturally winning praise. "Ignore it," seemed to be a leading thought about the proposed amendment, but closely related to this was the feeling that if it must be, "Every honest Southerner will reject with scorn the infamous condition, and despise the craven spirits that suppose us capable of such base submission."[14]

Many newspapers advocated calm behavior and the commission of no acts that would disturb Northern impressions of stability in the South.[15] "So long as Southern members are at last admitted, it makes but very little difference how they get into Congress," wrote one small-town editor.[16] Some questioned Johnson's leadership, but most subscribed to the opinion of the *Macon Daily Telegraph*: "The people of the Southern States, who have looked with confidence to President Johnson to deliver them from the machinations of their enemies in Congress, will have no reason to regret the faith that they have reposed in him." That paper regarded his 22 June message to Congress as effective as a veto. "It will kill the Amendment," it continued. Calculations to support this conclusion listed Maryland and Indiana as certain to reject, as would Delaware and Kentucky. The

---

[12]*Georgia Journal and Messenger*, 18 July 1866.

[13]*Tri-Weekly Constitutionalist*, 1 June 1866.

[14]*Georgia Telegraph*, 18 June 1866.

[15]*Georgia Journal and Messenger*, 18 July 1866.

Southern voting block plus these four states would mean its defeat in spite of Tennessee.[17]

Northern newspapers that praised the President's desire for the amendment's defeat received wide circulation by quotation in the Southern press.[18] Tennessee's admission had been given close attention and was generally regarded as both high-handed and illegal. "They have admitted the State of Tennessee simply because, under the system of suffrage restrictons imposed by a usurped government, the power is in the hands of a knot of radicals like themselves."[19]

The full text of Secretary of State Seward's message telling the governors of all states of the proposed Fourteenth Amendment was published. Objections voiced by Johnson in his congressional message were also repeated.[20] Support for the President was recommended and part of this support was seen as participation in the Philadelphia convention called for 14 August. "The President desires it and our interests demand it," wrote one editor.[21] Northern papers were quoted as being in favor of this meeting, and Democratic support was noted.[22]

Some of the newspapers were less than enthusiastic.[23] Montgomery Blair, believing strongly that Alexander H. Stephens could do much good, had written the former vice-president of the Confederacy urging that he come to the convention.[24] Neither of the Stephens brothers was enthusiastic and at first preferred not to waste money

[16]*Washington* (GA) *Gazette*, 27 July 1866.

[17]*Macon Daily Telegraph*, 1 July 1866.

[18]See quotations from *New York Times, New York News* and *Cleveland Herald* in *Macon Daily Telegraph*, 18, 24, 27 July 1866.

[19]*Georgia Journal and Messenger*, 28 July 1866.

[20]*Tri-Weekly Constitutionalist*, 29 June 1866.

[21]*Macon Daily Telegraph*, 5 July 1866.

[22]Ibid., 6 July 1866.

[23]*Washington Gazette*, 27 July 1866.

[24]A. H. Stephens to his brother, Linton, 21 July 1866. Alexander H. Stephens Papers, microfilm, University of North Carolina Library.

on something in which they had so little faith.[25] Hershel V. Johnson had no intention of taking part and was highly critical of the convention idea.[26] His counsel was to avoid backing a weaker person than Grant, who, he was convinced would become the next president. He wanted to do nothing to push Grant "into the arms of the Black Republicans." The general, he felt, "certainly loves us as much as Johnson does."[27]

Others advised letting "the Northern men study out the problems for themselves and act upon it. Let Northern parties divide and vote upon it. But do not let Southern men dispute about it or divide upon, or mix up with Northern parties either to embarrass or to aid."[28] "Hereabout, nobody seems particularly interested in the matter," reported the *Washington Gazette.*[29]

Reconstruction of the cabinet on the basis of its members' stands for or against the Philadelphia convention and the Fourteenth Amendment was observed carefully. The feeling was that Johnson should have long ago dismissed those who had since resigned (Dennison, Harlan, and Speed). Stanton, who remained in office, should have gone with them.[30] Letters from those who remained were made public in the press as was that of the aging Edward Bates, former attorney general, who opposed the amendment.[31] The admission of Tennessee, with the President's comments challenging the right of Congress to exclude representation of any reconstructed Southern state, received much attention.

However, when all was said and done, Alexander H. Stephens and his brother, Judge Linton Stephens, were selected as delegates and set out to attend the Philadelphia convention. Herschel V. John-

[25]Linton Stephens to A. H. Stephens, 29 July 1866, Stephens Papers.

[26]Herschel V. Johnson to A. H. Stephens, 2 July 1866, Herschel V. Johnson Papers, Duke University Library.

[27]Ibid., 6 July 1866.

[28]*Tri-Weekly Consitutionalist*, 11 July 1866.

[29]*Washington Gazette*, 13 July 1866.

[30]*Macon Daily Telegraph*, 15 July 1866.

[31]Ibid., 18 July 1866.

son was named, but refused to serve.[32] Among those who accepted the responsibility was General John B. Gordon.[33] Stephens had concluded that the real purpose of the Radicals was continued Southern exclusion, reduction of Southern power, and the transfer of what was left "to men who will betray it." He believed that the opposition of such developments must recognize these purposes in order to defeat them.[34] Johnson still felt that the South should stay out of the struggle in the North. Only moral aid and comfort should be furnished, he advised, while the South silently submitted. "When we make the required concessions, it is but the pretext for further exactions." "We cannot do or say anything that is not converted into a weapon against us."[35] The unenthusiastic Alexander H. Stephens had, meanwhile, reluctantly endorsed the assembly in Philadelphia in a letter to Montgomery Blair that was published. On their travel to Philadelphia, he and other delegates spent a few days in Washington to test the political winds.[36]

The convention itself was fully reported in the press,[37] as well as were related and unrelated events nationwide. The New Orleans riots were recognized as ammunition for anti-Southern propaganda. To find cause to disfranchise whites and enfranchise blacks was interpreted as the method Radicals had in mind to obtain ratification by Southern legislatures.[38] Fears were expressed that Northern Democrats sought to use the convention for their own purposes.[39] As early as July, Alexander H. Stephens had voiced the opinion that Democrats of the North would "never abandon their own organization" in a new coalition. He was realistic enough to ad-

---

[32]Ibid., 28 July 1866.

[33]Tankersley, *John B. Gordon*, 232.

[34]A. H. Stephens to his brother, Linton, 30 July 1866, Stephens Papers.

[35]Herschel V. Johnson to Dr. T. Ridley, 10 August 1866, Johnson Papers.

[36]*Macon Daily Telegraph*, 2, 14 August 1866.

[37]Ibid., 19 August 1866 and other Georgia newspapers.

[38]Ibid., 12 August 1866.

[39]Ibid., 8 August 1866.

mit that "outside the Democratic party in the North we have but few friends."[40]

Senator Doolittle, chairman of the Central Committee, wrote a letter that tried to appeal to Southern enthusiasm for an opportunity to unite under the old flag in a new common allegiance to the United States and its Constitution. It was published as a means of rallying support for the convention.[41] News of delegates coming to Philadelphia from all parts of the South left its impression on Georgians. "The Convention next Tuesday will make a noise up North" exulted the *Milledgeville Federal Union*.[42]

The events and resolutions of the Philadelphia convention did indeed "make a noise" in both the North and the South. Most Southerners were encouraged by it. Georgia newspapers emphasized the news from Philadelphia and from other events that raised Southern hopes. Radical failures in Kentucky as well as the President's proclamation that peace existed in all of the former Confederacy improved their outlook.[43]

Henry Ward Beecher, a preacher of influence in the North, had been asked to be chaplain of a soldiers and sailors convention meeting in Cleveland. His letter declining the invitation was published in full. After lamenting the failure of Congress to readmit Southern states, he eloquently stated his position:

> For the sake of the freedmen, for the sake of the South and its millions of our countrymen, for our own sake, and for the great cause of freedom and civilization, I urge the immediate reunion of all the parts which rebellion and war has shattered.[44]

And this action came to pass. Resolutions urging early restoration of Southern states to their places in the Union were gladly read and

---

[40]Robert Toombs, Alexander H. Stephens, and Howell Cobb, *Correspondence of Robert Toombs, Alexander H. Stephens and Howell Cobb*, ed., Ulrich B. Phillips, *Annual Report of the American Historical Society* (1911) 2:681.

[41]*Macon Daily Telegraph*, 1 August 1866.

[42]*Milledgeville Federal Union*, 7 August 1866.

[43]*Macon Daily Telegraph*, 7 August 1866.

[44]Ibid., 4 September 1866.

passed by the Philadelphia convention. Indeed, special reports of "solid evidence of sympathy" from "prominent and substantial men of the several sections" were reported by a Washington newspaper correspondent.[45] It was believed that these Northern capitalists would assure money for restoration.[46] Georgia state bonds were to be sold in New York for ninety cents on the dollar.[47] Herschel V. Johnson even admitted that some good had resulted from the Philadelphia convention, "Though not all I could wish, yet more than I expected was done."[48]

More cautious groups counseled that even a victory in congressional elections could not change the Senate and probably could only reduce the Republican majority in the House. For many, it continued to be prudent to avoid taking part in national discussions.[49] Appeals to trust the President and remain patient were made: "Let us devote ourselves to our individual affairs, do or say nothing of a character which will give our enemies, the Radicals, anything to create sensation over."[50]

Other party conventions were being held as fall elections began to take place in different states at different times, Maine and Vermont in September, others in October, and the majority in November.[51] When the Radical-sponsored convention of Southern Loyalists was held in Philadelphia, delegates came from all over the South. A Georgia editor stated thankfully that there were none from his state and he hoped there would be none.[52] B. F. Butler, "Parson" Brownlow, Frederick Douglass, as well as Jack Hamilton of Texas, were grouped with others in attendance as "The Nigger Worship-

---

[45]Ibid., 6 September 1866.

[46]Ibid., 4 September 1866.

[47]Ibid., 1 September 1866.

[48]Percy Scott Flippen, *Herschel V. Johnson of Georgia: State Rights Unionist* (Richmond VA: Deite Printing, 1931) 276.

[49]*Georgia Journal and Messenger*, 22 August 1866.

[50]*Macon Daily Telegraph*, 31 August 1866.

[51]*Federal Union*, 5 September 1866.

[52]*Macon Daily Telegraph*, 5 September 1866.

pers Convention in Philadelphia."[53] It cheered some in the South to be able to quote the *States and Union* of Portsmouth, New Hampshire, that "There is not a man from any Southern State who has the shadow of a constituency at home."[54]

In Augusta, an editorial voice was raised in favor of compromise: no impeachment of the President and acceptance of the Fourteenth Amendment. Johnson's National Union Convention had been a blunder and the South could expect nothing; better to say and do nothing, advised the editor. He lost his position the next day.[55]

Even Alexander H. Stephens, who had not favored the President's meeting in August though he had given it grudging support, wrote privately in a critical vein in late September. He "did not think that the convention was well managed either in its getting up or in its organization." He considered Johnson's speaking tour in the North unfortunate and expected the elections to produce little, if any, change in the tone of Congress. Many sensibilities were offended by President Johnson's "swing around the circle." Johnson visited leading cities in the North and delivered speeches against the congressional proposals and in defense of his own plan for reconstruction. He responded to hecklers angrily and showed poor taste by using intemperate language. Patience, it seemed to Stephens, was the only course left to follow.[56]

In late September, depression characterized the attitudes of other opponents of congressional policy. The *New York Herald* called for Southern ratification though little willingness to do so was reflected in Georgia. Rather, active efforts to support the President's policies cropped up locally.[57] Results of early elections in New England gave little cause to hope that the Radicals would lose, yet the opinion was expressed that after a victory for the opponents of the President, the South would become an "unfit place of abode for any-

---

[53]*Georgia Journal and Messenger*, 12 September 1866.

[54]*Federal Union*, 18 September 1866.

[55]*Tri-Weekly Constitutionalist*, 19 September 1866.

[56]A. H. Stephens to H. V. Johnson, 27 September 1866, Johnson Papers.

[57]*Macon Daily Telegraph*, 14 September 1866.

thing but dogs of the lowest degree."[58] The fear that suffrage for blacks was the primary purpose of Radicals was a prominent component of this belief. If the black man should be given the vote, "on what principle shall we exclude the women of the country and children above the age of fifteen?" In the opinion of the writer, neither was less capable.[59]

Herschel V. Johnson, a close observer of Northern events, wrote that he saw no help from Conservatives in other sections. He believed that Johnson's forces had blundered badly and that the South was at the mercy of "fanaticism."[60]

The one principal objection that remained to ratification of the Fourteenth Amendment was that "No leading Republican in Congress means to admit the ten waiting States simply on the adoption of the Constitutional Amendment. These States are to be admitted on no condition short of the equal political rights of the loyal citizens without distinction of race."[61] A few days later that same paper was stating that the North was asking the Southern people to "cut our own throats." "The North has nothing to grant that would compensate us for the loss of self-respect, and surrender of all claims to the respect of mankind."[62] While such thoughts were being expressed, it was reported that "Parson" Brownlow, speaking in New Jersey, and John W. Forney in Pennsylvania had predicted that war would be renewed if the South should thwart the victors by defeating the amendment.[63]

With all the furor over the proposed Fourteenth Amendment, it is interesting to note that the first point-by-point analysis of the amendment in Georgia's capitol by the *Federal Union* appeared in early October. The disqualification section received the most criti-

---

[58]Ibid., 5 September 1866.

[59]Ibid., 21 September 1866.

[60]Herschel V. Johnson to A. H. Stephens, 25 September 1866, Johnson Papers.

[61]*Macon Daily Telegraph*, 27 September 1866.

[62]Ibid., 2 October 1866.

[63]*Georgia Journal and Messenger*, 26 September 1866.

cism.[64] The *New York Times* was quoted to support the *Federal Union*'s conclusions as was the *Charleston Courier*.[65]

Other Georgia papers picked up the discussion and reproduced the amendment in full. The *Augusta Tri-Weekly Constitutionalist* insisted that Georgia should be readmitted before any consideration be given to the proposal. It reminded its readers that no assurance of admission as the result of ratification had been given. If Congress should emerge victorious from its confrontation with the President, as seemed probable, that publication accepted the necessity of submission but added, "Still we can submit in silence, preserving self respect."[66]

Efforts in Oregon to rescind its earlier ratification gave new courage.[67] The *Augusta Chronicle and Sentinel* could not believe that anyone would support congressional reconstruction.[68] Moves for compromise were discounted and the defeat of Radicals in "Glorious Little Delaware" was hailed.[69] The recurring theme was to be quiet and wait—to follow a policy of "masterly inactivity."[70]

Early election returns had left Georgians displeased but still hopeful of contests to come. When later reports showed sweeping Republican victories, with only a few for Democrats, they tried not be disappointed. Radical gains in Pennsylvania and Ohio, as well as in Indiana, were not encouraging.[71]

Eventually, in the old capitol at Milledgeville, Governor C. J. Jenkins addressed the assembled Georgia legislators on the same day final rejection was registered by Texas. In the beginning of his speech, he stressed his opinion that the official transmittal of the proposal

---

[64]*Federal Union*, 2 October 1866.

[65]Ibid., 9 October 1866.

[66]*Tri-Weekly Constitutionalist*, 5 October 1866.

[67]*Macon Daily Telegraph*, 5 October 1866.

[68]*Augusta Chronicle and Sentinel*, 2 October 1866.

[69]*Macon Daily Telegraph*, 5 October 1866.

[70]Ibid., 9 October 1866.

[71]Ibid., 10, 11, 13, 16 October 1866.

according to the Constitution imposed an obligation "to consider it respectfully." It was, said the governor, like all recent proposals, designed to operate "especially on the Southern States."[72]

As he interpreted it, the first section not only made all black people who were born in the United States citizens, but deprived the states of all power over citizenship. The second section provoked stronger language:

> Whether the object in proposing this change be the extension of the elective franchise to persons of African descent, (nearly all of whom are notoriously unqualified for it) or a further diminution of the already relatively small weight of the Southern States in the administration of the Government, the adoption of this amendment will certainly force upon them a choice between those evils.[73]

Did such an amendment, which provoked unequal effects on the different sections of the Union, represent magnanimity? It would "fall upon citizens inhabiting one latitude like an avalanche from its mountain perch, crushing where it settles; whilst upon those of another latitude it will alight unfelt like a feather floating in still air."[74]

The third section, as *Frank Leslie's Illustrated Newspaper* had observed, was, with the second of the two parts of the omnibus amendment, most disturbing to the South.[75] Governor Jenkins pointed out that it was purely sectional and that pardons already granted might be of doubtful value to those proscribed leaders of the South. "Can Georgia spare all of these from her service?" he asked.[76]

After dismissing the fourth section as inconsequential, the Georgia governor declared that what might constitute "appropriate legislation" under the fifth section would be subject to the interpretation of a congressional majority. There had been nothing to give assurance "that even this concession will insure our restoration." Why then had states that had no part in the framing of this proposal been

---

[72]*Georgia Senate Journal* (1866) 6.

[73]Ibid., 7.

[74]Ibid.

[75]*Frank Leslie's Illustrated Newspaper*, 6 October 1866.

[76]*Georgia Senate Journal*, 6.

asked to give formal approval? "Should the States especially to be affected by this amendment refuse their assent to it, it cannot be adopted without excluding them from the count and placing its ratification upon the votes of three-fourths of the now dominant States." The governor considered the amendment "unconstitutional, null and void." Instead of ratifying, Governor Jenkins suggested, in language reminiscent of that used by the Texas governor in August, that it would be "Far better calmly [to] await a returning sense of justice."[77]

Newspaper analysis of the amendment that was now before the legislature raised no question about paying the national debt but was critical of the rest. The *Milledgeville Federal Union* said that the proposal was a "plan to tide over the shoals of the fall election", rather than a plan to restore the Union." The legislature was urged to do "as Texas has done, return it without their approval." "Let us wash our hands clean of this foul thing; and when it comes upon us, if come it must, our conscience will be clean as our hands, and even our worst enemies will respect our manhood."[78] The *Augusta Tri-Weekly Constitutionalist* declared that "This obnoxious measure is being coaxed upon us by parties exemplifying every shade of opinion." It suggested that new states would be admitted to help swell the number of those ratifying the amendment.[79] This was actually to come about.

The *Macon Daily Telegraph* declared that no benefit would accrue from ratification; that keeping Southern states from participating in the Union until after the 1868 elections seemed to be the Republican purpose. It could be done, but not legally, that paper declared.[80] Ratification, it added, would change the essential nature of the constitutional relationships.[81]

It was suggested that repudiation of state debts was a matter for the courts to decide rather than a matter for coerced state action. The

---

[77]Ibid., 8-9.

[78]*Federal Union*, 16 October 1866.

[79]*Tri-Weekly Constitutionalist*, 17 October 1866.

[80]*Macon Daily Telegraph*, 25 October 1866.

[81]Ibid., 31 October 1866.

Atlanta Intelligencer considered the same idea and the *Cincinnati Commercial* was quoted to support the Georgia view.[82] The *Washington Gazette* avoided the usual diatribes and pointed out that some Southern newspapers thought Georgia should ratify "as a matter of expediency."[83] "Better remain forever unrepresented than accept terms as humiliating," countered the *Abbeville Press*.[84]

Georgia newspapers reported the activities of the legislature faithfully. Comments of leading citizens, like those of Alexander H. Stephens, were also reported. In a private letter, Stephens had said that he believed the amendment should be rejected. Several papers had reported rumors of Stephen's favoring the adoption and that Governor Orr of South Carolina had also advised this action. These allegations were denied. Many papers clamored for a swift rejection of the amendment, but the *Savannah Daily Republican* urged caution. It pointed out that the results of elections in the North were evidence of the people's disposition there. Undue haste was criticized in a most outspoken way:

> There has been too much blundering already through this damnable haste in rushing upon evils without counting the cost—before their real nature is perfectly understood by the people, and it was the duty of the representatives whose grave responsibilities made it incumbent upon them to approach the amendment with calmness and moderation; to show in this way, if in no other, that they are sincerely desirous of appeasing, and not of inciting the passions of the dominant party.[85]

Even the *Georgia Journal and Messenger*, no radical paper, counseled against rejection. "To refuse the Amendment is a new act of rebellion, which no doubt, in due time will bring its appropriate punishment." Nevertheless, that journal predicted unanimous rejection.[86]

---

[82]*Federal Union*, 30 October 1866.

[83]*Washington Gazette*, 19 October 1866.

[84]Quoted in *Washington Gazette*, 26 October 1866.

[85]*Savannah Daily Republican*, 12 November 1866.

[86]*Georgia Journal and Mesenger*, 9 November 1866.

On 5 November, the proposed amendment was referred to a Joint Committee on the State of the Republic.[87] The report of this committee discussed reasons for not considering the merits of the amendment and for not bringing up the matter for final decision at all.[88] However, on 9 November, the Senate unanimously passed a resolution declining ratification.[89] In the House, there were only two votes against rejection.[90]

With the elections in the North resulting in complete control of the new Congress by Radicals and with Georgia's rejection of the congressional plan in the form of the Fourteenth Amendment, the *Augusta Tri-Weekly Constitutionalist* summed up the prevailing sentiment in this manner: "Our duty, however, is plain. We can take no backward steps for dishonor. We must stand united and undaunted, in spite of threats and actual violence."[91] Georgians wished to survive economically and to retain as much of their self-respect as was possible after their devastating defeat, but, like others in the South, they were ready to accept the inevitable. Some understanding sympathy and support from friends in the North was welcome. Executive pardons from President Johnson fell into this category, but it was difficult to maintain a hopeful spirit under the circumstances.

Particular decisions that vexed them more than others included nonpayment for slaves and repudiation of the war debt. They found it hard to distinguish in many cases the costs of ordinary governmental operation from debt for war. They objected to black suffrage most of all, for they believed that largely uneducated population incapable of governing. Disqualification of recognized leaders added to the problem. The above objections, loss of power and prestige, and deeply imbedded racial prejudices, combined to leave them confused and demoralized.

---

[87]*Georgia House Journal* (1866) 42.

[88]Ibid., 61-67.

[89]*Georgia Senate Journal*, 72.

[90]*Georgia House Journal*, 68.

[91]*Tri-Weekly Constitutionalist*, 16 November 1866.

When Georgians asked themselves what could be done, the answer was usually "Nothing." To remain calm and allow the North to settle their fate was the usual advice of former leaders. Few expected much from the efforts of President Johnson, and even less was expected from the efforts of the National Union Convention. Whether Georgians should follow Johnson, in view of his uncertain position in the North, was something to consider. They did hope that some Northern capitalists might help furnish the means to rebuild their ruined economy.

Newspapers kept Georgians aware of leading events. They were surprised that they were to be permitted to approve or disapprove the Fourteenth Amendment. Nobody really expected that Georgia would approve it, and not many thought it would become a part of the Constitution. After its anticipated defeat, other, sterner measures would be demanded. Comments of participants indicated that there was no reason to act on the proposal, except to express their unwillingness to humiliate themselves further. By exercising their option to reject, they believed they were retaining some part of their honor and integrity.

Chapter Eight

Murky
Southern Skies

While the Georgia legislature had been preparing its act of rejection, Governor Isaac Murphy of Arkansas was presenting the proposed amendment to that state's legislators. On 8 November, he reported that Northern elections had just approved the congressional plan of reconstruction as presented in the Fourteenth Amendment. Whereas none could say that the proposal was what former Confederate states desired, he declared that "it becomes a very grave question for the legislature to decide whether any terms more favorable are likely to be obtained by opposition." The alternative would be to accept the amendment "and thus secure the prompt reconstruction of the State," bringing it back into a position of equality with others in the Union.

In Governor Murphy's opinion, better terms were not to be expected. Economic recovery would have to wait for more settled conditions that only political restoration could bring. "The effect of rejection on the prosperity and happiness of the people of the State, demands solemn consideration."[1]

The remarks of the Arkansas governor are notable for his emphasis on economic recovery, which was the most important issue to many during the reconstruction period in the South. There were those in most Southern states who were willing to accept almost any terms so that economic recovery could begin. Such views were not successful in 1866, in the face of strong insistence by their leaders that Southerners maintain their self-respect and and uphold traditional Southern honor. The other noteworthy point in Murphy's statement was his willingness to accept the implied promises of restoration on the basis of ratification. Lack of a definite Congressional commitment was a formidable stumbling block to the amendment's ratification throughout the South.

During the month of consideration given the amendment by the committees of the Arkansas legislature, a resolution of thanks to President Johnson was offered for his effort to stand between the citizens of that state and the "unholy legislation of radical majorities." On the same day that the Committee on Federal Relations made its report to the Senate, 10 December, a resolution showing the practical approach taken by some members was introduced and referred to that same committee. It endorsed the recommendations of Governor Murphy to ratify the constitutional amendment "to calm the troubled waters of our political atmosphere."[2]

The committee, however, made a full report to the Senate and proposed a resolution "That the General Assembly of the State of Arkansas declines to ratify the amendment." Reasons given for this position included: (1) lack of proper constitutional procedure in its proposal and in its failure to submit the proposal to the President for his approval by a Congress representing only two-thirds of the states; (2) the unwise delegation of power in the first section; (3) the unacceptable attempt to enforce suffrage for blacks in section two; and (4)

---

[1] *Arkansas Senate Journal* (1866-1867) 50-51.

[2] *Annual Cyclopedia* (1866) 27.

the unwise and unacceptable provision in the third section that would disfranchise "many of our best and wisest citizens."[3]

As in Georgia, little attention was given to the fourth section. Particular note was taken, however, of the "due process" clause of the first section. It was almost the identical language of the Fifth Amendment, observed the committee, "and if this provision already in existence will not secure the object designed, what assurance have we that a similar one will not be disregarded." The proposed section's restrictions on state action rather than on the federal government, as in the Fifth Amendment, seemed to have escaped notice, though in the same resolution an objection to the first section was made because it would "take from the States all control over their local and domestic concerns."[4] Likewise, it is interesting to note the objection to procedures that prevented the approval or disapproval of the President. Even in Congress this question had been aired, though it was generally recognized even by President Johnson that the executive had no discretionary power in the transmittal of congressional proposals to amend the Constitution.

The committee resolution recommended that the legislature decline to ratify the Fourteenth Amendment. However desirable early restoration might be, the people of Arkansas could never accept it "at a sacrifice of principle, dignity and self respect." It would be better to accept harsher terms at a later time and bear whatever might happen in the meantime "than commit an act of disgrace, if not annihilation, such as would result from the adoption of this amendment by the legislature."[5] The Senate approved the resolution that same day, 10 December, by a vote of twenty-four to one.[6]

In the House, where various resolutions both for approval and rejection had been referred to committee, the report of the Federal Relations Committee was received on 17 December. Wasting no time, the decision of the chair to adhere to the order of business was

---

[3]*Arkansas Senate Journal* 258ff.

[4]Ibid.; *Annual Cyclopedia* (1866) 27.

[5]*Annual Cyclopedia* (1866) 27.

[6]*Arkansas Senate Journal*, 262.

overruled and action called for. The Senate resolution was read three times and approved on that same day. The vote was sixty-eight to two.[7]

Other states of the former Confederacy were also taking up the "Howard Amendment," a name often given to the Fourteenth Amendment. Action in several of them took place during December. Especially noteworthy is the situation in North Carolina where many crosscurrents were at work. Among these was the influence of President Johnson, an ever-present factor in all Southern states but more obvious in the "tar heel" state. The North Carolina Proclamation of 29 May 1865 had inaugurated Johnson's executive plan of reconstruction and was to call down the wrath of the Radicals and, with other influences, to lead to the Fourteenth Amendment.

Special consideration had been given North Carolina by the Johnson administration, including direct financial assistance to the provisional government led by Governor William W. Holden, editor of the *Raleigh Daily Standard*.[8] Lewis Hanes, private secretary to Governor Holden, was elected to Congress though never seated.[9] He was to be important in the attempt of a small group close to Johnson to propose a modified Fourteenth Amendment early in 1867. These men in 1865 had worked through an agent in Washington to obtain pardons for leading North Carolinians.[10] Despite Holden's use of pardons for political purposes, he was defeated by Jonathan Worth, who became governor in December 1865. Worth was reelected in the fall of 1866.[11]

Holden's newspaper was quoted in the *Chicago Tribune* in June of 1866 in a discussion of the practical advantages of ratifying the Fourteenth Amendment. The third section seemed to be the strongest issue, because it raised the question of how long North Carolina could

---

[7]*Arkansas House Journal* (1866-1867) 291.

[8]Jonathan T. Dorris, *Pardon and Amnesty Under Lincoln and Johnson: The Restoration of the Confederates to their Rights and Privileges* (Chapel Hill: University of North Carolina Press, 1953) 188.

[9]Ibid., 197; *Wilmington Journal*, 10 August 1866.

[10]Dorris, *Pardon and Amnesty*, 191.

[11]Ibid., 216.

afford to remain outside the Union "on account of these persons and because we may not want to exclude them from office." The conclusion was that the terms offered in the amendment "are the very best the Southern States can obtain." If rejected, harsher terms would surely follow.[12]

This theme was continued in the ensuing weeks with some repetition of the refrain that the amendment offered "the best we can get." The *Raleigh Sentinel* did not so much question such a description of the proposal as it did voluntary approval, which it termed a form of suicide. The amendment would give legal authority for the Civil Rights Act, force suffrage for blacks, and disfranchise five-sixths of all male citizens in the South.[13]

It seemed better to the *Wilmington Journal* to allow the state to revert to a provisional government than to surrender "honor and manhood" voluntarily. It raised the question of what states could form the three-fourths necessary for ratification of the proposed amendment. It charged that the congressional proposal was "intentionally shamefully offensive to the Southern people" and had only partisan advantage as its purpose.[14] "No Southern state, where the people are free to vote, will adopt it," wrote Jonathan Worth.[15] To aid in opposition, attendance at the August convention in Philadelphia was urged.[16]

The same arguments about suffrage and disfranchisement, and the concern that the amendment would change the whole character of American government were voiced by the *North Carolina Argus* of Wadesboro.[17] The *Sentinel* claimed that the right to representation in Congress had nothing to do with the ratification of the Fourteenth Amendment. Johnson was praised for approving the admission of

---

[12]*Chicago Tribune*, 13 June 1866.

[13]*Raleigh Sentinel*, 26 June 1866.

[14]*Wilmington Journal*, 22 June 1866.

[15]Jonathan Worth to Benjamin S. Hedrick, 1 July 1866, Benjamin Hedrick Papers, Duke University Library.

[16]*Wilmington Journal*, 29 June 1866.

[17]*North Carolina Argus*, 5 July 1866.

Tennessee and for denouncing the methods used. Peculiar circumstances prevailing in that state indicated that the ratification had not been legal, and North Carolina should not "voluntarily accept the infamous Constitutional Amendment."[18]

By September, agitation for and against ratification brought about mass meetings. One such assembly in Raleigh opposed Governor Worth's reelection and nominated General Alfred Dockery to oppose him; he refused to run. He, nevertheless, expressed a preference for accepting the "Howard Amendment" with its indirect approach to the question of black suffrage "than to risk the next Congress, which in all probability will pass a more stringent law upon that subject." He also preferred the restrictions on officeholders to a more "general proscription, with the confiscation of our lands." There was a very real danger of this development, he said, if the proposal were rejected. Worth, meanwhile, addressed a convention of blacks, advising hard work and the avoidance of politics in order to improve their condition and avoid strife.[19]

The *Tri-Weekly Standard* indicated support for the amendment in a somewhat hesitant way. It had previously published the proposal several times without comment. Now it urged saving the South from "further impoverishment and calamity, by promptly accepting the proposed Constitutional Amendment." This paper asserted, as had others in the North, that "there is not a principle in the Amendment which has not received the approval of President Johnson."[20]

While opposing the amendment, the *Wilmington Journal* initially advised against agitation that would arouse Northern sentiment against the South. At the same time, that newspaper advised against "attempts to appease the hatred of our enemies by placing upon the statute books these nefarious and unconstitutional demands." It seemed better to obey rather than appear to embrace what the people of North Carolina despised.[21] A few days later the same journal illus-

---

[18]*Raleign Sentinel*, 6 August 1866.

[19]*Annual Cyclopedia* (1866) 552.

[20]*Raleigh Weekly Standard*, 20 September 1866.

[21]*Wilmington Journal*, 20 September 1866.

trated the strong, effective influence of President Johnson by reversing its stand, stating that "As long as the President stands by them, the South will refuse to ratify these Amendments."[22]

New courage to resist in North Carolina also emanated from the action of other states in the South. The legislative committee report in Texas was much publicized. A Salisbury, North Carolina paper, urging rejection, asserted that the real purpose of the amendment was to deprive the South of representation since there was no chance of voluntary suffrage for blacks.[23]

An analysis of the proponents of ratification, published in the *Sentinel* included criticism of those who merely pointed out that it really was not so bad. In fact, the writer declared, the amendment would take away the reserved rights of the states and give Congress power to legislate in those fields.[24] The different groups endorsing the amendment were classified in this way: (1) disappointed politicians seeking revenge and new offices; (2) those convicted of crimes during the war and now claimed to be Union men victimized by Confederates; (3) true Radicals; (4) those who really wanted black suffrage; (5) Northern men who had settled in North Carolina; and (6) some honest but frightened men.[25] The *North Carolina Argus* called for candidates for or against "this monstrous proposition"[26] who could make a decision possible.

Lewis Hanes, who had assisted Governor Holden and who was close to President Johnson, published with great respect in his Salisbury newspaper the letter of Judge Sharkey of Mississippi to Governor Humphreys of that state. His editorial pointed out the dangers of the amendment to state rights and expressed confidence that several Northern states would reject the proposal. Kentucky and Delaware were expected to reject, and the efforts of Oregon to withdraw

---

[22]Ibid., 27 September 1866.

[23]*Carolina Watchman*, 1 October 1866.

[24]*Raleigh Sentinel*, 8 October 1866.

[25]Ibid.

[26]*North Carolina Argus*, 11 October 1866.

its ratification were mentioned. Again the old refrain was voiced that Southerners must not be the instruments of their own degradation.[27]

Failure of Congress to promise admission of excluded state representatives after ratification was frequently mentioned. The implication of such a policy in the admission of Tennessee was the only sign that approval would bring a solution to any problems. Opposition to the amendment recognized that the arguments in favor of approval usually asserted the failure of Johnson's policy, assuring North Carolinians that the proposal was essentially the same as the presidential plan. Fear of harsher treatment upon rejection was always included.

Analysis of the amendment by its friends seldom recognized any danger in the first section while its opponents showed that it provided for the transfer of substantial power from the states to the federal government. Suffrage for blacks would be forced on the South while few states in the North allowed resident blacks to vote. The fourth section would be acceptable since it established nothing that was not already general practice.[28]

To join in changing the Constitution would be a disgrace, claimed the *Wilmington Journal*. It challenged the statements of the *Watchman* of New York, which had a large circulation in the South, in its position that ratification would restore the country. "If indeed the Constitution is to be continually set aside and trampled upon, what is to be hoped for by amending it?" The Wilmington paper specifically pointed out what seemed to be an important point: that an option was implied just by the act of referring it for adoption by Southern states.[29] This approach of reconstruction, that of offering a choice, was characteristic of all proposals for restoration and casts some light on attitudes in the North toward the Union and the status of ex-Confederate states.

When Northern elections produced despondency in the South, hope was still extended in the possibility of defeat of the amendment not only in the South but in Kentucky, Delaware, and Maryland. The

---

[27]*The Old North State*, 11 October 1866.

[28]*Raleigh Sentinel*, 15 October 1866.

[29]*Wilmington Journal*, 25 October 1866.

old appeal not to vote their own degradation continued.[30] Georgia's rejection added to such convictions.[31] In fact, David L. Swain, president of the University of North Carolina, wrote to Provisional Governor B. F. Perry of South Carolina that if Northern friends of the amendment knew the bare facts of the South, they would not urge adoption. The essence of his message was that few able leaders would be left who could or would take the loyalty oath and qualify for office.[32]

Against such a backdrop of North Carolina attitudes and election results in the North, Governor Jonathan Worth addressed the legislature. He reviewed at length the efforts of the state to bring about its restoration in the Union by meeting various requirements insisted upon by the federal government through the President. Now Congress had asked them to approve constitutional changes, "some of them altogether incongruous to be ratified as a *whole*, or rejected as a *whole*." There would probably be no objection to some of its provisions. "To others, or to the heterogenous whole, it is hoped the State will never give the assent."[33]

As usual, section three seemed particularly distasteful, for in disqualifying those mentioned they would be disqualifying "the great body of the intelligence of the State." In summary, Governor Worth declared that "the advocates of the Amendment urge that if we ratify it, representation in Congress will be conceded us; and if we reject it, we must expect, from the dominant party in Congress, calamities still more dire than we have yet felt." He considered it degrading to ratify under threats. The proposal should be considered solely on its "fitness to form part of the fundamental law of a country claiming high position among enlightened and Christian nations."

It was acknowledged that the amendment would transfer the protection of the individual from the state and its courts to the federal government and its courts. States would cease to be "self-governing

---

[30]Ibid., 15 November 1866.

[31]*Carolina Watchman*, 15 November 1866.

[32]David L. Swain to B. F. Perry, 19 November 1866, B. F. Perry Papers, University of North Carolina Library.

[33]*North Carolina Executive and Legislative Documents* (1866-1867) 1-12.

communities as heretofore." No definite time was set for restoration. Indeed, Worth could see in the proposal "nothing calculated to perpetuate the Union. . . ." Unhesitatingly he recommended that the proposed Fourteenth Amendment not be ratified.

A joint committee was moved and approved in the Senate on 22 November and in the House the following day.[34] When it made its report, this committee covered most of the same ground as the committees of a similar character in Texas and Georgia. Action of the legislature of North Carolina coincided with consideration of the amendment in Florida, Alabama, and Arkansas.

The North Carolina legislative committee was ready with its report on 6 December. Initial criticism was that the procedures used in submitting the amendment were of very doubtful validity. North Carolina was recognized for the purpose of ratification, but not for representation in the Congress that proposed it. It seemed a dangerous precedent as did the failure to secure presidential approval. This last point was unfounded but had been advanced by Southern legislatures beginning with Texas.

It was especially critical of the constitutional changes proposed in the first section. The proposal referred to privileges and immunities without defining them. Suffrage for blacks and racially mixed marriages might be included by interpretation. The effect of the amendment if approved would be to "break down and bring into contempt the judicial tribunals of the States, and ultimately to transfer the administration of justice, both in criminal and civil cases, to courts of federal jurisdiction."

The committee considered the threat of black suffrage real and indirectly included in the amendment. The idea of voter representation was "inconsistent with the theory of our political system." The third section was designed to affect only the South. Its practical influence would be "to destroy the whole machinery of our State Government." In conclusion, the committee claimed that those disqualified were as loyal as any, due to their complete acceptance of the outcome of the war. "Must we as a State, be regarded as unfit for fraternal association with our fellow citizens of other States, until after we shall

---

have sacrificed our manhood and tarnished our honor?" The state of North Carolina "can never consent to it,—Never!"

The fourth section was merely referred to as "useless." The Fourteenth Amendment as a whole seemed to the committee to add greatly to federal power, which it considered already too great. Yielding to threats, and ratifying would not lead to any guaranteed benefit to North Carolina. Acting on the committee's recommendation, the Senate approved rejection with only one dissenting vote.[35] The House received the Senate resolution and concurred with it that same day, 13 December, by a vote of ninety-three to ten.[36]

All these events were faithfully chronicled in the press. The *Wilmington Journal*, which had termed the committee report "a noble and honorable, if ineffectual, protest on the part of North Carolina," now reported "every member fully impressed with the importance of the occasion."[37]

Though Florida, and especially its capital, Tallahassee, was favored with very poor communication with the rest of the country,[38] the din of the election in the North had been loud enough to sporadically penetrate into that southernmost state. Meetings of Johnson's followers supporting the National Union Convention had been held at different places in the state. Loyalists also responded to Northern efforts to have a meeting of that group in September.[39]

In spite of moderate presentation by most newspapers, Florida was aware of the possible pressure for black suffrage.[40] Efforts at compromise and the fear of more radical demands if the proposed amendment failed were included in the news that sifted down from the North.[41] The progress of the amendment and Southern opposi-

---

[35]Ibid., 91-104.

[36]*North Carolina House Journal* (1866-1867) 182.

[37]*Wilmington Journal*, 20 December 1866.

[38]Susan Bradford Eppes, *Through Eventful Years: Reproductions of 1860 Editing of Starter Printing Co.* (Gainesville FL: University Presses of Florida, 1968) 340.

[39]*Annual Cyclopedia* (1866) 325.

[40]*New York Times*, 25 September 1866; *National Intelligencer*, 10 November 1866.

[41]Michael Perman, *Reunion Without Compromise: The South and Reconstruction, 1865-1868* (London: Cambridge University Press, 1973) 255-59.

tion to it as represented in nearby Georgia also had its influence.[42] Events in Tennessee and more recently in North Carolina and Georgia did not cause Floridians to move toward ratification. They were much aware of the lack of specific commitments for readmission on the basis of ratification and suspected purposes beyond that.[43]

The *New York World's* comment that the amendment was as "dead as Julius Caesar" was widely quoted. It gave Floridians comfort because it fitted their desires and lulled their fears[44] while the proposal was being presented for official action in November. Like other defeated Confederate states, Florida was more immediately concerned with practical problems of economic survival. Floridians were quite naturally more concerned with current reports of yellow fever in Key West and were fearfully inspecting for signs of it in other ports.[45]

Results of national elections were variously interpreted in the South. The *Montgomery Advertiser* attributed Republican victories "more to the credit of opposition to the Democrats than to a decided expression of disapprobation of the party of restoration."[46] The *Richmond Enquirer* reported that the results of the elections were not unanticipated, but still wanted the amendment to be rejected.[47] W. A. Graham of North Carolina wrote that it was folly to expect Southern rejection to be overruled by elections in the North.[48] In general, the Southern press reflected the encouraging words of the *New York World* that Congress had done its worst and that the Radicals had been blocked.[49]

---

[42]Harold M. Hyman, *The Radical Republicans and Reconstruction, 1861-1870* (Indianapolis: Bobbs-Merrill Co., 1967) 351-54; Eppes, *Through Eventful Years*, 340.

[43]Martin E. Mantell, *Johnson, Grant and the Politics of Reconstruction* (New York: Columbia University Press, 1973) 22.

[44]*New York World*, 17 November 1866.

[45]J. N. Shofner, *Nor Is It Over Yet: Florida in the Era of Reconstruction, 1863-1877* (Gainesville FL: University Presses of Florida, 1974) 82.

[46]*Montgomery Advertiser*, 9 November 1866.

[47]*Richmond Enquirer*, 1 November 1866.

[48]W. A. Graham to Governor Swain, 6 November 1866, W. A. Graham Collection, University of North Carolina Library.

[49]*Jackson Clarion*, 25 November 1866.

Conservative voices in the North blamed Johnson's speeches and looked forward to winning the next national elections in 1868. Senator J. R. Doolittle of Wisconsin wrote Thomas Ewing of Ohio that the South would "reject the constitutional amendments." "The Rads [sic] will propose provisional governments or enabling acts based on negro suffrage."[50]

Governor David S. Walker of Florida was aware of this kind of comment when he addressed the Florida legislature on 14 November. He reviewed the record of his state in complying with presidential requirements. "But still," he said, "our constitutional representation is denied us" and military rule continued. No part of the blame for this violation of what he considered the pledged faith of the nation could be attributed to President Johnson. "So far as he is concerned, he has endeavored to comply with our reasonable expectations."[51]

In another reference to what he considered broken faith, Governor Walker claimed that those in "the dominant party are fearful that the admission of the Southern members might transfer the balance of power from themselves to their opponents." "It is true," he added, "that they have passed a joint resolution proposing an amendment to the Constitution of the United States, but they have nowhere said that upon the adoption of this amendment our members will be admitted." The overall impression was that ratification would not end reconstruction.[52] Even if admission should follow, the governor ventured to express the opinion that his people would scarcely purchase something they considered already their right at "so terrible a price."[53] Nevertheless, the lack of a definite commitment to readmission doubtlessly played a part in Southern rejection.

Less than a month after Governor Walker's speech, which professed uncertainty as to whether the Southern states would be admitted upon ratifying the Fourteenth Amendment, James G. Blaine

---

[50]J. R. Doolittle to Thomas Ewing, 5 November 1866, Thomas Ewing Papers, Library of Congress.

[51]*Florida Senate Journal* (1866) 2d session, 5-13; *Annual Cyclopedia* (1866) 325.

[52]Shofner, *Nor Is It Over Yet*, 102.

[53]*Florida Senate Journal*, 7.

of Maine expressed the view of an influential group in the House of Representatives in Washington in this way:

> The popular elections of 1866 have decided that the lately rebellious States shall not be readmitted to the privilege of representation in Congress on any less stringent condition than the adoption of the pending amendment; but those elections have not determined that the privilege of representation shall be given to those States as an immediate consequence of adopting the amendment.
>
> But even if the Constitutional Amendment should be definitely accepted, South as well as North, as the condition on which the rebel States should regain the privilege of Congressional representation, the actual enjoyment of that privilege would of necessity be postponed until the terms of the amendment could be complied with, and would involve a somewhat uncertain period of time.[54]

The press reported about this same time that a caucus in Washington of the dominant group in Congress had agreed to pass a bill excluding from the 1868 electoral college all states not then represented in Congress,[55] so it is small wonder that leaders in the South had little confidence in the Fourteenth Amendment as a means of restoration. President Johnson exerted a strong influence in this regard by continuing to urge confidence in himself. It is certainly possible that with the President promoting the amendment as the sole condition for readmission, public pressure on the Republican party might have achieved restoration, but it is by no means certain in view of certain widespread desires for stronger measures against the South. These desires were enormously strengthened by Southern rejection of the amendment.

Governor Walker had unhesitatingly recommended rejection to the Florida General Assembly. In his list of reasons, many points made in earlier state debates are reflected with perhaps the influence of more recent national agitation. First, the constitutional two-thirds of Congress had not proposed the amendment, nor had it been submitted to the President for approval. Second, the first and fifth sections "taken together, give Congress the power to legislate in all cases touching the citizenship, life, liberty or property of every individual

---

[54]*Congressional Globe*, 39th Cong., 2d sess., 53.

[55]*Cincinnati Commercial*, 6 December 1866.

in the Union, of whatever race or color, and leave no further use for the State governments." It would completely change the form of American government. Third, the representation section was intended to diminish the political power of the South by substituting a voter basis of representation for one of population. This theory was not in harmony with the theory of representation that was firmly established in the Constitution.[56] The amendment quite carefully avoided completely substituting a voter basis because of uneven results predicted in the North, but such an inexact interpretation was frequently encountered.

Fourth, the third section had been inserted to punish a certain class in the South, one that was not more guilty than the others. Those who accepted a congressional pardon under this section would be tools of their benefactors. The governor had little to say about the section on debt other than it was a makeweight; it was only objectionable because it was useless.[57]

In the House of Representatives, the Joint Committee on Federal Relations of the Florida legislature presented on 23 November its recommendation in the form of a joint resolution not to ratify. To a large extent this report dealt with the same points that the governor's analysis did, emphasizing the second, third, and fourth sections. In a challenge to the alternatives of suffrage for blacks or reduced representation as presented in the second section, the committee claimed that "No sane man would desire to extend the right of suffrage to these people without 'abridgement'. . . ." Such action would "result in no practical good either to them or to others."[58]

As to the detested third section, the committee expressed a willingness to do anything honorable to secure reunion, but "we will bear any ill before we will pronounce our own dishonor." Like the governor, the House committee approved the fourth section. In summing up its case for rejection, however, the committee succinctly stated a basic constitutional argument: "We are recognized as a State for the

---

[56]*Florida Senate Journal* (1866) 2d session, 7-8.

[57]Ibid., 13.

[58]*Florida House Journal* (1866) 2d session, 75-80.

highest purpose known to the Constitution, namely, its amendment; but we are not recognized as a State for any of the benefits resulting from that relation." In fact, the committee reported that the state was recognized "for the single and sole purpose of working out our own destruction and dishonor."[59]

On 1 December the Florida House voted unanimously to reject the Fourteenth Amendment.[60] Two days later the Senate took up the report of the Joint Committee on Federal Relations and that same day concurred on the House resolution with no dissenting votes.[61]

The situation in California is indicative of what those in the far West were thinking while those in the deep South were pondering their course of action. It is particularly interesting to note that the Republican governor of California, F. F. Low, adopted a wait-and-see policy and did not give in to urgings of many in the East to call a special session of the legislature to ratify the proposed amendment.

On 16 November, Governor Low wrote to E. B. Washburne of Illinois, one of the framers of the proposal, to inquire about the uncertainty surrounding the Fourteenth Amendment. The California governor explained that, because of the amendment's doubtful future, he was not calling the legislature into session. He did promise that "when the action of this State will decide the matter, or the weight of its action will be productive of good in this direction, I will see that it is done." He was wondering in November what leading men in the East would do, "whether they will simply adhere to the proposed constitutional amendments as the basis of re-construction, or whether other and additional guarantees will be demanded."[62] Small wonder that those concerned in the South should ask similar questions.

The unusual ratification by the border state of Tennessee was not the beginning of similar movements in the South. November and December of 1866 saw further action, as Texas and Georgia refused to

---

[59]Ibid., 79-80; Walter L. Fleming, *Documentary History of Reconstruction* (Cleveland: Arthur H. Clark Co., 1906) 1:236; *Annual Cyclopedia* (1866) 326.

[60]*Florida House Journal* (1866) 2d session, 149.

[61]*Florida Senate Journal* (1866) 2d session, 101-11.

[62]F. F. Low to E. B. Washburne, 16 November 1866, E. B. Washburne Papers, Library of Congress.

approve the amendment. Then Arkansas, North Carolina, and Florida declined to ratify. Southern states were, in general, influenced by similar facts, ideas, and motivations, with each state basing its decision on its own particular view of these influences.

The governor of Arkansas was the only executive besides Madison Wells of Louisiana to recommend ratification. He took his position on purely pragmatic grounds, favoring the substance of the amendment no more than those who strongly opposed it. Economic survival needed political peace in which to develop, and many Southerners favored ratification if it would bring about that vital stability. With no definite promise of restoration and with little confidence that it would in fact follow ratification, few were willing to accept the amendment. As this document was composed of five sections that were not closely related, many referred to it as "the amendments." They did not consider the fourth section, which guaranteed the national debt, as important but to varying degrees, strongly denounced the other sections.

In general, Southerners felt that they could not voluntarily bring humiliation and dishonor upon themselves by approving the proposal. They also objected to what they believed to be unconstitutional procedures used in proposing the amendment. It seemed better to leave things as they were or to await more severe demands that seemed sure to come.

Chapter Nine

Troubled
Southern Waters

During that November in 1866, South Carolina was also moving toward a decision on the proposal. As early as June, the motives of Republicans in submitting the proposal had been questioned in the *Charleston Daily News*. "The leaders of the Republican party do not expect to have this Constitutional Amendment accepted by the Southern States, and are doubtful moreover of some of the States of the North." That paper questioned the readiness of either section to seriously consider unqualified, universal suffrage and equality of the races. For the present, a policy of "watch and wait" was advocated.[1]

After the August convention sponsored by the Johnson forces, General Wade Hampton declared his open gratitude to the Presi-

---

[1] *Charleston Daily News*, 28 June 1866.

dent for his efforts and extended his "cordial support."[2] None of these expressions indicated any belief in the efficacy of any action on the part of the South. The South's destiny seemed, to the editor of the *Charleston Daily News* on the eve of national elections, altogether a matter for Northern decision.[3]

Former Provisional Governor B. F. Perry, who remained in touch with President Johnson, wrote on 10 November that he believed "the Amendment will be unanimously rejected by the Legislature. Worse terms may be imposed by Congress, but they will be *imposed* and not *voluntarily accepted*."[4]

Governor James L. Orr felt much the same some two weeks before he recommended rejection to the assembled legislature. In writing to Herschel V. Johnson, he seemed greatly discouraged by the election results in the North, but concurred with the beliefs of Governor Jenkins of Georgia and the action of that state. "Our true policy in my judgment," wrote Orr, "is to assent to no further conditions that are tendered by our conquerors." Each concession would merely lead to further demands, and "Negro suffrage is to be the pet measure" of the new Congress. The South could resist no anarchy imposed by that body. Nevertheless, he predicted, his South Carolina legislature would "with the same unanimity as yours [Georgia] repudiate the Constitutional Amendment." Threats should not deter them from such a course. If further degradation should follow, the South could with self-respect say "thou canst not say I did it."[5]

A newspaper exchange illustrates the legislature's state of mind. B. F. Perry wrote an open letter to the *New York Herald* defending his position against ratification and maintaining his devotion to the South:

---

[2]Wade Hampton, *Family Letters of the Three Wade Hamptons*, ed., C. E. Cauthen (Columbia SC: University of South Carolina Press, 1953) 124.

[3]*Charleston Daily News*, 12 October 1866.

[4]B. F. Perry to Andrew Johnson, 10 November 1866, Andrew Johnson Papers, Library of Congress.

[5]James L. Orr to Herschel V. Johnson, 11 November 1866, Herschel V. Johnson Papers, Duke University Library.

How can you expect, sir, a brave and honorable people to voluntarily vote their own inferiority, dishonor and destruction? . . . If it should be imposed upon them by others they would have to abide by it and submit but never could they impose it on themselves.

Perry stated that he had never thought that Radical leaders expected it to be adopted and that universal black suffrage was the purpose of these people. "Their object is to establish the permanent rule of the Radical party. . . ."[6]

The same day that the legislature assembled to consider the amendment, the *Charleston Daily Courier* took a similar position editorially.[7] "Acceptance of events is one thing. The subversion of the Constitution is quite another." That organ advised unequivocal rejection "with calmness and dignity."

Whether we consider the manner of its proposal or the nature of its provisions, it is alike inconsistent with statesmanship or policy. It can not bring repose. Its elements are those of agitation, discord and penalties. It changes the character of the Government by transferring to Congress the supreme power over the States.[8]

Governor Orr, when addressing the South Carolina legislature, followed a procedure comparable to that of Governor Walker of Florida in first listing and emphasizing the efforts of the state to comply with all requirements of the federal government. "History furnishes few examples of a people who have been required to concede more to the will of their conquerors than the people of the South. Every concession we have made, however, so far from touching the magnanimity or generosity of the victors, has sharpened their malice and intensified their revenge."[9]

States of the North, said Orr, did not provide for the security and rights of black men in ways that they seemed about to thrust upon the South. As to procedure, the amendment had not been proposed by the requisite two-thirds of Congress. The South Carolina governor

---

[6]B. F. Perry to *New York Herald*, quoted in the *Charleston Daily News*, 27 November 1866.

[7]*Charleston Daily Courier*, 27 November 1866.

[8]Ibid.

[9]*South Carolina House Journal* (1866) 32.

then challenged the congressional attempt to usurp the pardoning power of the executive by the terms of the amendment. Furthermore, there was no guarantee of admission on the basis of ratification, but there were "unmistakable indications that they would still be excluded." With the background of such an analysis, it was natural that Governor Orr should conclude his address with a recommendation for rejection as a means of retaining self-respect.[10]

The proposal was referred to the Committee on Federal Relations, which delayed making its report till the middle of December. It was soon known that Colonel T. C. Weatherly had been deputized by the legislators to visit Washington to see what factors there needed to be considered. He reportedly spoke to Republican congressmen and visited the President. Johnson was said to have told Colonel Weatherly that the South Carolina legislators should "remain firm in their position as regards the Constitutional Amendment and steadfastly reject it."[11] Johnson denied trying to influence the legislators.[12]

Newspaper comment was to the effect that no disagreement existed except that concerning the manner of expressing legislative disapproval.[13] The *Annual Cyclopedia* claimed disagreement about the desirability of a national convention.[14] If true, this disagreement might have been an early hint of strategy that emerged the next month in a Southern compromise offer.

Only one man in the entire General Assembly of South Carolina was reported willing to suggest that "the amendment should be swallowed."[15] The committee made its report on 13 December, but it was not considered until the next day.[16] Final passage of a resolution of

---

[10]Ibid., 33-35.

[11]*Charleston Daily Courier*, 21 December 1866, 22, 25.

[12]Eric L. McKitrick, *Andrew Johnson and Reconstruction* (Chicago: University of Chicago Press, 1960) 491; 1866.

[13]*Charleston Daily Courier*, 4 December 1866.

[14]*Annual Cyclopedia* (1866) 705.

[15]*Charleston Daily Courier*, 4 December 1866.

[16]*South Carolina House Journal*, 204.

rejection was finally achieved on 19 December when all except one (possibly the person referred to above), voted for it. The vote was ninety-five to one.[17] The Senate concurred with the House action the next day with no recorded vote.[18] A Charleston paper reported that the Senate rejected the Fourteenth Amendment by a unanimous vote.[19]

Even before the elections in the North, Virginia was also trying to plot its course. In late June the *Richmond Whig*, realizing that Southern legislators would not meet until after voters in the North had expressed their views, urged the South to declare its intention not to approve the proposal until representation in Congress was given.[20] Throughout the summer and fall, the elections were watched with apprehension.[21] Many individuals, like General Robert E. Lee, took particular, positive interest in the Philadelphia convention sponsored by the President and declared their support for efforts to heal "the lamentable divisions of the country."[22]

Some Northern sentiment also reflected this same yearning for an end to strife. The people voted "not negro suffrage—not confiscation—not harsh vindictive penalties; but the plan of restoration dictated by Congress, and designed to be a final adjustment of our national difficulties."[23] Some, like Chief Justice Chase, as he continued his efforts to gain the presidency, tried to unite Congress with the President in a program that would include adoption of the Fourteenth Amendment together with other items such as universal suffrage and general amnesty.[24] Many who had been willing to

---

[17]Ibid., 284.

[18]*South Carolina Senate Journal* (1866) 230.

[19]*Charleston Daily Courier*, 21 December 1866.

[20]*Richmond Whig*, 30 June 1866.

[21]*Richmond Daily Examiner*, 10 August 1866.

[22]R. E. Lee to H. C. Saunders, 20 August 1866, quoted in Douglas Southall Freeman, *R. E. Lee* (New York: Charles Scribner's Sons, 1935) 4:240.

[23]*New York Times*, 29 September 1866.

[24]Michael Les Benedict, *A Compromise of Principle: Congressional Republicans and Reconstruction, 1863-1869* (New York: W. W. Norton and Co., 1974) 212.

compromise earlier now responded so differently that they produced a wider, deeper chasm than compromise could bridge. Religious people could be persuaded that the amendment was really a wise, even magnanimous, offer on which questions born in blood could be settled.[25]

Once the Northern elections were over, some believed that the political air had been cleared.[26] A kind of uneasy impasse had settled down, with Democrats still opposed to the amendment and the South totally unwilling to ratify even if it remained unrepresented. There seemed no way to make Southerners show the desired contrition and return cooperatively to a weakened position within the Union.[27] While some Northerners like John Quincy Adams wrote that the proposed amendment was "impossible for any decent Southerner ever to vote for it,"[28] a correspondent of Senator Zachariah Chandler of Michigan demonstrated the opposing view by recommending that at least a hundred of the traitors be hanged and others punished."You undertook to pacify them by half measures such as the Amendment. You can now see the result."[29] A comparable attitude is found in the correspondence of one of the framers of the proposal, Elihu B. Washburne of Illinois. The writer advocated action "to reduce the rebellious States to Territories if they wont [sic] adopt the Constitutional Amendment and behave themselves generally."[30]

Elections in Delaware and Maryland, added to rejection of the amendment in the South, "rendered the passage of the proposal by

---

[25]G. L. Prentiss, "The Political Crisis," *American Presbyterian and Theological Review* (October 1866), pamphlet reprint.

[26]W. E. Chandler to D. Cross, 19 November 1866, W. E. Chandler Collection, New Hampshire Historical Collection.

[27]Martin E. Mantell, *Johnson, Grant and the Politics of Reconstruction* (New York: Columbia University Press, 1973) 21-22.

[28]J. Q. Adams to Montgomery Blair, 29 November 1866, Gist Blair Papers, Library of Congress.

[29]Samuel Harris to Zachariah Chandler, 5 November 1866, Zachariah Chandler Papers, Library of Congress.

[30]Cyrus Aldrich to E. B. Washburne, 27 December 1866, E. B. Washburne Papers, Library of Congress.

Northern States alone impossible."[31] Radicals saw this not as a defeat, but as even more reason to push for the black vote, which would be a means of keeping political power.[32]

It may well be, as Professor Avery Craven has suggested, that Radicals in Congress assumed that their victory meant more than the voters had intended.[33] The average Northern voter was certainly race conscious and still devoted to white supremacy as a practical matter. Representative George W. Julian of Indiana touched a tender nerve when he stated that "The real trouble is that we hate the negro. It is not his ignorance that offends us but his color."[34] One implication of such analysis is that many in the North wanted rights and votes to be recognized in the South in order to induce people of that race to stay there, or even to return there.[35]

When victorious Republican congressmen assembled that December, knowing they would be even stronger when the next Congress convened in March, President Johnson avoided mentioning the amendment in his initial message. He did criticize the Congress for not readmitting Southern states.[36]

Although it attracted attention, the Supreme Court opinion in the Milligan case involving military rule was not emphasized as much as its implications might have justified. The able document written by Justice David Davis was available on 14 December and was joyously received by Southern opponents of military rule.[37] The war-

---

[31]*The Nation*, 25 November 1866.

[32]Carl Schurz, *Reminiscences of Carl Schurz* (New York: Doubleday, Page and Co., 1908-1909) 247-49; McKitrick, *Andrew Johnson and Reconstruction*, 455-56.

[33]Avery Craven, *Reconstruction: The Ending of the Civil War* (New York: Holt, Rinehart and Winston, 1969) 260; C. Van Woodward, "Seeds of Failure in Radical Race Policy," in *New Frontiers of the American Reconstruction* (Urbana IL: University of Illinois Press, 1966) 125.

[34]Woodward, "Seeds of Failure," 125-26.

[35]Craven, *Reconstruction*, 263.

[36]James D. Richardson, *A Compilation of the Messages and Papers of the Presidents, 1789-1897*, 10 vols. (Washington DC: Bureau of National Literature and Art, 1896-1899) 6:447-48; McKitrick, *Andrew Johnson and Reconstruction*, 451.

[37]Charles Fairman, *Reconstruction and Reunion, 1864-1888* in *History of the Supreme Court of the United States*, ed., Paul A. Freund (New York: MacMillan Co., 1971) 201.

time dispute originating in Indiana was decided with a condemnation of military tribunals operating within an area not involved in actual hostilities while the civil courts were open and functioning. It was natural that people in the South would consider turning to the courts as another possible source of relief against the powers of Congress. This trend was to bear fruit in the important *ex parte* McCardle case that would soon be before the Court and would create a problem for Congress's program of reconstruction. In January 1867, two other cases struck down parts of state and congressional laws concerning test oaths that persons were required to make if they wished to function in various capacities in recently rebellious states.[38]

Senator John Sherman of Ohio, looking forward to the newly-elected Congress that would assume power after 4 March, ominously wrote during the Christmas season that "The South has two months more in which to accept the Constitutional Amendment."[39] Sherman had already publicly stated his opinion in Congress and in the campaign that ratification would be all that was required for readmission. He criticized the President for encouraging rejection by Southern legislatures.[40] More radical spokesmen like Wendell Phillips feared that "the wily South will adopt the Amendment before your session closes and work its way into the next congress."[41]

In congressional debate, the old argument as to what, if any, pledge had been made to readmit on the basis of ratification was still going on with new significance since the election. In answer to the conservative Senator James Doolittle's question on this point, both Senators Sumner and Wilson of Massachusetts avoided answering directly by insisting that three-fourths of those states already repre-

---

[38]Mantell, *Johnson, Grant and the Politics of Reconstruction*, 22.

[39]John Sherman to W. T. Sherman, 27 December 1866, W. T. Sherman Papers, Library of Congress.

[40]*Congressional Globe*, 39th Cong., 2d sess., 128; Roger Bridges, "The Constitutional World of John Sherman" (Ph.D. diss., University of Illinois, 1970) 263.

[41]Wendell Phillips to Charles Sumner, 27 December 1866, Charles Sumner Papers, Harvard University Library.

sented in Congress would be sufficient for ratification.[42] W. P. Fessenden of Maine wanted to wait for ratification action before Congress should face that issue. Then the legislative branch could pronounce whether unrepresented states were competent to perform the ratification function. According to him, they were not legally competent until Congress so declared.[43]

Ben Wade of Ohio was already openly threatening to put the rebellious states "under the strong arm of military power." On the other hand, he enunciated his position that "If they will take the terms we offer in a reasonable time I am bound to stand up to my agreement." In answer to the question of how long was "reasonable," Wade replied that he meant until the legislatures had met and considered ratification.[44]

James G. Blaine of Maine, a member of the framing committee, refused to be committed as has already been shown. Even if all excluded states ratified, they would still need to comply with its terms, and that, he understood, "would involve a somewhat uncertain period of time."[45]

Before final rejection in South Carolina, the legislature of Virginia heard a long analysis of the considerations involved in ratification by the governor of the recognized government, Francis H. Pierpoint. This wartime Unionist had led the new government formed at Wheeling during the war and later transferred to Alexandria. Now, in the old capitol of the original Virginia, with West Virginia now recognized by Congress, he outlined reasons for accepting the amendment. Pierpoint did not give it a solid endorsement, but thought rejecting it would serve no practical purpose. Victory in twenty-six states of the North in recent congressional elections gave no basis for believing that hope of better terms had any foundation at all. "The practical question for your consideration now is, whether by the rejection of the proposed amendment, you are likely to place

---

[42]*Congressional Globe*, 39th Cong., 2d sess., 191-93.

[43]Ibid.

[44]Ibid., 125.

[45]Ibid., 57.

the people of our state in a better condition. If the views I have presented be correct," the governor concluded, "there is no hope of better terms." Tranquility would follow submission to the conqueror; harsh action by Congress would surely follow rejection.[46]

A motion to refer the matter to a Joint Committee on Federal Relations was defeated in the Senate by a vote of ten to four. Then on 7 December that body sent the proposed amendment to its own Committee on Federal Relations.[47] On 9 January, this committee reported in favor of rejection. By a unanimous vote, its recommendation was accepted just as the House resolution also rejecting the proposal, arrived for consideration. It was immediately referred to the Senate Committee on Federal Relations, which had just had its recommendation approved. This time, by special permission, the Senate authorized the committee to continue to sit during the regular legislative session. Very shortly, a favorable report was forthcoming and was unanimously approved.[48] Thus, the Senate had adopted both versions of the rejection resolution, but by accepting the House action last in preference to its own, made that action the official resolution. In the House the wording approved by the Senate had been passed seventy-four to one earlier that day. Now, to avoid further confusion, the House rejected the Senate resolution.[49]

Off-the-record reports indicate that some changes in sentiment may have developed during December and January. One account mentioned at least one member who spoke very hopefully of its possible passage.[50] Some were reported in favor of taking no action until the end of the session in March. Newspapers had urged prompt rejection, however, and sentiment moved solidly in that direction. Sur-

---

[46]*Virginia Senate Journal* (1866-1867) 28-34.

[47]Ibid., 47-48.

[48]Ibid., 101-103.

[49]*Virginia House Journal* (1866-1867) 101.

[50]Alexander Sharpe to E. B. Washburne, 19 December 1866, Washburne Papers.

prise was expressed that some of the members did not vote at all in the final count.[51]

According to Joseph Segar, all parts of the amendment were acceptable, or could be swallowed as surrender terms, except disqualification of Southern leaders. It would be practically impossible, testified Segar, to carry on state government, especially in the judiciary, with such a measure as law. He mentioned the concurrence of General John M. Schofield in such a conclusion. The general-in-command in Virginia had expressed the belief that the Fourteenth Amendment was unjust and unwise.[52] If state officers were exempt, Segar continued, the amendment might have been adopted.

Alabama's legislative consideration of the Fourteenth Amendment overlapped that of all the other Southern states except Texas and Tennessee. Deliberations there were long and tumultuous. As in all ex-Confederate states except Arkansas and Louisiana, the governor was opposed to ratification. Nearly all the newspapers of the state were aligned against approval by Alabama.[53] An example is the *Montgomery Daily Advertiser*, which in August had called participants from the North in the Philadelphia conservative convention, "our friends." It accused Radicals of trying to start another civil war and "throw the onus and responsibility of an event so calamitous on the South."[54]

In preparation for the Philadelphia meeting, a conservative meeting had assembled in Selma during July. There were Loyalists in the state who looked to Congress for support. These Loyalists were centered in the hills of northern Alabama.[55] Although Lewis E. Parsons had been governor when the Thirteenth Amendment had been approved with the urging of the President, he now traveled exten-

---

[51]Ibid., 10 January 1867.

[52]Joseph Segar to W. P. Fessenden, 9 February 1867, W. P. Fessenden Papers, Library of Congress; James L. McDonough, *Schofield, Union General in the Civil War and Reconstruction* (Tallahassee: Florida State University Press, 1972) 167.

[53]Walter L. Fleming, *The Civil War and Reconstruction in Alabama* (New York: Columbia University Press, 1905) 344.

[54]*Montgomery Daily Advertiser*, 28 August 1866.

[55]Fleming, *Civil War*, 401-402.

sively in the North and opposed not only congressional reconstruction, but the Fourteenth Amendment also.[56] When the *New York Herald* criticized the amendment in September, former Provisional Governor William L. Sharkey published a letter to Governor Benjamin G. Humphreys of Mississippi denouncing the proposal because it had not been passed by two-thirds of the Congress.[57]

The same forces headed by the President that had insured the passage of the Thirteenth Amendment were now allied against the Fourteenth. Loyalists looking for better times under the Radical Congress were an exception. Even so, all this might not have secured rejection if there had been a definite promise of restoration as a direct result of approval.[58] General Wager Swayne, regarded in Alabama as a fair man, was a factor throughout the critical days of legislative consideration of the amendment.[59] Early in the process, he urged Senator John Sherman of Ohio to "give us a little time."[60] He did maintain a constant pressure on Governor R. M. Patton,[61] an old-line Whig who had won over other conservatives.

The governor called the legislature into special session and addressed them on 12 November. In his analysis of the proposed constitutional amendment, he pointed out that it would change the jurisdictional limits between state and federal governments in a way that would cause the state courts to become overshadowed and weakened, if not nullified altogether. Most interesting is his remark that the principal danger lay in the words of section one beginning "No state shall deprive any person. . . ."[62] Few others seemed to sense so

---

[56]Ibid., 392.

[57]*New York Herald*, 17 September 1866.

[58]Albert Burton Moore, *History of Alabama* (University AL: University Supply Store, 1934) 466-68.

[59]McKitrick, *Andrew Johnson and Reconstruction*, 454.

[60]General Wager Swayne to John Sherman, 5 December 1866, John Sherman Papers, Library of Congress.

[61]Fleming, *Civil War*, 397.

[62]*Alabama House Journal* (1866) 34.

much potential danger in this most significant part of the Fourteenth Amendment.

According to the second section, said Governor Patton, the South would lose half its representatives if it refused to give the black man the ballot. Because unnaturalized foreigners counted in the apportionment quotas of states now represented in Congress, it was a case of voter representation in some states and population in others. This was most unfair, declared the governor.[63]

The third section would "establish a test of eligibility for office, both Federal and State, that is not only unnecessarily and unjustly proscriptive, but that might possibly lead to the most ruinous consequences." It was plainly ex post facto, Patton said. With such a section in force, state governments would cease to be governments at all.[64] The amendment was proposed, declared Patton, when nearly one third of the states were unrepresented, and "all of its harsh features are aimed directly at the States thus excluded." In summation, he pronounced himself "decidedly of the opinion that the amendment should not be ratified." Such approval could not possibly "accomplish any good to the country, and might bring upon it irretrievable disaster."[65]

Three days later David C. Humphreys addressed a message to E. M. Stanton, the radical secretary of war, stating that the Alabama legislature would never ratify as long as there should be "a strong party in the North agreeing with them" and offering a hope that ultimately they might gain control of the country. Humphreys urged that Congress and the President get together on a policy of restoration to eliminate delay that would be fatal to the economic recovery in the South.[66] Such ideas were part of the force that produced in January a movement for compromise—too late and too ineffective.

General Swayne had a slightly different opinion. He reported to Chief Justice Chase, who was very active politically, that on "The first

---

[63]Ibid., 34.

[64]Ibid., 35.

[65]Ibid., 36-37.

[66]David C. Humphreys to E. M. Stanton, 15 November 1866, E. M. Stanton Papers, Library of Congress.

day of the session the Amendment would have been defeated by a very large majority; since then, numerous individual changes have been privately announced, and . . . if it is plain that the amendment is a finality, and the only one, it will probably be ratified."[67]

Confirmation of this view is supported somewhat by the new executive's message submitted to the legislature on 6 December. Although he still endorsed the principles expressed earlier, the governor now saw conditions as being different. In order to gain representation again, ratification might be the practical thing to do; surely the matter should be given careful consideration. If, after ratification, Alabama should not be admitted to representation, it would serve as a warning to the other states. Thus a kind of test case was proposed. If it did not work favorably, the action would certainly speed the defeat of the amendment.[68]

An added impetus to compromise could be seen in the growing doubt in the North that the proposal could be ratified. Indicative of this is the comment of the *Nation* on 29 November. Election results in Delaware and Maryland seemed to spell defeat for the amendment; this would certainly be the case if its passage depended on unanimous approval in Northern states. Rejection in the South thus posed the question of what to do. Should not the present proposal be given up in favor of something more acceptable?[69] Other magazines and newspapers were saying somewhat the same thing. If there lingered any hope in the South, it would insure the defeat of the present form of the proposal. All this voiced doubt was paving the way for the obvious strategy of offering a compromise early in 1867 by Johnson and some of his supporters.

Under these conditions, an earlier proposal of Nevada Senator William M. Stewart of a simple program for both universal amnesty and universal suffrage was gaining support. Radicals still opposed it, for even if it did achieve one of their principal objectives, suffrage for blacks, failure to disfranchise former Confederates would nullify

---

[67]Wager Swayne to S. P. Chase, 27 November 1866, S. P. Chase Papers, Library of Congress.

[68]*Alabama Senate Journal* (1866) 176; *Annual Cyclopedia* (1866) 12.

[69]*The Nation*, 29 November 1866.

this advantage. "Universal suffrage with universal amnesty won't do—the disqualifying clause must be retained," wrote James Speed of Kentucky,[70] who had opposed Johnson's plans even when he was still in the cabinet. Speed's position coincided neatly with the conclusions of *Harper's Weekly*, that the "consequences of one process may very easily paralyze the intended results of the other."[71]

December also brought forward new ideas for changes in the Fourteenth Amendment by members of Congress. Even among the majority, moves were afoot to change the first plan. One of these ideas was presented by James M. Ashley of Ohio on 10 December. The main point of the proposal was a frank and complete institution of universal citizen suffrage, not just a restriction to men. A requirement for adequate public schools was added, entirely logical as a support for the sweeping proposal.

"No man was more thankful than I," said Ashley, "that they rejected our propositions. Only by their rejections were we saved from a doom as certain as the coming of November, 1868." The Ohio congressman recognized that unanimous ratification by the North would be insufficient to claim a constitutional change.[72] *Harper's Weekly* also adopted the idea that three-fourths of those states represented in Congress was not enough for ratification.[73]

As can be seen, far from disturbing some Radicals, pending defeat for the amendment that was no product of theirs relieved them of embarrassments in its formal adoption. Their objective had been partly the winning of the elections of 1866 and later, when opinion might be more ready to accept it, suffrage for blacks as a means of staying in power and preventing the return of Southern and other groups to power. Charles Sumner still maintained that ratification in the North was enough, since the South was not recognized as a part of the Union when it was proposed. Keeping the Southern states in limbo could accomplish the same results. Fessenden's statement pur-

---

[70]James Speed to Charles Sumner, 28 November 1866, Sumner Papers.

[71]*Harper's Weekly*, 6 December 1866.

[72]*Congressional Globe*, 39th Cong., 2d sess., 117-19.

[73]*Harper's Weekly*, 29 December 1866.

porting the legal impotence of the South without congressional approval, though the expression of an opponent of Sumner, tended to support him in this position. The administration had sent the amendment to the Southern states; Congress had not specifically requested that procedure.[74] Theorists in Congress had been voicing opinions all along concerning what would happen to the South should it refuse to ratify, and now that an unofficial deadline was emerging, the end of the Thirty-ninth Congress in March 1867, they were going to see whose opinion had been right.

While all this jockeying was transpiring, Alabama's legislature took up the Senate's resolution to reject the amendment after hearing the governor's revised statement referring to a changing situation. The same day, the Senate acted by a vote of twenty-eight to three.[75] In the House, after defeating motions to amend, to lay it on the table, to refer it to the people for a decision, and to refuse action because the amendment had been unconstitutionally proposed, the Senate resolution to reject was accepted sixty-nine to eight.[76]

General Swayne's version of what happened is graphic. After the governor's message had been received with "a marked sensation," it seemed that those in favor of ratifying might win out. "The strain, however, was severe, such as only could be due to the threatening programs of Territorial government with definite results. For it was undeniable that the people, ignorant, proud, and without mail facilities, were not up to the necessity and would be severe upon whoever should act favorably without consulting them. And yet so vivid was the memory of '60-'61 that this dread would have been overcome."[77]

"Unfortunately," continued General Swayne, "a dispatch had gone to Governor Parsons[78] asking counsel. It came, emphatic that the amendment be at once rejected, and that the Legislature meet

---

[74]*Congressional Globe*, 39th Cong., 2d sess., 191-93.

[75]*Alabama Senate Journal*, 183.

[76]*Alabama House Journal*, 213.

[77]Wager Swayne to S. P. Chase, 10 December 1866, S. P. Chase Papers.

[78]Former Provisional Governor Parsons was speaking and traveling in the North. From time to time he also conferred with the President.

again in January. I don't believe this had the inspiration of the President, yet it was openly asserted that it had. The cry was raised 'we can't desert *our* President,' and quite soon it was plain that a vote was unavoidable, and that the measure would be lost."[79]

Others thought it not at all remarkable that Alabama had refused to ratify the amendment. With sister states in the South rejecting for their own good reasons, it seemed entirely proper for other ex-Confederate states to follow their lead, especially in the absence of a pledge to readmit if they approved.[80]

Influenced by the rejection of the Fourteenth Amendment in its neighboring states of North Carolina and Georgia, South Carolina added its disapproval in late December. Election results from the North had already brought events to a crisis point. In this setting and amid much confusion over the issue, Virginia also rejected the amendment. This was a Virginia that had lost the territory and people that were now recognized as the state of West Virginia.

New factors in the ratification picture included a judicial one. The Milligan case, originating in Indiana during the war, was now formally reported. It involved the power of military tribunals to act in an area free of hostilities where civil courts were operating. The McCardle case from Mississippi had not yet reached the Supreme Court, but it, too, would open a new door in the ratification fight.

The situation had now reached a stage in which even its advocates believed the amendment would not pass. Attitudes in the North contributed to a new view of the importance of compromise. Radicals were pleased that the amendment seemed lost and made plans for furthering their own aims in March when the newly-elected Congress would add to their strength. Before that time there was a period when a modified plan, or a new one, might be considered. It was a timely opportunity for opponents of the Fourteenth Amendment to offer a positive approach to new terms of settlement.

After discussing and debating the amendment longer than any other state, Alabama finally came to a decision and rejected the proposal. The event was dramatic, but actually only added another to the growing list of Southern states refusing to ratify.

---

[79]Wager Swayne to S. P. Chase, 10 December 1866, S. P. Chase Papers.

[80]*New Orleans Bee*, 9 December 1866.

Chapter Ten

Another Tack

The Alabama situation was not regarded as completely settled by either side, nationally or locally. As such, it offered the possibility of beginning a new movement to submit a more acceptable
amendment with the backing of President Johnson. This idea was already gaining headway in various parts of the country including the
North, as has been shown. An example is the comment of the *New
Orleans Bee* in early December on proposals to that effect in the *New
York Times*.[1] Now, before Congress could harden its attitude because
of Southern uncooperativeness, seemed the time to act. Although
there were several movements in various parts of the country aimed
at achieving a workable compromise and thus ending the paralysis in
national life by restoring the Union, one line of development seems
particularly significant.

---

[1]*New Orleans Bee*, 8 December 1866.

If a press report is to be believed, President Johnson met at the Willard Hotel on 14 December with Provisional Governors Marvin of Florida and Parsons of Alabama. He met later the same day with Provisional Governor Sharkey of Mississippi, unseated Congressman Foster of Alabama, and the two elected Texas senators. The purpose of these meetings was supposedly to arrange for a conference in Washington on 20 January.[2] Other attempts were made by leaders of the South to negotiate with Radicals.[3] These leaders, with coordinated efforts of Northern Conservatives, opened a new approach to restoration problems.

Not long after the Washington initiative was begun and while pressure continued for reconsideration of the amendment's rejection in Alabama, Richard P. L. Baber submitted a most interesting proposal to Senator Doolittle of Wisconsin, a conservative leader and close associate of the President in opposing congressional reconstruction in the form of the Fourteenth Amendment. Baber was an Ohio Republican who had supported Johnson and Conservatives throughout. He was particularly critical of the Radical proposal to grant black suffrage. He wrote to Seward, Doolittle, and other leaders from his vantage point in Ohio politics.[4] As he expressed it, the time seemed ripe to create a diversion. He suggested that Southern legislatures ask Congress to call a national convention under the constitutional provisions for amending the national charter. They would indicate their willingness to ratify the result of such a shared approach without asking Congress to repudiate its earlier proposal.

His proposal, an alternative to the proposed Fourteenth Amendment, would meet the Radical challenge by indicating a willingness to furnish guarantees. Best of all, from the Midwest's point of view, it might constitute an opening wedge for attacking the New England-backed tariffs, regarded by many in the Midwest and West as contrary

---

[2]*New Orleans Times*, 15 December 1866.

[3]See Governor Jenkins of Georgia to Governor Orr of South Carolina, 26 December 1866 in South Carolina Archives.

[4]Richard P. L. Baber to Seward, 4 November 1865, Seward Papers, Library of Congress; to J. R. Doolittle, 28 February 1867, J. R. Doolittle Papers, Library of Congress.

to the best interests of agricultural regions.[5] We can interpret this reasoning as an attempt to revive the former alliance of agricultural sections against the industrial Northeast. The national convention idea had already been discussed at some length when the South Carolina legislature considered the Fourteenth Amendment in December.[6]

In support of his idea that now was the time to strike, Baber pointed out that "The present amendment was merely shaped as a bridge to get over the elections, knowing that it would be rejected, for it is obvious that representation should either be based on population exclusively, or upon political power, namely voters."[7]

It was the Baber plan to have the Alabama legislature, in which the matter was still under consideration, submit the proposal to Congress as an official resolution.[8] In this manner, the countermovement for an acceptable Fourteenth Amendment would be launched. The actions of the influential former Governor Parsons of Alabama, who was in close touch with the President, may or may not have played an early part in the movement. Parsons and Johnson did play major parts in the later phases of a countermovement along with Doolittle and associates.

Because a close comparison of Baber's proposals with later documents will be in order, the full text is reproduced here. It was to follow a preamble indicating that it could be regarded "as a final settlement of the controversies which have grown out of the late civil war," and as a pledge of good faith on the part of the South.

Sec. 1. No State shall make or enforce any law which shall abridge the privileges, or immunities of Citizens of the United States, nor shall any State deprive any person of life, liberty or property without due process of law, nor deny to any person within its jurisdiction the equal protection of its laws.

Sec. 2. Representatives shall be apportioned among the several States which may be included within this Union according to the number of male citizens of the United States, not less than 21 years of age, possessing the qualifications of electors for the most numerous branch of the State Legislature in pursuance of the Constitution and laws of each State. Direct taxes shall be

---

[5]Baber to J. R. Doolittle, 11 January 1867, Doolittle Papers.

[6]*Annual Cyclopedia* (1866) 709.

[7]Baber to Doolittle, 11 January 1867, Doolittle Papers.

[8]Ibid.

apportioned according to the value of property, real and personal in each State, to be ascertained by laws, but no State shall be admitted into the Union, until it contains at least Citizen voters sufficient, for one representative under the existing apportionment.

Sect. 3. No person shall be a Senatorial [sic] Representative in Congress, or elector of President or Vice President, or hold any office, civil or military, under the United States, who having previously taken an oath as a member of Congress, or as an officer of the United States to support the Constitution of the United States, shall have engaged in insurrection or rebellion against the same, or given aid and comfort to the enemies thereof. But the President, may on a vote of three fifths of each house of Congress, remove such disability by a special pardon.

Sect. 4. The validity of the public debt of the United States authorized by law, including debts incurred from payment of pensions and bounties for services in suppressing insurrection shall not be denied, but neither the United States, nor any State shall assume or pay any debt or obligation incurred in aid of insurrection or rebellion against the United States, or any claim for the loss, or emancipation of any Slave, but all such debts, obligations and claims shall be held void.[9]

It should be noticed that most of the objectionable items to the pending amendment are omitted here. In the first section, there is no definition of citizenship; in the second, a clear voter basis of representation is substituted for the clumsy alternate choice as provided in the congressional proposal. However, careful provision is made for continued control of voter-qualification by the states. Also, the choice of words here would eliminate in calculations for representation any voter who by state law was not a citizen of the United States. The change from population to voters as the basis for representation made necessary the statement concerning the basis for taxation. An innovation in the written constitution is the provision for minimum population requirements for new states. This provision had always and was to continue to be a point of debate and of unofficial standards such as the one suggested here. It was especially pertinent at this time because of movements to add to Republican strength by admitting new states in the West.

Although there are minor variations, aside from apparent errors in saying precisely what he had in mind, the proposal from Baber in its third section is primarily concerned with restricting the disqualification of ex-Confederates to those who had held federal office be-

---

[9]Ibid.

fore the war and to disqualify them only for further service in the United States government. This would leave them free to be selected for state office. It will be remembered that one of the chief objections to the Fourteenth Amendment in the South was this section and the practical handicap to the operation of state government that it would impose. Three-fifths is substituted for the two-thirds as the vote of each house of Congress necessary to remove this disability. The President still retains final power to initiate pardons, although Baber's proposal certainly would curtail his complete pardoning power. The proposal, however, would avoid a clear grant of pardoning power to Congress.

The last section, to which there was no objection in the South, was left intact. Even though no practical result was achieved by proposals for a substitute amendment, the one presented here is important in that it shows in a positive way what was acceptable by its inclusion and what was unacceptable by its omission.

Whether or not Senator Doolittle discussed with the President the proposals from Baber, we do not know. Circumstantial evidence would cause us to believe that he did. On the night of 29 January, not much more than two weeks after the letter to Doolittle was written, the Wisconsin senator met with cabinet members and others to discuss a proposal for a substitute amendment presented by Governor Orr of South Carolina. Others in attendance at this meeting in a club room at Fifteenth and F Street were O. H. Browning, Secretary of the Treasury Hugh McCulloch, Attorney-General Speed, Postmaster-General Randall, a Mr. Dickinson of Texas, General James Steedman, General Daniel Sickles, General George Este, and possibly Secretary of the Navy Gideon Welles. Although Welles was mentioned in Browning's diary as being present, Welles does not allude to it in his, and his account of a later conference with the President would indicate his lack of knowledge of what transpired there.[10]

The next day another meeting took place at the Ebbitt House with the knowledge and approval of President Johnson. This meeting included Governor Orr of South Carolina, Governor Marvin of Flor-

---

[10]Orville Hickman Browning, *The Diary of Orville Hickman Browning, 1865-1881*, ed., Theodore C. Pease and J. G. Randall (Springfield IL: Collections of the Illinois State Historical Library, 1933, 1938) 2:127.

ida, former Governor Parsons of Alabama, as well as Lewis O. Hanes, and Nathaniel Boyden of North Carolina. The group framed and approved certain proposals for a constitutional amendment to be submitted by Southern legislatures. At that time Florida was selected to take the lead in passing the proposal, with other states to follow suit.[11]

During the afternoon of 30 January, proposals for modifications of state constitutions and the proposed compromise for a national constitutional amendment were drafted in the handwriting of Lewis O. Hanes. After a "protracted discussion" with the President, parts of these documents were modified. It was agreed that North Carolina, instead of Florida, would initiate the movement.[12]

On 31 January, the President sent his secretary to call on Orr, Hanes, and Boyden at the Ebbitt House with suggested changes.[13] The names of all those consulted by Johnson are not known with certainty, but Secretary Welles recorded such a conference with the President as taking place on the night of 31 January. After emphasizing the importance of an early restoration of the Union and declaring that the policy of Congress as stated in the pending Fourteenth Amendment was a failure, Johnson said that it was necessary to redirect their thinking. He then asked Welles his opinion of a possible proposal in the nature of a compromise coming from one or more of the excluded states, demonstrating his concern with its possible reception in the North.[14]

Welles did not commit himself, saying the reaction would depend upon what was proposed. He added that in his opinion nothing could be rightfully expected of the South but that it observe the Constitution. Of course, Johnson agreed to that, but pressed Welles for his opinion concerning "whether in the excited condition of the country and the party feeling which prevailed, it would not be well to take some steps which might be considered a compromise." If these pro-

---

[11]Notes of Colonel W. G. Moore, secretary to President Johnson, 30 January 1867, transcription of shorthand notes in Library of Congress.

[12]Ibid.

[13]Ibid.

[14]Diary of Gideon Welles, 31 January 1867, Gideon Welles Papers, Library of Congress.

posals should come from the rebel states themselves in the form of a constitutional amendment that might be acceptable to all and thus form a basis for uniting all, how would this be received?[15]

The President then went into his library and emerged with a paper to illustrate his point. Handing it to Welles, he asked him to read it aloud. North Carolina, said Johnson, would adopt the resolutions as stated on the paper in Welles's hand. A committee, he said, awaited some "expression in regard to them." For that reason, the President was asking his opinion.[16]

Whatever Welles's reaction proved to be, he was impressed that Johnson liked one of his ideas, which was to change that part of the proposal renouncing the right to secede and declaring outright that the Union is perpetual. The substance of this proposed change seems to have been accepted with the additional change that no state could voluntarily withdraw from the Union or be deprived of its constitutional right to representation in it.[17] Whether the exact wording of the proposal at this point came from Welles, it is impossible to say, but the first section of the proposed substitute originally read as follows:

> The Union under the Constitution shall be perpetual. No State shall pass any law or ordinance to secede or withdraw from the Union, and any such law or ordinance shall be null and void.

After incorporating presidential suggestions, it was changed to this:

> Sect. 1. No State under the Constitution has a right of its own will to renounce its place in, or to withdraw from the Union. Nor has the Federal Government any right to eject a State from the Union, or to deprive it of its equal suffrage in the Senate, or of representation in the House of Representatives. The Union under the Constitution shall be perpetual.[18]

---

[15]Ibid.

[16]Ibid.

[17]Ibid.; Col. Moore's Notebook, 31 January 1867, transcription of shorthand notes.

[18]Col. Moore's Notebook. The full document is to be found in W. L. Fleming, *Documentary History of Reconstruction* (Cleveland: Arthur H. Clark Co., 1906) 1:238.

The other sections of the substitute measure framed in private conferences in Washington with approval and participation of President Johnson are as follows:

Sect. 2. The public debt of the United States authorized by law, shall ever be held sacred and inviolate. But neither the United States nor any State shall assume or pay any debt or obligation incurred in aid of insurrection or rebellion against the Government or authority of the United States.

Sect. 3. All persons born or naturalized in the United States and subject to the jurisdiction thereof, are citizens of the United States, and of the State in which they may reside, and the citizens of each State shall be entitled to all the privileges and immunities of citizens of the several States. No State shall deprive any person of life, liberty or property without due process of law; nor deny to any person within its jurisdiction the equal protection of the laws.

Sect. 4. Representatives shall be apportioned among the several States according to their relative numbers, counting the whole number of persons in each State, excluding Indians not taxed. But when any State shall, on account of race or color, or previous condition or servitude, deny the exercise of the franchise at any election for the choice of electors for President and Vice-President of the United States, Representatives in Congress, members of the Legislature, and other officers elected by the people, to any of the male inhabitants of such State, being twenty-one years of age, and citizens of the United States, then the entire class of persons so excluded from the exercise of the elective franchise shall not be counted in the basis of representation.[19]

Orr told Colonel Moore, the President's secretary, that John Bingham of Ohio had informed him (Orr) that the article to exclude from office leading ex-Confederates was the work of Thaddeus Stevens and had been put through the committee that framed the amendment when Fessenden and Washburne were absent.[20] The implication was that there was some aid or comfort being given members of the framing group by some in Congress who wished to compromise. The feeling of the group responsible for the compromise proposal was that if their work should be presented and supported by the entire South, "they would operate as a flank movement against and defeat the Radical program, which as was then supposed, it had

---

[19]Fleming, *Documentary History*, 1:238.

[20]Moore, W. G., "Notes of Colonel W. G. Moore, Private Secretary to President Johnson, 1866-1868," in *American Historical Review* 19 (October 1913): 104.

already been demonstrated could not be adopted by a vote of the States."[21]

At several different points in the compromise proposal, variations occur at different phases of the framing.[22] Without going into these matters in detail, it is fair to say that most are the result of careless error and were eliminated in the corrected final draft. One or two deliberate changes that are highly significant are on record. For example, in the fourth section of the substitute measure the words, "deny the exercise of the elective franchise," were the result of a change from "deny the right to vote," a wording that compares with that of the original congressional proposal. In the same spirit of exactness and of taking care to avoid any suggestion of voting as a legal right, the wording of the same section in the substitute contains "class of persons so excluded from the exercise of the elective franchise." This version is different from the earlier one in that it inserts "exercise of" into the wording that had been "class of persons so excluded from the elective franchise."

It should be noted that the order of the sections is greatly altered. After the entirely new section 1, there appears the changed version of the debt section that had been section 4. Citizenship and personal guarantees are now in section 3 instead of section 1. Representation is made the fourth and last section, rather than section 3. There is no fifth section at all, nor any provision that compares with the grant of power to Congress.

Upon reading the debt section, one quickly observes that the words of the congressional proposal that specifically guarantees pensions and bounties as well as those that outlaw claims for loss of slaves are omitted. There can be no doubt that this omission was intentional. It is difficult to see why the framers of the substitute would make such a change when great emphasis had been placed in recent

---

[21]Ibid.

[22]Interesting comparisons may be made, using the "Notes of Col. W. G. Moore," the finished document indicating changes in Fleming, *Documentary History of Reconstruction*, 1:238, and the proposals introduced into the legislatures of North Carolina and Alabama as reproduced in *Annual Cyclopedia* (1867). Also the proposals are to be found reproduced and summarized in leading newspapers throughout the country.

Northern elections on the fear that Southerners and Johnson's friends in the North intended to endanger pensions and to pay for emancipated slaves. Even if there seemed no reason to retain such clauses from the viewpoint of law or logic, any practical analysis of the political situation would still support caution. Neither can it be argued that law and logic constituted the only basis of the proposal, for by such standards, the entire section on debt might have been omitted. By placing the debt section near the top of the proposal, the framers emphasized its importance.

At first glance it might be thought that no change was suggested in the first section of the congressional proposal, for the definition of citizenship is verbatim and much of the wording of the rest is similar. Highly significant, however, is the omission of the words, "No State shall make or enforce any law which shall abridge the privileges and immunities of citizens of the United States." In place of this wording so deliberately incorporated in the congressional plan appears "the citizens of each State shall be entitled to all the privileges and immunities of citizens of the several States." The latter wording, adopted by framers of the substitute measure, is an exact reproduction of the first part of Article 4, section 2 of the original Constitution. The use of these words seems to have been done to avoid the future difficulties foreseen by O. H. Browning and published in his open letter during the recent election campaign. Browning and those who had approved of his analysis of the congressional plan had important roles in the framing of the counterproposal. Since it was a reproduction of a part of the existing Constitution, the only reason for its inclusion would seem to be a realization that something must be said on this point.

It is difficult, however, to reconcile such an analysis with the fact that the highly objectionable due-process section with its guarantees to "any person" of equal protection was retained as a direct prohibition of state action. It is true that the fifth section with its grant to Congress of power to enforce the amendment by "appropriate legislation" was omitted, but what Browning had seemed to fear most, and what has actually come about, is the use of these sections to review actions of state courts and hence to place them under the dominance of the federal judiciary.

The omission of the section to disqualify leading ex-Confederates certainly was calculated to please the South, but it is hard to see how it involved much of a compromise. As has already been shown, many Southerners were prepared to go much further, though it is certainly true that this section, more than any other single part, brought about the proposal's rejection by the South. The most that can be said for the resolutions framed in Washington that January is that they represented a positive statement by those who had opposed the Fourteenth Amendment as to what was acceptable to them. Obviously they sought to parallel the amendment, which now seemed to be defeated, as closely as sentiment in the South would permit and as closely as the attitudes of those in the North who had opposed the congressional proposal in 1866 would approve.

This much is certain. Johnson had played an important part in the defeat of the amendment up to this time. He had not been successful in the North, but his influence can be said to have been decisive in Southern states. One bit of evidence will illustrate. In Alabama, where the amendment had been defeated in December largely through the leadership of those who worked with ex-Governor Parsons and who had used Johnson's name freely, pressure of events and uncertainty of the future had caused a reconsideration in January. In the midst of this situation, this same Lewis Parsons wired President Johnson relating the rumors reaching Alabama from Washington about a possible compromise, saying "We do not know what to believe." The President had replied immediately, "What possible good can be attained by reconsidering the Constitutional Amendment?" In his opinion the people would not sustain such a change in their government.[23] In less than two weeks the recipient of this message was in Washington conferring on the substitute proposals.

The story of the new approach through a new amendment was presented in the *New York Times* of 5 February as a possible "basis for reconstruction which will be adopted by the Southern people, meet

---

[23]Lewis E. Parsons, to Andrew Johnson, 17 January 1867, Andrew Johnson Papers, Library of Congress; Andrew Johnson to Parsons, 17 January 1867; copies in Stanton Papers indicate the source of much antiadministration information about presidential plans.

the views of the President, and at the same time receive the approval of the majority of Congress."[24] Other papers published its text with varied comments.[25] The new plan was duly introduced into the North Carolina legislature, and friends of Johnson in Raleigh labored to bring it to a favorable result. There was constant communication between the President and his aides working in North Carolina in an effort to spur the legislature to propose the changes as a Southern compromise offer.[26]

In Congress, Senator Dixon had presented the compromise offer on 6 February.[27] Little interest was shown. The North Carolina Senate referred the plan to its Committee on Federal Relations on 11 February.[28] Then began a series of delays. Governor Orr of South Carolina expressed his regret that North Carolina was not acting speedily.[29] W. L. Sharkey wrote Governor Humphreys of Mississippi that President Johnson thought that if the measure prevailed, it could split the Republican party. He hoped that it would. As Parsons of Alabama began to doubt its success, he informed Governor Patton that even if the Radicals should kill the proposal, "it will put our friends on much better ground for ultimate success."[30]

By the middle of February, the action of states where the plan was stalled was being pushed by President Johnson and his supporters. In Alabama the governor had sent the proposal to the legislature on 4 February. Its purpose was stated as being a Southern plan to be submitted to Congress. Because the proposal had been referred in each house to the Committee on Federal Relations, that committee made

---

[24]*New York Times*, 5 February 1867.

[25]Examples are *Raleigh Sentinel*, 5 February 1867, and *Richmond Enquirer*, 6 February 1867.

[26]Communications in Johnson Papers between Lewis Hanes and Nathaniel Boyden in Raleigh and Col. W. G. Moore in Washington.

[27]*Congressional Globe*, 39th Cong., 2d sess., 1045.

[28]*North Carolina Senate Journal* (1866-1867) 260.

[29]Orr to Alexander H. Stephens, 21 February 1867, Alexander H. Stephens Papers, Duke University Library.

[30]Michael Perman, *Reunion and Reconstruction: The South and Reconstruction, 1865-1868* (London: Cambridge University Press, 1973) 262-63.

its report to the House on 18 February. Recognition was respectfully given to announcements from "persons high in authority" that Congress would seriously consider any proposals from Southern states, but the committee had seen no reason to submit the proposal and, therefore, respectfully recommended no action. This position was unanimously approved in the House and sustained in the Senate fourteen to four.[31]

By the middle of February, President Johnson was urging impartial suffrage rather than universal suffrage, for there was no longer any doubt concerning the necessity of accepting some kind of vote for the black man. State legislatures had been asked to pass some kind of limited grant at the same time they endorsed the counterproposal. The plan was receiving a good deal of discussion in and out of legislatures in the South. The crucial question still seemed to be whether or not the constitutional proposal would be accepted as the final terms for restoration. Most reaction was in terms of continued inactivity rather than activity for or against any plan. Possibly, the feeling of being caught between Congress and the President caused such inaction.[32] Much seemed to hinge on the movement in North Carolina initiating movement elsewhere. In South Carolina, the "Orr-Sharkey" amendment would be placed before a special session of the legislature as soon as North Carolina should act.[33]

Delay followed delay and soon the new Fortieth Congress was assembling in Washington, ready to pass stringent rules for an unreconstructed South in the coming month of March. Its actions might even have been taken sooner than otherwise would have been the case because of knowledge that Southern proposals, once launched successfully, might weaken the position of Congress.

All efforts for the compromise proposal proved to no avail. In legislative debate in North Carolina, it was finally withdrawn in favor of

---

[31]*Alabama House Journal* (1866-1867) 456, 472-73; *Alabama Senate Journal* (1866-1867) 363, 409-10; *Annual Cyclopedia* (1867) 15-16; *New York Times*, 10 February 1867.

[32]*Atlanta Intelligencer*, 20 February 1867; *Augusta Constitutionalist*, 8 February 1867; *Charlotte Observer*, 8 February 1867; *Southern Watchman* (Athens GA) 13 February 1867; *Raleigh Sentinel*, 26 February 1867; *Jackson Clarion*, 17 February 1867.

[33]*New York Times*, 17 February 1867.

a resolution for a national convention.[34] By the lack of positive action in that state and in Alabama, the moves to take strategic advantage of a fleeting situation by taking the offensive came to a disorganized end.

Of all the dramatic and interesting episodes within the larger story of the ratification of the Fourteenth Amendment, that of the counterproposal is one of the most fascinating. It has all the elements of grand strategy, discussed and planned in small secret sessions, with the potential for significant results. It failed.

What went wrong? Success of the plan depended on timing, and possibly the idea was tried too late. A strategic approach might have had a better chance before the results of Northern elections had made clear that Radicals would be stronger in the Fortieth Congress. By the time the counterproposal had been publicized, its possibility of success was limited. Perhaps a little earlier, even a month or two, would have made a difference.

Southern support, which Johnson and his advisers had counted on, was never enthusiastic, and the plan depended on the new proposal being launched by a Southern legislature. This launching was never brought about; either Southern leaders had lost confidence in Johnson, or they reacted against the parts of the counterproposal to which they had objected strongly in the original amendment. To succeed, it had to be a compromise, but what points were to be conceded by each side? There must have been miscalculation. Dependable leaders in the North who could carry public opinion with them were not found.

If concessions had been made when the amendment was being framed, or when it was being launched, congressmen might have been convinced. At that time they were trying to cultivate the President. Any acceptable modification at that time would most certainly have been ratified in the South if it had been urged by Johnson. Whatever went wrong, the effort made an interesting story.

---

[34]*North Carolina Senate Journal*, 365, 377, 387-91; *North Carolina House Journal* (1867) 434-35.

Chapter Eleven

Still
on Course

The last of the "Insurrectionary States"[1] rejected the proposed Fourteenth Amendment as if there had been no hesitation in the steady march to refuse ratification. Final rejection came in Mississippi in late January and in Louisiana in early February. Little note was taken of these actions except to emphasize the circumstances producing the counterproposal on the one hand and to increase the Radicals' push for strong congressional acts that were to take place in March.

Mississippi had been the exception to Southern states in regard to the Thirteenth Amendment. All others had followed presidential advice and ratified; Mississippi simply refused despite considerable

---

[1]Edward McPherson, *Political History of the United States of America During the Period of Reconstruction* (Washington DC: Philip and Solomons, 1871) 194.

pressure from Johnson. Three-fourths of all the states quickly completed constitutional requirements for ratification, and the anti-slavery amendment became law while Mississippi continued to refuse even to file a token approval after its adoption.

Laws passed to deal with the problem of the freed black were unusually harsh in Mississippi, being reminiscent of slave regulations. Military commanders set aside some of the worst features of this law with the backing of the President but against appeals of the provisional governor. In the face of deteriorating relations between the President and Congress, Mississippi had little choice, and like other Southern states, depended on Johnson for protection. It seemed only natural to choose executive reconstruction policies in preference to threats of unknown dangers in congressional control. Provisional Governor Sharkey had specific proof of presidential support in Johnson's actions when clashes with objectionable military orders arose.[2]

Newspapers in Mississippi and neighboring Louisiana expressed optimism not only because of presidential support but because of the sympathetic attitude of Northern Democrats.[3] Benjamin G. Humphreys was elected governor even though he had not received a pardon and was, therefore, ineligible. He was actually inaugurated before President Johnson's pardon, probably already in process, was delivered to him ten days later.[4] Other leading Mississippians had gone to Washington to request, and usually to obtain, pardons. One of these, James L. Alcorn, was elected senator, but the majority in Congress did not seat him, and he returned home.[5]

The proposal for the Fourteenth Amendment was duly reported in Mississippi with criticisms of the Congress that framed it. "We trust that no Southern state will ever give its sanction," declared one editor. It would be better to remain unrepresented, claimed the *Natchez Daily*

---

[2]James W. Garner, *Reconstruction in Mississippi* (New York: MacMillan Co., 1901) 99-103.

[3]*New Orleans Picayune*, 17 September 1865.

[4]Garner, *Reconstruction in Mississippi*, 94-96; *Vicksburg Herald*, 4 October 1865.

[5]Lillian A. Pereyra, *James Lusk Alcorn: Persistent Whig* (Baton Rouge: Louisiana State University Press, 1966) 81-85.

Courier. The editor of that paper, Giles Hilyer, wrote that the "Radical Rump" that initiated the Fourteenth Amendment hated the South and loved New England and blacks. It sought to stay in power by control of the franchise. The action of Congress signified that Mississippi had been right in rejecting the Thirteenth Amendment.[6]

Local papers analyzed in detail the plan for a new constitutional amendment. According to them, it had been proposed solely to keep out the South, for Congress knew that the South would not accept the disqualification section. There was no real need for a change in the federal Constitution to protect the rights of blacks. They, like all citizens of Mississippi, had rights guaranteed in the state constitution.[7] The *Jackson Clarion* spoke for the entire South when it stated vehemently that Southern people "should not cooperate in our own humiliation."[8]

Like others in the South, leading Mississippians had attended and participated in the National Union Convention of August 1866. Provisional Governor Sharkey addressed a letter to the newly elected Governor Humphreys advising against ratification of the amendment. The letter was published all over the South and even in the North. The proposal merely offered a choice between evils, wrote Sharkey.[9]

Mississippians were relatively well informed of events and speeches in the North, always interpreted by their press to suit their outlook on their predicament. From the Soldiers and Sailors Convention in Cleveland, Ohio, came an interpretation of the Fourteenth Amendment: "Substantive propositions, without connection have been united in one amendment, and the people have been denied opportunity of free choice concerning each." States could not accept other parts of the Fourteenth Amendment without swallowing that section that disqualified the natural leaders of the South from all opportunity to lead. Even if all Southern states would ap-

---

[6]*Natchez Daily Courier*, 5, 9 June 1866.

[7]*New Orleans Picayune*, 18 June 1866; *Natchez Daily Courier*, 17 June, 13 September 1866.

[8]*Jackson Clarion*, 20 June 1866.

[9]*New Orleans Bee*, 30 September 1866.

prove the amendment, there was no guarantee that they would be allowed representation in Congress. The real purpose of the proposal was to secure the black vote.[10]

When the legislature of Mississippi assembled in October, Governor Humphreys, still without his pardon, informed the legislators that the Radical Congress had proposed amendments "which if adopted will destroy the rights of the States and of the people and centralize all the powers of government in the Federal Head." The South could have no voice; it could only submit. Only time could heal the nation, said Humphreys. As for the Fourteenth Amendment, it had been proposed unconstitutionally by a Congress of less than three-fourths of the states in violation of the rights of those absent. He termed the proposal an "insulting outrage" that usurped the rights of states, and would centralize all power in the federal government. He concluded that "I presume, a mere reading of it, will cause its rejection by you."[11]

It is interesting to note the view of Adelbert Ames, a military officer from Maine who was to take a leading part in radical reconstruction in Mississippi. Returning from a European tour, he lamented the divisions taking place in the Republican party. "The extremists," he wrote, "seem to me to be almost crazy on many points." He had earlier said that he thought Johnson "more nearly right than the majorities in the two houses of Congress."[12]

Mississippi opinion was not unanimous by any means, but some is reflected in the *Aberdeen Daily Sunny South*. The editor wrote that Mississippians wanted to get back into the Union, but were "not prepared to become parties to their own degradation."[13] Congress could not be trusted to admit former Confederate states even after the ex-

---

[10]*Natchez Daily Courier*, 27 September 1866.

[11]*Mississippi Senate Journal* (1866-1867), 7ff; *Macon Daily Telegraph*, 18 October 1866; *Natchez Daily Courier*, 23 October 1866.

[12]Blanche Ames, *Adelbert Ames, 1835-1933: General, Senator, Governor* (New York: Argosy Antiquarian Ltd., 1964) 225-35; Blanche B. Ames, ed., *Chronicles of the Nineteenth Century: Family Letters of Blanche and Alderbert Ames (Clinton MA: Colonel Press, 1957)* 1:31.

[13]December 1866.

ample of Tennessee. The statement of the *New York News* that the proposal was unconstitutionally presented was read in Mississippi with interest, especially its indication that if adopted, the amendment would be repudiated by the South as an innovation "in the passage of which they were neither consulted nor allowed the privilege of a vote." What good would it do to be admitted under the terms of the proposal? A natural question was "by whom can she be represented?"[14] Obviously the disqualification section, the most detested part of the amendment in the South, was uppermost in that editor's mind.

In the House of Representatives of the Mississippi legislature, the Standing Committee on State and Federal Relations reported on the proposed amendment at some length. In summary, members of the committee saw nothing in the amendment to "commend its ratification." The words of O. H. Browning of Illinois, published throughout the country, apparently influenced at least one statement in the committee report: "This Amendment would disturb, to a degree which no jurist can foresee, the established relation between the Federal and State Courts." It would cause a large number of cases to be transferred to federal jurisdiction, to say nothing of appeals from state courts. From a Mississippi point of view, "It inculcates in the colored population a distrust of State law and authority for the protection of persons and property. . . ." The amendment provided new rules for United States and state citizenship and would compel black suffrage with no qualifications permitted. These non-whites could not be said any longer to be "incompetent to vote."

It was the statement of the committee that "The 3rd section degrades and disfranchises a most useful, intelligent and respectable class of our citizens—in a form the most odious and tyrannical—by *ex post facto* law." The precedent of the Thirteenth Amendment, the committee pointed out, was that the votes of the South counted in ratification. They concluded that twenty-five states could not continue to govern eleven as they should see fit, just as one party could not exclude others.[15]

---

[14]Quoted in *Natchez Daily Courier*, 15 December, 27 December 1866.

[15]*Mississippi Senate Journal*, 196.

The vote of the House on 25 January to reject was unanimous,[16] and the Senate took up the measure the next day. On 30 January at three o'clock in the afternoon, the Senate also registered its unanimous disapproval.[17]

Alcorn, who had been elected by the legislature to the United States Senate, was asked to address them just before these votes. That practical, yet popular, leader advised against a coalition with factions of either party of the North and warned that Democrats there were in no position to help the South. On the merits of the proposal, he advised rejection, but as a basis for restoration and political adjustments, he counseled "diplomacy and expediency" in much the same way that Joseph E. Brown of Georgia did. He was opposed to the hated section three regulating the holding of office but would accept even that if there was a basis for national consensus. The South needed restoration so that it could work for peace, order, and prosperity.[18] There were men in most Southern states who looked upon the troubled scene as did Alcorn, but few were in a position to be heard or to be influential.

Soon Alcorn was telling an audience in Bolivar County that the legislature had made a mistake in rejecting the amendment. Such reactions at this point could achieve nothing and represented a "childish display of spite." He pointed to President Johnson's loss of influence in the North. Harsher measures would surely follow through action by Congress. The South, by rejecting, was simply furnishing its enemies with an excuse to launch an extreme course of action that would further injure the region.[19]

Louisiana was the last of the Southern states to register its opposition. People of that state had followed national and regional discussions on the merits and politics of the proposal since it began to emerge in Congress. During the period of the fall elections, the idea

---

[16]Ibid., 202.

[17]*Mississippi Senate Journal*, 196.

[18]Frank Johnson, "Suffrage and Reconstruction in Mississippi," in *Mississippi Historical Society Publications* 6 (1902) 141-243; Pereyra, *James Lusk Alcorn*, 89; *Annual Cyclopedia* (1867) 514.

[19]Pereyra, *James Lusk Alcorn*, 87-88.

of approving the proposal in order to dampen the power of Radicals was considered and dismissed. An attitude of waiting and watching prevailed in Louisiana as elsewhere.[20] Some, like General James Longstreet, who had been quoted in a New York interview, advocated moderation, forbearance, and submission even to approval of the Fourteenth Amendment. "We cannot afford to be made the objective point of Northern fanatics," was Longstreet's argument.[21] The *New Orleans Bee* commented after the elections that it should no longer seem "a matter of surprise that our people should desire to remain passive when unable to act according to their convictions upon matters of public welfare." Remaining quiet and "taking no part in these tamperings with the Constitution" would make it difficult for Radicals to carry out their purposes. "Stand aloof from them altogether" was another way of suggesting the inactivity advocated elsewhere in Southern states.[22] The radical *New Orleans Tribune* expressed delight that the amendment was being rejected in the South.[23] This once again indicated the prevailing view that suffrage for blacks was the ultimate objective.[24]

The legislature that Governor J. Madison Wells addressed on 28 January was elected under the Louisiana Constitution of 1864, framed according to suggestions by President Lincoln.[25] It was still conservative, though Wells was currying favor with the Radicals and had played all sides of the situation to maintain his position in Louisiana politics. For these reasons, the governor, like Governor Isaac Murphy of Arkansas, recommended ratification, knowing full well that the amendment would not be approved.[26] "I believe your minds

---

[20]*New Orleans Bee*, 19 September, 27 September 1866.

[21]Thomas Robson Hay, *James Longstreet: Politician, Officeholder and Writer* (Baton Rouge: Louisiana State University Press, 1952) 329.

[22]13, 16, 22 November 1866.

[23]3 October 1866.

[24]*New Orleans Picayune*, 30 October 1866.

[25]Walter J. Suthon, Jr., "The Dubious Origins of the Fourteenth Amendment," *Tulane Law Review* 28 (1953): 31.

[26]*New Orleans Picayune*, 7 February 1867.

to be made up how you should vote on it, and nothing I could say would have any weight with you for or against."[27] He accepted the idea that ratification would, in any case, not be a finality but that black suffrage would follow.[28]

On Friday, 1 February, the Senate suspended its rules and considered the Fourteenth Amendment, referring it to the Committee on Federal Relations.[29] Four days later the committee reported and recommended "that the State of Louisiana refuses to accede to the Amendment of the Constitution of the United States proposed in Article 14." The recommendation was unanimously adopted.[30] The House took up the Senate resolution the next day, 6 February, and endorsed it with no dissent.[31] None of these events were a surprise to anyone, but interest was sufficient to cause the full legislative record to be published in the press.[32] The *New Orleans Times* observed that "A Governor without a single supporter in the legislature is without precedent in the political annals of the country."[33]

The last two states in the South to reject the Fourteenth Amendment did so in the first two months of 1867. They rejected it after the elections in the North were held, knowing that their actions would have no effect on either ratification or the national political scene.

Mississippi had never ratified the Thirteenth Amendment and exhibited the same kind of unrepentance shown in that situation. It especially objected to disqualification of its leaders and the pressure for black suffrage. Even in Mississippi, however, there were those who, like James Lusk Alcorn, advocated ratification on purely pragmatic grounds. It was more important to reestablish peace and stability so that the state could begin economic recovery than to hold out

---

[27]*Louisiana House Journal* (1867) 4; *Documents of the Second Session of the Legislature of the State of Louisiana* (1867) 4; *Louisiana Senate Journal* (1867) 5-10.

[28]*New Orleans Bee*, 29 January 1867; *Annual Cyclopedia* (1867) 452.

[29]Louisiana Senate Journal, 17.

[30]Ibid., 29.

[31]*Louisiana House Journal*, 28-31.

[32]*New Orleans Bee*, 8 February 1867.

[33]*New Orleans Times*, 8 February 1867.

for abstract principles when drastic measures would surely follow at the hands of Congress.

Louisiana rejected the amendment unanimously in spite of the recommendation of Governor Madison Wells for approval. General James Longstreet, who had settled in Louisiana, supported ratification also. Others joined him in his "practical" advice. They wanted to offer as little resistance as possible to Northern pressures in order to return to normal relations as soon as possible.

No two states were more solidly against the amendment than Mississippi and Louisiana. They both knew that rejection was futile and would in all probability lead to something they both bitterly opposed, suffrage for blacks. Despite this knowledge, they joined the other eight states of the South in opposing the Fourteenth Amendment. They were convinced that they had no real choice.

Chapter Twelve

Shifting
Winds

Even as the concept of a counterproposal for the Fourteenth Amendment waxed and waned, and even after ten of the ex-Confederate states had rejected the congressional plan, Delaware stepped forward to do the same. A strongly Democratic state, it had resisted the surge of Republican victories in 1866 and now had a good working majority of Democrats in both houses of its legislature and a Democrat in the governor's mansion.[1] In these ways it was distinctly different from the areas outside the defeated South.

Governor Gove Saulsbury, who, like Democrats of the two southern counties and his brothers, had close ties with the South[2] predictably advised rejection. "It is believed," said he, "that a faithful

[1]*Annual Cyclopedia* (1866) 264.

[2]Harold B. Hancock, "Reconstruction in Delaware" in Richard O. Curry, ed., *Radicalism, Racism, and Party Realignment: The Border States During Reconstruction* (Baltimore: Johns Hopkins University Press, 1969) 191-99.

observance of its [the Constitution's] provisions would now more effectively secure the just rights of all, than can be effected by amendments such as that now proposed." He expressed serious doubts about the right of Congress to propose constitutional amendments while representing only part of the Union. He claimed that the ultimate purpose of the dominant group in Congress was to obtain suffrage for blacks. Saulsbury objected to the Radicals' acknowledged purpose to reduce the political power of the South; a balance among the sections must be maintained, he claimed. Because the congressional majority was seeking permanent control, it had wanted to reject the amendment "that it might be made the pretext for usurped consolidation of power."[3]

Not before February did the committee to which the proposal had been referred make its report. Then the recommended resolution declared "their unqualified disapproval." In its special report, the minority of two claimed that "the proposed Amendment is an eminently just and feasable basis of reconstruction, and one upon which the present unhappy differences could be adjusted."[4] This minority statement was indefinitely tabled by a vote of eleven to ten and the resolution of rejection was approved by the House, fifteen to six.[5]

On 7 February the Senate concurred with the House resolution by a vote of six to three.[6] Thus Delaware became the first state outside the former Confederacy to register its disapproval of the Fourteenth Amendment. Together with the number of Southern rejections, this action helped to make ratification seem impossible.

New York began its legislative consideration of the proposed amendment about the same time as Delaware. There the Republican convention had declared the previous September "That the pending amendment of the Constitution . . . is essential to engraft upon the organic law the legitimate results of the war, commends itself by its justice, humanity and moderation, to every patriotic heart." It also

---

[3]*Delaware House Journal* (1867) 19-20.

[4]Ibid., 223-25.

[5]Ibid., 226.

[6]*Delaware Senate Journal* (1867) 176.

passed resolutions favoring universal amnesty and impartial suffrage. It is significant that in a close election, Republicans of New York had pledged "that when any of the late insurgent States shall adopt that Amendment, such State shall at once . . . be permitted to resume its place in Congress."[7]

Democrats, also meeting in state convention a week later, affirmed the principles expressed by the National Union Convention in Philadelphia in opposition to centralization and in favor of reunion.[8] Their candidate for governor, John T. Hoffman, a regular Tammany Democrat, declared that the issue was whether, after secession and slavery had been put down and after the defeated South had submitted to federal authority, "the Southern states shall be represented in the Congress of the United States by loyal men."[9] Later Hoffman specifically approved the representation section of the Fourteenth Amendment, but denied that Congress had the authority to demand its approval as a condition of readmission. Congress had never wanted the amendment adopted, claimed the Democratic standard bearer, stating that Republicans planned to keep the South out until after 1868.[10] The nomination of Hoffman had marked the exit from power of Thurlow Weed who had made the mistake of following the President "into the ditch."[11]

Henry Ward Beecher, eminent orator and pastor of the Plymouth Church in Brooklyn, speaking at the Brooklyn Academy of Music in October, took much the same position—he favored the amendment, but not as a condition precedent to readmission.[12] It was what he had consistently advocated.[13] Also, before the fall voting, Hamilton Fish stated his reservations about the amendment, most of

---

[7]*Annual Cyclopedia* (1866) 545-46.

[8]Ibid., 546.

[9]*New York Herald*, 13 September 1866.

[10]Ibid., 29 September 1866.

[11]Thurlow Weed to Seward, 15 September 1867, Seward Papers, Library of Congress.

[12]*New York Herald*, 11 October 1866.

[13]*New York Times*, 13 September 1866.

which he favored. Fish could not "give a cordial approval to that part of the proposed Amendments which restricts the control of each state over the laws regulating suffrage within its limits by making the exercise of that control the price of representation in the Federal Congress." He did not like interference with such decisions in his own state of New York.[14]

In the subsequent elections, the Republican party managed to squeak to a narrow victory by a vote of 366,315 to 352,854 in the gubernatorial race. They retained control of both houses of the legislature,[15] which was critical to the ratification of the Fourteenth Amendment.

In both houses of the legislature a resolution was introduced but laid on the table pending the address of the governor, Reuben E. Fenton.[16] The new executive, in this speech on 2 January, urged the legislature to act speedily, reminding his listeners that the provisions of the proposed amendment "are understood, appreciated and approved." "Never before in the history of the government," said Fenton, "has there been such unanimity in the expression of the popular will." Realizing that the proposal might fail in the South, and apprehensive that the failure of the proposal in the South and rejection of the amendment might lead to possible compromise proposals, the governor emphasized that there was no other plan before the people and that the elections had indicated no desire for another. However, he openly took stock of the probability of total rejection in the South and concluded that in such an eventuality, "it will then be the duty of the Congress, by more stringent measures, to give effect to the popular will."[17]

The Senate lost no time in passing its resolution of ratification the next day by a vote of twenty-three to three.[18] Not until 10 January did

---

[14]5 October 1866, Hamilton Fish Papers, Library of Congress.

[15]*Annual Cyclopedia* (1866) 545-46; Glendon G. Van Deusen, *Horace Greeley: Nineteenth Century Crusader* (Philadelphia: University of Pennsylvania Press, 1952) 347.

[16]*Annual Cyclopedia* (1866) 546.

[17]*New York Senate Journal* (1867) 7-8; *New York Times*, 3 January 1867.

[18]*New York Senate Journal*, 73-77.

the House receive from committee and adopt the Senate resolution. The vote was seventy-seven to forty. A motion to reconsider the ratification was made that initiated some lively debate and, still later, a motion was made to table it until reconsideration. The tabling was refused sixty-six to thirty-nine and the main motion to reconsider approval was turned back by a vote of eighty to twenty-six. Other dilatory appeal motions appeared at once. A motion to adjourn failed as did one to postpone until 22 January. Then, a new vote on the resolution to ratify passed by a vote of seventy-one to thirty-six.[19] Obviously, ten legislators who had voted in the first ballot failed to cast their ballot in this count. Perhaps the changing direction of the political winds that brought Democratic victory in state elections of 1867 was already apparent to some in New York as demonstrated by such vacillation after the vote.[20]

In the Ohio legislature that met in January of 1867, there were Republican majorities in both houses with a ratio of about two to one. These members were meeting after the election previously discussed in which the resolutions of party conventions in Ohio referred to the amendment. Republicans had endorsed it fully, while Democrats had favored restoration under the leadership of President Johnson that included admission of Southern states into Congress "unless on the degraded condition of inferiority in the Union, and of negro political and civil equality enforced by the Federal Government."[21]

Governor Jacob D. Cox recommended ratification of the amendment in his address to the legislature of 2 January. He was complimented by the *Cincinnati Commercial* for not being "one of those Republicans who thought the amendment good enough before the election as a basis for an appeal to the people, but now repudiate it as patch-work."[22] The governor, who had been elected in 1865, took an approach that was somewhat out of the ordinary.

---

[19]*New York House Journal* (1867) 7.

[20]Republicans lost control of the House and major state offices the following November. See *Annual Cyclopedia* (1867) 545-46.

[21]*Annual Cyclopedia* (1866) 603-604.

[22]*Cincinnati Commercial*, 3 January 1867.

Although Governor Cox declared that "a single statement of these propositions is their complete justification,"[23] he proceeded to analyze them in some detail. The first section, said he, "was necessary long before the war, when it was notorious that any attempt to exercise freedom of discussion in regard to the system which was then hurrying on the rebellion, was not tolerated in the Southern States; and the State laws gave no real protection to immunities of this kind, which are the very essence of free government." As to the effect of this part of the proposal, Cox continued, "If these rights are in good faith protected by State laws and State authorities, there will be no need of federal legislation on the subject, and the power will remain in abeyance; but if they are systematically violated, those who violate them will be themselves responsible for all the necessary interference of the central government."[24]

Other sections of the amendment were dismissed by the Ohio governor with much less analysis. On representation, he claimed that the proposal merely corrected an old and unfair compromise. Any diminution of political power resulting from this section would only take away excess power and prevent domination of the Union by the South as in the past. Disqualification of Confederate leaders was a burden that loyalty could remove. The debt section was completely ignored in Cox's address to the Ohio legislature.[25]

The very next day following the executive message, the Senate took up the report of the Committee on Federal Relations.[26] It cannot be said that there was debate, for Republicans, sure of their strength, made no speeches and let all discussion come from the opposition. Senator Hurd opposed adoption of the Fourteenth Amendment because of its birth in the passion and prejudice of civil war. Such interference with the basic rights of the states should not be permitted by three-fourths of the members of the Union. The amendment, Hurd said, would take away the right of a state to determine who should be

---

[23]*Ohio Executive Documents* (1867) 1:282.

[24]*Cincinnati Commercial*, 3 January 1867.

[25]Ibid.

[26]*Ohio Senate Journal* (1867) 7.

its citizens and would make blacks citizens of the state arbitrarily. Injustice was certain to result from giving up the population basis of representation. Disqualification in the amendment was ex post facto and most ungenerous. The debt section, claimed Hurd, was a blow at freedom of the press and speech because its purpose was to prevent discussion relating to the validity of the public debt. Other lengthy speeches were made by Democrats in the Ohio Senate before the ballots were cast.[27] The vote was twenty-one to twelve to ratify.[28]

The House received the Senate resolution of ratification on 4 January.[29] The same strategy used by Republicans in the Senate was followed in the House. Democrats talked away the afternoon, while Republicans merely waited to vote. After one particularly strong speech of opposition, a resolution was introduced amid laughter that a copy of the address be sent to Jefferson Davis to console him in retirement.[30] A count of votes showed fifty-four to twenty-five in approval.[31]

In the neighboring state of Pennsylvania, the amendment was also considered that January of 1867. Previously the Democrats of thirty counties had met in July to discuss the approaching Philadelphia meeting of the Johnson-inspired National Union Convention as the regular state convention had already been held prior to the proposal of the Fourteenth Amendment. This group of Democrats passed a resolution registering the strongest kind of opposition to the amendment. Their nominee for governor asserted that it was a choice between continued constitutional government and "a central consolidated government, bound by no constitutional restraints, and in which the liberties of the people would be at the mercy of a bare majority of Congress, controlled by a self-constituted and irresponsible central directory." The amendment was declared "nothing but

---

[27]*Cincinnati Commercial*, 4 January 1867.

[28]*Ohio Senate Journal* (1867) 9.

[29]*Ohio House Journal* (1867) 12.

[30]*Cincinnati Commercial*, 5 January 1867.

[31]Ibid.; *Ohio House Journal* (1867) 12.

the offer of a reward to the states for granting negro suffrage, and the threat of a punishment in case of refusal."[32]

Despite this bold talk, the Democrats went down in defeat, the Republicans winning the governorship by a majority of only 17,678 votes and continuing their majority in both houses of the legislature.[33] John W. Geary, the successful candidate for governor, took the position that suffrage for blacks was not a civil rights question but a political one. Black people could not vote in Pennsylvania and could not do so until an amendment to the state constitution was passed.[34] After the election in his inaugural address, Geary praised the North for its forbearance and mercy toward the rebellious South.[35] Former Governor Andrew Curtin said more about the amendment's being magnanimous and made necessary by the recent rebellion. He also wanted the question of suffrage left to the states.[36]

Of course, in the election of 1866, Pennsylvania's radical congressman, Thaddeus Stevens, had demonstrated his strong opposition to President Johnson, which necessarily included his support of the Fourteenth Amendment, though it was well known it was not radical enough to suit him. He was more enthusiastic about its guarantees of civil rights than any other part. In Pennsylvania, he was shrewd enough to point out carefully that the amendment would not touch political rights that had been left to the states.[37]

Ratification was taken up by the state senate first, and approved by a vote of nineteen to twelve on 2 January.[38] The resolution was not acted on in the House until 14 January. Four days later the committee

---

[32]*Annual Cyclopedia* (1866) 614.

[33]Ibid.

[34]Harry Martin Tinkcom, *John White Geary, Soldier-Statesman* (Philadelphia: University of Pennsylvania Press, 1940) 114.

[35]*New York Times*, 17 January 1867.

[36]William H. Egle, ed., *Andrew Gregg Curtin: His Life and Services* (Philadelphia: Avil Printing Co., 1895) 193-95.

[37]Speech at Bedford PA, 4 September, reported in *Cincinnati Commercial*, 11 September 1866.

[38]*Pennsylvania Senate Journal* (1867) 13-22.

reported favorably. On 25 January it was read a second time, and on 6 February the House passed it sixty-two to thirty-four.[39]

In the final debate, a motion was made to amend the resolution of ratification by adding a statement that the Southern states should be considered in the number necessary for ratification. However, it was rejected fifty-seven to thirty-one.[40] Not only is it of interest that such a matter was considered and that as many as thirty-one favored the motion, but the vote tabulation shows fewer legislators voting on the issue than on the final approval of ratification. It would seem that some were uncertain about committing themselves. The ratification resolution was sent to the governor after legislative adjournment and hence could not be signed until mid-February when the legislature reassembled.[41]

Missouri also formally ratified the Fourteenth Amendment in January under pressure. By substantial majorities each house voted approval after listening to Governor Thomas C. Fletcher on 4 January.[42] A border state where feelings ran unusually deep and where armed conflict actually occurred between local factions as well as organized troops during the Civil War, Missouri was full of bitterness and continued frictions. Under military control during the war and with only a skeleton government recognized in Washington, Missouri was never unrepresented or considered legally eligible for reconstruction.

Although Johnson supporters in Missouri had contributed to his campaign efforts in 1866 including attendance at the Philadelphia convention, they had suffered a stunning defeat in the elections. One who found that defeat hard to accept was Edward G. Bates, Lincoln's attorney general.[43] He wanted the Constitution to remain as it was

---

[39]*Pennsylvania House Journal* (1867) 276-78.

[40]Ibid., 228.

[41]*New York Times*, 8 February 1867.

[42]*Missouri Senate Journal* (1867) 14.

[43]Marvin R. Cain, *Lincoln's Attorney General, Edward Bates of Missouri* (Columbia MO: University of Missouri, 1965) 330.

and white supremacy to continue.[44] When Tennessee had been read-mitted to Congress, on 21 July 1866, he wrote "I am glad that *poor, ignorant*, Mr. Stevens has found out at last that there is really such a state as Tennessee."[45]

Because there had been military control of Missouri and disfran-chisement of many supporters throughout the Confederacy,[46] Rad-ical strength went back to war-torn conditions and "bloody-shirt" tactics but also to recognition of the faction in the National Union Convention of 1864. They had profited from Lincoln's victory and from the war itself. Conservatives were squeezed out, becoming Democrats in many instances.[47] It will be remembered that the test-oath cases affecting professions had originated in Missouri.

The test oath for voters was not a part of these cases, and the wide latitude given registrars, plus the presence of state troops and some federal soldiers under General W. T. Sherman to keep down violence in the election of 1866, was claimed to have influenced the results.[48] The Radical legislature elected in 1866 had tried to instruct repre-sentatives in Congress to oppose Johnson measures.[49]

When Governor Thomas C. Fletcher presented his views to the legislature in January he said little that was new. The first section, he asserted, would prevent a state "from depriving any citizen of the United States of any rights conferred on him by the laws of Congress, and secures to all persons equality of protection in life, liberty and property under the laws of the State." The second section would give "representation to every person of the class permitted to vote." The debt section, continued the governor, provided against repudiation

---

[44]Edward Bates, *Diary of Edward Bates, 1859-1866*, ed., Howard K. Beale, vol. 4, *Annual Report of the American Historical Association for the Year 1930* (Washington DC: Government Printing Office, 1933) 512-13.

[45]Ibid., 566.

[46]Norma L. Peterson, *Freedom and Franchise, The Political Career of B. Gratz Brown* (Columbia MO: University of Missouri Press, 1965) 158.

[47]William E. Parish, *Missouri Under Radical Rule, 1865-1870* (Columbia MO: University of Missouri Press, 1965) 4-6.

[48]Ibid., 15-16.

[49]Peterson, *B. Gratz Brown*, 157.

and would prevent "repeal of laws giving pensions and bounties for services rendered in suppressing the rebellion." It would also guarantee "exemption from taxation at any future time for the payment of the debt made by rebels in their efforts to destroy the Union."[50]

On 5 January, the Senate approved its select committee's report recommending approval by a vote of twenty-six to six, the identical vote by which an attempt to amend it was defeated.[51] In the House, the ratification resolution introduced on 4 January was brought up 8 January, but its consideration was defeated. Later that day it was read a second time and tabled. Eventually, it was approved by a vote of thirty-four to three.[52]

In Kentucky that January, the governor, Thomas E. Bramlette, presented the Fourteenth Amendment for appropriate action.[53] Although Kentucky was a border state, it was decidedly not in the same situation as Missouri. Like Missouri, it had never actually been out of the Union, although much of the state with its Southern traditions and connections sympathized and even fought for the Confederacy. Also like Missouri, it was never organized as a state to be reconstructed by either the President or Congress, and it retained representation in Congress throughout with much less interference by the military.

In contrast to Missouri, returning Confederates were honored and respected in much of the state, thus gaining influence in Kentucky politics immediately. Naturally they worked with President Johnson and his more moderate approach to the South, supporting his anti-Radical position on legislation and sharing his opposition to the Fourteenth Amendment. They elected Democrats to local and state offices or at times worked in a coalition with conservative Republicans. The influence of ex-Confederates was so great that it seemed to many that in Kentucky, adherents of the Southern position had won instead of lost politically by virtue of the war and recon-

---

[50]*Missouri Senate Journal* (1867) 14.

[51]Ibid., 32.

[52]*Missouri House Journal* (1867) 50.

[53]*Kentucky House Journal* (1867) 19-23.

struction. Rights tempered by a desire to avoid violent change were granted the black man. In these ways the influence of the Freedmen's Bureau was avoided.[54]

Governor Bramlette had offered a resolution in the Philadelphia National Union Convention in August of 1866 in support of the President.[55] The legislature had already removed disabilities of ex-Confederates.[56] As early as December 1865, the *Cincinnati Gazette* characterized the Kentucky legislature "as disloyal as any that ever met in Richmond or in South Carolina."[57] At least their policies permitted persecution of Union men and the reinstatement of ex-Confederates.[58]

In his message to the legislature, the Kentucky governor expressed his disapproval of the Fourteenth Amendment in no uncertain terms. Although he registered his opposition to the subject matter of the proposal, his main objection was to what he considered its illegality.[59] Even if the provisions of the amendment are "as acceptable as they are objectionable," said Bramlette, "the fact that they are not proposed in conformity with the requirements of the Constitution would be sufficient to compel their rejection, and more especially so, when they are held out as a condition precedent to admitting rights already secured by the existing Constitution."[60]

As to the content, Governor Bramlette declared that

> The just balance of powers between the State and Federal Government is sought to be destroyed, and the centralization of powers to be established in the Federal Government through amendments to the Constitution, which,

---

[54]Ross A. Webb, "Kentucky, Parish Among the Elect," in Curry, ed., *Radicalism, Racism and Party Realignment*, 119-20.

[55]Ibid., 122.

[56]E. M. Coulter, *Civil War and Readjustment in Kentucky* (Chapel Hill: University of North Carolina Press, 1926) 292-93.

[57]*Cincinnati Gazette*, 15 December 1865.

[58]Coulter, *Civil War and Readjustment in Kentucky*, 295.

[59]*Kentucky House Journal*, 19-23.

[60]Ibid.; Also reproduced in full in *Cincinnati Commercial*, 5 January 1867 and in *Annual Cyclopedia* (1867) 426.

if successful, will destroy those rights reserved to the States and people, and which are essential to the preservation of free government.[61]

In the Kentucky House, a resolution to reject the proposal was offered on 7 January. The next day an amendment to this resolution, substituting one of ratification for that of rejection, was voted down sixty-seven to twenty-seven. Then by exactly the same vote, rejection was approved.[62]

That same day the Senate received official notification of the House rejection. Again, a substitute measure to ratify was proposed but rejected. The Democratic majority then proceeded to pass the House resolution by a vote of twenty-four to nine.[63] The speed of this action indicates that although there existed a minority, there was little debate and no serious opposition to rejection.[64] It took only until 18 January for the official action to be received and incorporated into the records of the Congress.[65]

In Illinois as in some other states, there had been some discussion, even before final clearance of the amendment in Congress, about the possibility of calling a special session of the legislature to register early approval and thus help the proposal on its way to ratification. With the probability that the campaign of 1866 would deal primarily with the proposal, however, there seemed no reason to hurry and act on "snap judgement" without adequate consultation.[66] Despite issues still heavily tinged with war feeling, the *Chicago Tribune* expressed misgivings about the adequacy of the civil rights guarantees. "Moreover," this newspaper editorialized, "it may be doubted by the friends of impartial suffrage, whether the Amendment itself is such a stupendous prize that it is worthwhile to steal a ratification of it in the manner proposed."[67]

---

[61]*Kentucky House Journal*, 23.

[62]Ibid., 54-61.

[63]*Kentucky Senate Journal* (1867) 62-64.

[64]*Cincinnati Commercial*, 9 January 1867.

[65]*New York Times*, 19 January 1867.

[66]*Chicago Tribune*, 1 June 1866.

[67]Ibid.

Later that month the same paper reported that there was little satisfaction with the amendment among legislators. "It is felt that the Amendment is the cunning headwork of politicians, providing for the present, rather than building up, regardless of considerations of expediency, a sane foundation for the lasting internal peace and prosperity of the Republic."[68]

Senator Trumbull was reluctant to work with the Radicals. He voted for the proposed amendment but without enthusiasm, for he felt it unnecessary except to emphasize ideas that could benefit by repetition. Rejection in the South pushed him further into opposition to President Johnson, and he eventually campaigned vigorously for the Republican ticket.[69] Despite his feeling that Radicals wanted delay to keep the South from returning to Congress, thus helping them to keep power, Trumbull was gradually drawn into making stronger speeches.[70] By late summer he was inviting none other than B. F. Butler of Massachusetts to come to Illinois and speak in the fall. "Our people require strong meat," he wrote to the Radical who he knew could supply it.[71] Still he did not hesitate to claim that states should be readmitted as soon as ratification of the Fourteenth Amendment was complete.[72]

Governor Richard Oglesby waited to speak out until the regular session of the Illinois legislature convened in January of 1867. He then sent his message on the Fourteenth Amendment.[73] In accord with his party's position taken in its August convention, he recommended it. Majorities in the election had sanctioned the party decision over the Democratic convention's stand in opposition.

---

[68]Ibid.

[69]M. M. Krug, *Lyman Trumbull, Conservative Radical* (New York: A. S. Barnes and Co., 1965) 246-50; *Cincinnati Commercial*, 3 September 1866.

[70]Horace White to Lyman Trumbull, 24 July 1866, Lyman Trumbull Papers, Library of Congress.

[71]Lyman Trumbull to B. F. Butler, 29 August 1866, Trumbull Papers.

[72]Speech in Evanston, 31 August 1866 quoted in *Cincinnati Commercial*, 3 September 1866.

[73]*Illinois Reports* (1867) 1:29-30. The message is also to be found in the Journals of the Illinois House and Senate.

Democrats had not been very specific, to be sure, but they had indirectly criticized the amendment in discussions about taxation and debt.[74]

The Illinois governor in his 7 January message recommended ratification on the basis of "a most emphatic approval and endorsement by the people of the State." Oglesby then proceeded to make this unusual statement:

> While in some sense it may be supposed the necessity for this amendment grew out of the late rebellion, and that it was framed with direct reference to the state of facts resulting from the war, it is candidly submitted that there is not a principle asserted, a right declared, or a duty defined by it, that might not, with great propriety, have been engrafted upon the Constitution, without any reference to the war, and independently of and antecedently to it.[75]

If this proposal, so necessary to guard against future insurrection, should fail adoption, he added, other safeguards would be adopted to establish the government on the basis of unity, supremacy of laws, and equal liberty of all citizens in every state.

It is not easy to explain the governor's words. The emphasis seems to be on states' rights, and yet, considering the position of Senator Trumbull, who was the principal author of the Civil Rights Bill made law over a veto the previous year, perhaps he merely thought it could be brought about by an act of Congress. He did speak even before the war of the need for constitutional change. Did other safeguards have to do with an impartial suffrage to include blacks? Or was he merely referring to more drastic military reconstruction to follow?

In the Senate, a resolution was introduced on 9 January to ratify the Fourteenth Amendment. Two days later debate was held on the proposal, and by a vote of seventeen to eight, the resolution was approved.[76] In the House, the Senate resolution was presented and finally approved on 15 January by a vote of sixty to twenty-six.[77] The decision was reached only after women's suffrage had been injected

---

[74]*Annual Cyclopedia* (1867) 399-400.

[75]*Illinois Reports* (1867) 1:29-30.

[76]*Illinois Senate Journal* (1867) 48-76.

[77]*Illinois House Journal* (1867) 154.

into the discussion,[78] and an amendment to the state constitution to permit black suffrage had been proposed and passed by a vote of fifty to twenty-one.[79] The difference in the total number of votes cast on these different measures is worth noting. It would appear that some did not wish to be committed on the issue of black suffrage, a delicate matter throughout the Midwest.

It is also interesting and perhaps significant that while the ratification of the Fourteenth Amendment was pending before the legislature, regulation of monopolistic railroad corporations was discussed with no connection between the two apparently recognized. This fact is especially important in view of later developments and the wording of a resolution to authorize a legislative committee on railroads to investigate the question of monopolies. The committee was "to enquire into the power of this legislature to control the railroad corporations of this state, by direct legislation, on the subject of charges for passengers and freight to secure the private citizens of the state from inordinate and extortionate demands, and to assert the sovereignty of the state over all persons, natural and artificial, within its limits, for the general good...."[80]

The question was raised directly in subsequent discussion whether or not the state had a right to regulate these chartered bodies. The charters were referred to as contracts. "Unreasonable" rates were already subject to review by the courts, which had the power to redress.[81] All this is familiar constitutional discussion that goes back through the days of the Supreme Court led by Taney and even earlier by Marshall. Rights of corporations were secured and defended as contracts long before the use of "due process" in the Fourteenth Amendment. Of course, the place of "public interest" is also part of this heritage—a heritage that was still very much alive in Illinois on the eve of the passage of the Fourteenth Amendment, which was to change the emphasis and meaning of corporate rights and those of

---

[78]Ibid., 153.

[79]Ibid., 137.

[80]Ibid., 45-46.

[81]*Illinois Daily State Journal*, 16 January 1867.

the state to regulate them. The interesting thing is that no connection was noted by those who passed on the ratification of the Fourteenth Amendment.

The legislature of Kansas, which was now called upon to ratify the constitutional proposal, was elected in 1865 but was largely Republican as were those of other states elected in 1866.[82] Governor S. J. Crawford sent his message to the Kansas lawmakers on 9 January. Although the amendment was not all that the governor "might desire," nor what he believed "the times and exigencies demand," he claimed that "in the last canvass, from Maine to California, it was virtually the platform which was submitted to the people." The popular verdict at the polls had been such that as "servants of the people" the present duty of the legislature was plain; it should accept it without delay.[83]

Issues in the amendment were closely related to the black suffrage issue of Kansas. On this the governor expressed himself clearly. He wanted to drop the word "white" from the Kansas constitution and went so far as to join this recommendation to one that would disquality those in the states who gave aid to the Confederacy.[84] Suffrage for blacks did appear in the Kansas election the following fall; it was defeated by a large majority.[85]

The next day, 10 January, after listening to the governor's message, the House passed a resolution of ratification by a vote of seventy-six to seven.[86] The following day the House resolution was pushed through the Senate and was approved unanimously on a roll-call vote.[87]

In Maryland, Democrats had won the election of November 1866 and elected at least two-thirds of the legislators in each house. In preparing for this test, they had met in convention, complimented Pres-

---

[82]*Annual Cyclopedia* (1866) 422.

[83]*Kansas Senate Journal* (1867) 45.

[84]Ibid.; Address of Governor also in *Kansas House Journal* (1867) 64-65.

[85]*Annual Cyclopedia* (1867) 420.

[86]*Kansas House Journal* (1867) 79.

[87]*Kansas Senate Journal*, 76.

ident Johnson, and maintained that the Constitution could not be rightfully amended until all the states had a vote in Congress.[88]

Governor Thomas Swann, a transplanted Virginian who had been elected in 1865, was a committed Democrat. He worked closely with Montgomery Blair, who was close to the President, and with Senator Reverdy Johnson, able foe of the Fourteenth Amendment, on the committee that framed it.[89]

Republicans found the Fourteenth Amendment a source of embarrassment in Maryland, especially since they could not obtain suffrage for blacks, and the state would surely lose representation in Congress because of it.[90] Unionists had, nevertheless, held an integrated convention and called on Congress to help guarantee a Republican form of government. It urged the abolition of "any legal distinction on account of color" and advocated black suffrage not only in Maryland but throughout the nation.[91]

The issues of the black vote and social amalgamation provoked much bitterness; strong prejudice was dominant. One newspaper declared, "Be not deceived; our very firesides are threatened."[92] There were rumors of a coup d'etat to prevent the disfranchisement of the majority of Maryland citizens. Montgomery Blair was useful in securing executive patronage to help shore up conservative sentiment. Radicals claimed their opponents would compensate former owners for freed slaves with tax money. The campaign result at the polls was at least a two-thirds majority for Conservatives in each house of the new legislature.[93]

---

[88]Charles L. Wagandt, "Redemption or Reaction, Maryland in the Post Civil War Years," in R. O. Curry ed., *Radicalism, Racism, and Party Realignment*, 167-69; *Annual Cyclopedia* (1866) 470-71.

[89]Jean H. Baker, *The Politics of Continuity; Maryland Political Parties from 1867 to 1870* (Baltimore: Johns Hopkins University Press, 1973) 470-71.

[90]Ibid., 162.

[91]Ibid., 176-78.

[92]*Frederick Republican Citizen*, 22 June 1866.

[93]Wagandt, "Redemption or Reaction," 167-69.

There, resolutions of ratification were referred to a joint committee on federal relations. It did not report until 23 March.[94] In the meantime, Congress had launched its own drastic program of reconstruction in the acts of that month. As early as 22 February, however, the committee had made its decision and its chairman had begun to write its report. In his words, it was to be "a firm and unequivocal protest against it, in every form—against all the usurpation of Congress." It would, Chairman Isaac D. Jones continued, "counsel patient endurance in the faith that at the next return to the ballot box, the awakened people, who have been deceived and betrayed, will right the wrongs to the cause of Constitutional Government in this land."[95]

The report itself was, in fact, quite voluminous. Its first part consisted of the quoting of the preamble to the Constitution. "We have to confess that we are unable to discover any possible tendency in the proposed amendment to promote any of these indispensable requisites of good government," the committee concluded. On the contrary it seemed that people were being called upon by ratification "to strip themselves and their State Governments of powers most vital to their safety and freedom, yea, even to their continued existence in any useful or practical operation; and to bestow those powers upon the Federal Government."[96]

The border state position, which no doubt entered into the Delaware and Kentucky rejections, is illustrated well in the Maryland committee report:

> There are several striking incongruities in this proposition. The first is, that while this demand for additional powers to be conferred upon the Federal Government is presented in the report, as if made upon the so-called Confederate States only, and as a punishment to them, it is in fact made upon every State in the Union.[97]

---

[94]*Maryland House Journal* (1867) 1139; *Maryland Senate Journal* (1867) 808.

[95]Isaac Jones to Andrew Johnson, 22 February 1867, Andrew Johnson Papers, Library of Congress.

[96]*Maryland Senate Journal*, appendix, 5.

[97]Ibid., 8-9.

Maryland, like rebel states, was to be punished also.

Furthermore, the Maryland committee echoed statements of Southern states in listing objections. The Fourteenth Amendment had not been proposed by any true two-thirds of Congress. No legal excuse existed for excluding those not participating. There was no obligation of a state to uphold the federal law, for the federal government was set up to deal with the citizen directly, bypassing the state. If there was indeed a real purpose in preserving the Union, it was decidedly unwise to upset the balance between state and federal government, always an essential ingredient.[98]

As for the particular provisions of the amendment, there was no need for the guarantees of life, liberty, and property, for that was already in every state constitution. "The proposition to vest in Congress the power of supervision, interference and control over State legislation affecting the lives, liberty and property of its citizens and persons subject to its jurisdiction is virtually to enable Congress to abolish the State governments."[99]

Every state, declared the committee of the Maryland legislature, has its own qualifications for voters. The object of this amendment was to confer upon blacks the power to vote or to deprive fifteen states of a large number of their present constitutional representatives. The congressional committee that proposed the amendment must have ranked the Southern ability high to fear it to such an extent,[100] declared the committee report.

The third section on disqualification of the leading ex-Confederates was so repugnant to the Constitution, in the opinion of the Maryland committee, that it doubted the right of a state to ratify it. To call the acts of these men crimes would be hard to establish due to general approval of the right to secede not too long before the fact. It had even been taught at West Point, the national school for army officers attended by many of the men concerned.[101]

---

[98]Ibid., 10-13.

[99]Ibid., 14.

[100]Ibid., 15-16.

[101]Ibid., 16-22.

The necessity to declare the validity of the national debt could not be found by the committee. Certainly there was nothing to indicate that money loaned to the government could be made more secure by it. "In truth, your committee is of the opinion that the agitation of such a question is calculated rather to create apprehensions than to prevent or delay them."[102] Before the Fourteenth Amendment had been born, such sentiments had been expressed by Hugh McCulloch, the secretary of the treasury, who seemed genuinely concerned.[103]

From the foregoing arguments there was no doubt that the Maryland committee would recommend rejection of the Fourteenth Amendment. It did so and filed its long majority report with a minority statement. The House of Delegates on 22 March 1867 voted to refuse ratification by a vote of forty-seven to ten.[104] On the same day, the Senate concurred in this action thirteen to four.[105]

That part of Virginia that had been recognized by Congress as a new state was considering ratification of the Fourteenth Amendment as the state of West Virginia. Procedures followed in the highly irregular birth of this loyal member of the Union were of dubious constitutionality, but up to now no challenges of their legality has been made. In the elections of 1866 an overwhelming Republican majority of the legislature was selected.

Governor Arthur I. Borman called attention to the "wise" measures proposed by Congress. These terms were not "vindictive" or "even unkind." They were truly moderate and, as the Fourteenth Amendment, were the condition for restoration. Tennessee's admission was proof of the intent of the people and Congress. Governor Crawford recommended ratification that was accomplished by a large vote.[106]

---

[102]Ibid., 22.

[103]Hugh McCulloch to Charles Sumner, 22 August 1865, Charles Sumner Papers, Library of Congress.

[104]*Maryland House Journal*, 1139-41.

[105]*Annual Cyclopedia* (1867) 425; *Maryland Senate Journal*, 808.

[106]*West Virginia Senate Journal* (1867) 24, 78.

Delaware was Democratic and a border state. Its action on the Fourteenth Amendment reflected both of these facts. Even Republicans could not support suffrage for blacks or other parts of the proposal that would undermine states' rights. Delaware's rejection was anticipated, especially after the election had given Democrats a working majority in both houses.

Another border state that shared many views with its neighbor was Maryland. Though it never actually seceded, its strong Southern sympathies had given Abraham Lincoln many anxious moments. Debate in its legislature reflected Southern objections to the Fourteenth Amendment and led to rejection as expected. Legal slaves in both Delaware and Maryland had been freed by the Thirteenth Amendment without compensation to their owners. The ideas of these former slaves voting was not popular. Maryland leaders were cooperative with the Johnson administration in Washington, and the majority committee report of the legislature was withheld until late in March in an effort to influence national affairs. The report was long and eloquent in the defense of states' rights, adding to the worries of the new Republican-dominated Fortieth Congress.

New York politicians were also careful in discussing the rights of states, especially the right to regulate suffrage. Republicans had won after a close election that left sharp differences of opinion and a respect for voter attitudes. Despite this caution, the governor's message went so far as to support more stringent measures if the amendment should be rejected. New York did approve it as expected. Nearby Pennsylvania, though divided, ratified after lively debates centering on states' rights. Democrats charged that the amendment was intended to reward blacks with the vote and punish states that refused it. Even Thaddeus Stevens, in supporting ratification, was very careful to avoid suggesting any interference with the right of states to regulate suffrage. His influence in framing the amendment had not been paramount.

To the south, West Virginia added its ratification. It will be remembered that that part of Virginia had been recognized by Congress during the war as a new state. The skeleton legislature that claimed to approve the division of Virginia in the name of the parent government, and the fictional character of this situation, raises constitutional questions that have been allowed to remain unanswered.

Ohio and Illinois represented the voice of the Midwest and demonstrated awareness of sectional differences in the North and South. Republicans in Ohio used an interesting strategy in their legislative plan to ratify. They remained silent, leaving Democrats to voice their arguments against the amendment. Then the dominant Republicans registered ratification without stating individual views. The suffrage issue was also dangerous in Illinois, as was the issue of states' rights in general. Opinions were shifting, but ratification had been foreshadowed by election returns.

Missouri and Kentucky were both border states but quite individual in their thinking and reasoning. Actual hostilities had taken place in both states, and some federal troops still remained in Missouri. According to Democrats, their presence influenced the election. The legislature, definitely radical in tone, successfully ratified in procedures noteworthy only for their emotional oratory. Kentucky, like Missouri, had never seceded, but large numbers of its citizens had fought for the Confederacy. Now these citizens were returning home to outvote Loyalists and to dominate the governmental process. This situation was unique and caused much concern in Washington. Eventually Kentuckians rejected the amendment, criticizing it as harshly as did any state of the deep South.

The troubled history of Kansas in prewar times is a familiar story. Now the governor, S. J. Crawford, reminded the legislature that the Fourteenth Amendment had been the principal issue in elections "from Maine to California." He wished to go further and enlarge rights for blacks in Kansas by dropping the word "white" from the state constitution. Black suffrage did later appear on the ballot and was defeated. The Fourteenth Amendment, however, was approved in January 1867.

By the end of March, three border states had joined the unrepresented Southern states in rejecting the amendment. The weight of numbers of Northern states under Republican control was beginning to be felt. Beginning in early 1867, a wave of Northern states rapidly added their ratifications to those already registered.

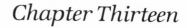

Chapter Thirteen

Uncertain Currents

In Massachusetts as in Maryland there was a delay in voting upon the amendment but for different reasons. Overwhelming control of the legislature elected in November 1866[1] would seem to give Republicans an open opportunity. However, they had to get it past that state's group of extreme Radicals. As has been seen, this group was opposed to the amendment as a final condition of restoration and looked upon the proposal as much too timid in what it demanded. Charles Sumner was known for his "suicide theory" of the position of Southern states and did not feel that they needed to be consulted about the passage of the Fourteenth Amendment. Others sought stronger guarantees before readmission to representation. Fre-

---

[1] *Annual Cyclopedia* (1867) 478. The Senate was one hundred percent Republican, and the House had only eleven Democrats of 240 members. There were two black members.

quently, suffrage for blacks was indicated as the most essential additional demand.

As early as 13 September, when the Republican state convention assembled in Boston, black suffrage was seen as a desirable insurance for the future, which should be required of the South.[2] Benjamin F. Butler presided over this Republican body and asked, "Shall the people who saved the Union not control it?" In introducing the tempestuous "Parson" Brownlow of Tennessee, who was making many speeches in the North, he shouted, "Shall all the fruits of the war now be thrown away and all the good results now lost at the call of personal ambition or selfishness?"[3]

The state platform included resolutions endorsing the black vote and specifically approved the resolutions of the Loyalist convention recently concluded on 3 September in Philadelphia. Senator Henry Wilson told the convention that the black vote must be had by any means, though he had earlier sought a middle ground and had spoken less bitterly in other places during the campaign then in progress.[4]

The retiring governor, John A. Andrew, had disagreed with Massachusetts Radicals in Congress on reconstruction requisites. He tended to support the proposal for universal amnesty and universal suffrage advanced by Senator William M. Stewart of Nevada. Andrew was quite moderate in his views toward the restoration of the South. He recognized the intricate nature of the many-sided problem. Concerned about economic recovery of the South, he held counsel with Southern leaders.[5]

Richard Henry Dana, who had resigned a diplomatic post because of his disapproval of Johnson policies, was now a candidate for

---

[2]*Boston Daily Transcript*, 13 September 1866.

[3]Martin E. Mantell, *Johnson, Grant, and the Politics of Reconstruction* (New York: Columbia University Press, 1973) 17; Michael Les Benedict, *A Compromise of Principle: Congressional Republicans and Reconstruction, 1863-1869* (New York: W. W. Norton and Co., 1974) 201.

[4]Ernest McKay, *Henry Wilson: Practical Radical, A Portrait of a Politician* (Port Washington NY: Kennikat Press, 1971) 206.

[5]Henry Greenleaf Pearson, *The Life of John A. Andrew, Governor of Massachusetts, 1861-1865* (Boston: Houghton Mifflin Co., 1904) 2:312.

the state legislature.[6] Congressman George S. Boutwell, who had served on the committee that framed the Fourteenth Amendment, urged its ratification. He had contempt for Senator Sumner, who seemed to him to be much too impractical[7] as he thought most Radicals were.

Massachusetts had been slow to accept suffrage for blacks as an issue. Henry Wilson had tried to work with Johnson as had Sumner himself in his arrogant and pedantic fashion.[8] Wilson had concluded that the people simply were not ready to support that issue in 1865. In his home state he argued that the Fourteenth Amendment would eventually bring black suffrage about,[9] but he still was not sure of popular support. He now followed his first arguments against early admission of the South by saying that it would have to accept black suffrage or simply remain unrepresented.[10]

In Boston, Southern papers were quoted to show that no pledge to admit on the basis of ratification had been made or understood. The only reason no specific pledge had been made, however, as editorially explained by the *Boston Advertiser* was because of controversy concerning the date representation would become effective—after the individual state action or when official ratification of the amendment should be completed.[11]

Sumner maintained his absolutist position after the Massachusetts Republican convention. In an address in the Boston Music Hall on 2 October, he urged black suffrage as the best guarantee. "Their ballots will be needed in time to come much more than their muskets

---

[6]Charles Frances Adams, *Richard Henry Dana* (Boston: Houghton Mifflin Co., 1890) 336.

[7]George S. Boutwell, *Reminiscences of Sixty Years in Public Affairs* (New York: McClure, Philips Co., 1902) 46.

[8]Henry Wilson to Charles Sumner, 7 September 1865, Charles Sumner Papers, Harvard University Library.

[9]Richard H. Abbot, *Cobbler in Congress: Life of Henry Wilson, 1812-1875* (Lexington: University of Kentucky Press, 1972) 169; *Boston Daily Transcript*, 11 August 1866.

[10]Abbot, *Cobbler in Congress*, 175.

[11]*Boston Advertiser*, 29 September 1866.

were needed in time past." There must be more guarantees for the future, he urged.[12]

In Washington, Sumner was at last tasting victory after his unswerving insistence on imposing black suffrage on the South. His membership on the special Senate committee headed by Sherman of Ohio gave him an opportunity to win Republican caucus approval on 17 February for his proposal to require such suffrage. He still demanded more reformation of Southern institutions than his more moderate colleagues could accept.[13] Meanwhile, the National Union State Convention and the Democratic State Convention were held in Boston on 3 October. Conservative Republicans and Democrats in these meetings pledged support of the National Union Party ticket in the 6 November election.[14]

Overwhelming Republican control of the legislature resulted from the balloting.[15] With this group in power, it would seem that passage of the amendment was certain when Governor Alex H. Bulloch recommended it on 4 January. But as has been seen in other similar situations, extreme Radicals were opposed to immediate adoption of the proposal. Wendell Phillips wrote Sumner that February, "Can't you write to some of your friends (Bird or Loring or some one, Stone the speaker) in the House or Senate here advising them *to reject* or *postpone* action on the amendment?"[16]

Whether in answer to a letter of Sumner's or on his own initiative, George B. Loring suggested that admission of new states must be based on universal suffrage and that Massachusetts "consider the proposed amendment not as a finality, but simply an advancing step in the work of reconstruction."[17]

---

[12]Charles Sumner, *Works of Charles Sumner* (Boston: Lee and Shephard, 1870-1883) 11:22.

[13]David Donald, *Charles Sumner and the Rights of Man* (New York: Alfred A. Knopf, 1970) 281-87, 298.

[14]*Annual Cyclopedia* (1867) 478.

[15]Ibid.

[16]Wendell Phillips to Charles Sumner, 1 February 1867, Sumner Papers.

[17]George B. Loring to Charles Sumner, 9 February 1867, Sumner Papers.

For whatever reason, action was postponed by many dilatory tactics. The Joint Committee on Federal Relations did not report until 1 March. F. W. Bird and George B. Loring, specifically mentioned in Phillips's letter to Sumner, were members[18] and undoubtedly played a part in the delay. During the interval between reference and report, other resolutions concerning the amendment were turned over to the same committee,[19] as were objections and petitions during January and February.[20]

When the 1 March committee report was read, it recommended postponement until the next session.[21] The majority report pointed out that only New York had failed to omit any endorsement of readmission to representation for the South when ratification should be complete. Congress was in an excellent position to require guarantees with or without the amendment.[22] In fact, the first of several reconstruction acts was at that time receiving approval in Congress. It was abolishing presidential methods and establishing military control in the South as a means of beginning the congressional approach to restoration of the Union with added conditions to those already advanced in the Fourteenth Amendment.

As for Massachusetts, ratification would become a final condition for admission on approval. The committee recognized that the South was expecting the courts to set aside the amendment because of alleged unconstitutional procedures used in proposing and counting states for ratification. The majority indicated that Massachusetts disfranchised certain classes such as paupers, those under guardianship, nonresidents, and tax delinquents. These exclusions might well cost the state representatives or at least cause trouble in the courts.[23]

---

[18]*Massachusetts House Journal* (1867) 66.

[19]Ibid., 125-54.

[20]Ibid., 181-201.

[21]Ibid., 166.

[22]*New York Times*, 2 March 1867.

[23]Ibid.

Section three seemed to fall short of meeting the need. Nowhere did the amendment really enlarge congressional powers because the fifth section applied only to the amendment. Court rulings on definition of citizens as native born or naturalized seemed a better way to deal with that question. Much of what was proposed in the amendment was already covered by the Constitution thus making the provisions of the Fourteenth Amendment "mere surplusage." Section two would permit continued disfranchising of black citizens and the penalty for not giving these people the vote was too little. There seemed no real reason to ratify, at least at that time.[24]

A minority report[25] recommended adoption of the Fourteenth Amendment and a motion to accept its recommendations as a substitute for those of the majority was adopted in the House on 13 March by a vote of 120 to 22.[26] This action was followed the next day by a resolution to ask Congress for a constitutional amendment prohibiting the disqualification of any citizen because of color. It was defeated 130 to 14.[27]

On 14 March the proposed Fourteenth Amendment was ordered read a third time by a vote of 197 to 21. After objections about a suspension of the rules, the ratification motion was passed on 15 March. The vote was 120 to 20.[28] The House resolution was received in the Senate[29] where the Joint Committee's report was already on the agenda. On the following Monday, 18 March, before the House's resolution was to be taken up on Tuesday at 2:30 P.M., a Senate resolution was proposed for a constitutional amendment to change voting qualifications. This proposal was referred to the Judiciary Committee. A number of other motions relating to the recent war were clam-

---

[24]Ibid., 2 March 1867; Irving Brant, *The Bill of Rights* (Indianapolis: Bobbs-Merrill Co., 1965) 342.

[25]See *Massachusetts House Journal*, appendix, 12.

[26]*Massachusetts House Journal*, 207.

[27]Ibid., 202.

[28]Ibid., 211; Edward McPherson, *Political History of the United States of America during the Period of Reconstruction* (Washington DC: Philip and Solomons, 1871) 194.

[29]*Massachusetts Senate Journal* (1867) 377.

oring for attention, such as one demanding aid for disabled soldiers and sailors and their families as well as for families of slaves.[30]

On Tuesday, the Senate considered the House resolution on "an Amendment of the Constitution of the United States." As planned, the motion to defer action until the next meeting of the General Court was defeated five to twenty-six and further action was delayed until Wednesday, 20 March. At no point does the Senate journal refer to the proposal for the Fourteenth Amendment in those terms, but only as "an Amendment to the Constitution of the United States." However, under such a general label, the amendment was voted on and approved by a vote of twenty-four to six.[31]

Other states were acting more quickly. Nevada, hurriedly admitted into the Union only eight days prior to the 1864 election that it was intended to influence, helped the Republican majority in Congress, especially with the addition of its two senators. Now the governor of this overrepresented state recommended passage of the Fourteenth Amendment after giving it his hearty endorsement. This was on 10 January.[32] The very next day the House passed such a resolution of ratification by a vote of twenty-four to four.[33] Eleven days later the Senate gave its approval by a vote of eleven to three.[34] Needless to say, Republicans commanded large majorities in both houses of the Nevada legislature.[35]

The Wisconsin legislature, also overwhelmingly Republican,[36] convened in January of 1867. That state's Senator Doolittle had backed President Johnson and had been one of the national leaders against the Fourteenth Amendment. Senator Timothy Howe gave reluctant support, although it was not radical enough for his taste.[37]

---

[30]Ibid., 385.

[31]Ibid., 395, 401-402.

[32]*Nevada Senate Journal* (1867) 9-10.

[33]*Nevada House Journal* (1867) 21-25.

[34]*Nevada Senate Journal*, 14.

[35]*Annual Cyclopedia* (1866) 772.

[36]Ibid., 535.

[37]*Congressional Globe*, 39th Cong., 1st sess., appendix, 267.

It should also be noted that Wisconsin had been one of the states that had voted against black suffrage in 1865. Governor Lucius Fairchild, whose record on reconstruction had been relatively moderate, declared in his message of 10 January that the proposals for constitutional amendment had been before the people of the nation for months and that "the people of this state are thoroughly familiar with its provisions and, with a full understanding of them in all their bearings, have declared in favor of its immediate ratification." Such an issue had been the basis for the recent campaign throughout the North, said the Wisconsin executive.[38]

The demand for Southern ratification, declared Fairchild, "is not made with a desire to appropriate to ourselves undue political power, or to oppress or humiliate the Southern people. It is made because, in view of the terrible events of the past five years, we deem these guarantees necessary to the life of the nation, and we insist that those who saved the life have an undeniable right to demand all guarantees essential to its future preservation." At least two-thirds of the loyal states would ratify, he said. The time for compromise was now over and the people must be prepared to do right for right's sake.[39] It is interesting to see the modest claims concerning ratification that states put forward in this speech. Most of the Southern states had already rejected the proposal and there were some signs of disapproval in at least a few Northern states.

Wisconsin's Senate passed a resolution of ratification on 23 January by a vote of twenty-two to ten after some parliamentary maneuvering.[40] The Committee on Federal Relations had been in charge of it and other interesting material, including a resolution to request the resignation of Senator Doolittle. It had reported favorably on the ratification issue on 22 January.[41]

The minority filed a lengthy report worthy of some note.[42] In it the opposition claimed that the proposal was aimed at "the surrender

---

[38]*Wisconsin Senate Journal* (1867) 32.

[39]Ibid., 33.

[40]Ibid., 108-109.

[41]Ibid., 41-73.

[42]*Wisconsin House Journal* (1867) 96-104.

of certain rights and powers which the several states of the union now hold by their sovereign power in trust over the persons and property of their citizens to the federal government, so as to make it the arbiter between the states and the citizens and residents thereof." Such a development would disturb the harmony between federal and state governments. "Under the amendments Congress will have power to appoint commissioners and provide for courts that may be authorized to say if the state is depriving its citizens of his rights without due process of law."

All this, the minority claimed, was repugnant to the Republican platform of 1860. Population could be the only secure basis for representation. The disqualification section would eliminate from public life all the educated leaders of the South. Although the debt section could do no harm, "it may be questioned if it would do any good." The procedure used in proposing the amendment was improper, since not two-thirds had backed it in Congress.

Despite this reasoned statement and other active opposition that caused delay, the ratification by Wisconsin was formalized in the Senate on 23 January. The matter was then transferred to the lower house. However, not until 7 February was the proposal put to a final vote. It was then passed sixty-nine to ten with thirteen members not present.[43]

In another midwestern state, Indiana, the 1866 elections had been exceedingly animated, with strong language and even riots occurring during Johnson's visit to Indianapolis that September. Both state conventions had already met before the Fourteenth Amendment had cleared Congress, so there were no clearly defined party positions on that prime issue.

When the election was held in October, the legislature selected was decidedly Republican, but members were not so dominant as in many other states. The majorities were thirty to twenty in the Senate and sixty-one to thirty-nine in the House.[44] Then too, the attitude of most Republicans was much more moderate and less radical than the party label might indicate. These events resulted despite the attitude

---

[43]*Wisconsin Senate Journal*, 109; *Wisconsin House Journal*, 224.

[44]*Annual Cyclopedia* (1867) 404-406.

expressed that June in neighboring Ohio that "If you are determined that we should choose between Radicalism and Copperheadism, I fear there is danger of making Radicals of us all."[45]

Senator Hendricks and other Conservatives offered spirited opposition as has already been shown elsewhere. The prominent position of Schuyler Colfax as Speaker of the House helped Republicans, although even he did not sound extremely radical. Democrats attacked him in his own district, but with an ineffectual candidate. Colfax skillfully exploited reaction to Southern riots and the Irish vote, and carefully used the "bloody shirt" technique and made personal charges against his opponent in order to defeat the Democratic challenge that attacked the Fourteenth Amendment and favored immediate admission of Southern states.[46]

Governor Morton and other Republican leaders avoided the black-suffrage issue although it was openly urged by some.[47] The question of blacks' rights in conservative Indiana was made more prominent by a state-court decision that the 1851 law forbidding blacks "to come in or settle in the state" was unconstitutional. This decision was based on Article 4 provisions of the Constitution concerning privileges and immunities. The dilemma was pointed out by the *Chicago Tribune* in June when it declared that Indiana would have to choose suffrage for blacks or loss of Congressional representation if the Fourteenth Amendment became law.[48]

Governor Oliver P. Morton addressed the biennial session of the Indiana legislature on 11 January. Like other Republican governors, he made much of the last election as being a forum in which the voters had, with full understanding, passed on the desirability of the proposed Fourteenth Amendment. "No public measure was ever more fully discussed before the people, better understood by them, or received a more distinct and intelligent approval." There was urgency,

---

[45]*Toledo Blade*, 11 June 1867.

[46]Willard H. Smith, *Schuyler Colfax: The Changing Fortunes of a Political Idol*, vol. 23, Indiana Historical Collections (Indianapolis: Indiana Historical Bureau, 1952) 228-39.

[47]Ibid., 240-46.

[48]*Chicago Tribune*, 19 June 1866.

he claimed, because if no change in representation was made before 1870, the peace of the country would be affected by its inequality. Suffrage for blacks, Morton admitted, was repugnant to a large number of people, and its only justification was that it was impossible to maintain loyal republican governments without it.[49] One wonders if he should not have used the word *republican* with a capital *R* since his political purpose was so obvious.

The Indiana legislature responded by a vote to ratify as soon as possible. The select committee reported favorably on 18 January. The upper house approved by a vote of thirty to sixteen, demonstrating either some Democratic absentees or shifts from the opposing lineup.[50]

During the debate in the House, several interesting constitutional points were made. At one time, Representative Vawter offered a resolution that no state could be or had been out of the Union and to instruct Indiana's representatives and senators "to vote to admit, without delay, every loyal and legally qualified Senator and Representative from every State in the Union...." This resolution, like the proposal to amend, was referred to the Committee on Federal Relations.[51] When this committee was ready to report, it presented a recommendation to ratify with a specific amendment to the third section to change "or" to "and" between "President" and "Vice-President" (as it now reads). No issue was made of either idea, for the proposal to amend was laid on the table and no action was taken on the proposal to "instruct" congressmen.[52]

The meaning of the proposal to the amendment is not so important as the concept of a legislative committee appointed by a state legislature having the right to amend a proposed constitutional change before approval. The other suggestion to instruct the state delegation in Congress was an old idea dating back to the days of the Articles of Confederation. From time to time a state legislature tried to give

---

[49]*Indiana House Journal* (1867) 47-51.

[50]*Indiana Senate Journal* (1867) 98.

[51]*Indiana House Journal*, 92.

[52]Ibid., 101.

instructions to the representatives and senators of its state. There was more reason to think in this way about senators than representatives since before the Seventeenth Amendment was passed legislatures elected them. The idea was never accepted, and the concept that senators were federal officials paid by the federal government and not legally responsible to the legislature, which elected them but could not remove them, became the accepted interpretation.

Minority opposition in the committee produced an unusually violent minority report.[53] Beginning with the statement that the public mind was much too excited to consider radical changes in fundamental law, the committee reiterated the usual argument that Congress had been made up of only two-thirds of the states when it had proposed the change and that it had for its objective only partisan purposes that could not stand the test of time. These objectives were proposed merely "to impress upon the Constitution the political dogmas of a radical party, and to perpetuate power in the hands of a minority of the white people of this country, by forcing into our political system the odious doctrine of negro equality." This, we must remind ourselves, was Indiana in 1867, not some state in the deep South.

Regional rivalry is reflected in the minority criticism of the representation section by the statement that there was no more inequality with the South than there was with New England. The constitutional proposal was to enforce black suffrage, which was intended to strengthen the latter section. By so doing, the power of the agricultural West would be weakened. The disqualification section was ex post facto, the "offspring of passion." The fourth, or debt section, was labeled "a cheat and a fraud." It denounced a debt that did not exist legally, "that there may be a precept to fasten upon the people forever the present heavy burden of our public debt, with all its immunities and exemptions from any part of the weight of taxation, under which our people are laboring." This, said the minority, was a section for the sole benefit of capitalists. The entire amendment had been grossly misrepresented to the people, concluded the Indiana minority report.

---

[53]Ibid., 102-105.

The Midwest, only recently weaned from a Southern political alliance, was obviously, at this time, none too sure that New England would be acceptable in its stead. Clashes of economic interests were commonly recognized, but, as has been previously noted, social and intellectual liberalism was quite different in the two sections of the victorious North. Would the cooperation developed under the unusual circumstances of the past few years be able to survive more peaceful days? Republicans themselves recognized this to be a strategic problem in the political wars of the reconstruction era. New issues to cement the alliance would be necessary, but pending their development, the issues that had been effective during the crises of war could be perpetuated. Both parties were groping for a stable basis of support in this time of political flux.

After some delay in considering the Senate resolution endorsing ratification, due in part to a return of the document to the Senate to correct an error, the House finally voted on 23 January to approve by a majority of fifty-six to thirty-six.[54] Thus, as was usual after the thunder of debate and the delay of parliamentary maneuver, the vote generally followed predictable party lines.

The biennial meeting of Michigan's legislature also began in January 1867. The two houses were composed of large Republican majorities, thirty to two in the Senate and eighty-three to seventeen in the House. These men had been elected in a campaign that featured "bloody shirt" tactics. Republicans had passed a resolution in their 30 August convention in Detroit in favor of the proposed Fourteenth Amendment. Another part of this campaign document described the Democratic opposition in these words: "defeated in the field, the enemy has renewed the struggle through the ballot box, and by political machinations aims at the governance of that which it failed to destroy."[55] Thus the issues of constitutional change were exacerbated by the mingling of pure emotion related to other issues.

Senator Jacob M. Howard had been important in the congressional development of the proposal, and his involvement would naturally interest his fellow Michigan citizens in the Fourteenth

---

[54]Ibid., *Annual Cyclopedia* (1867) 507.

[55]*Annual Cyclopedia* (1867) 508.

Amendment, often called the "Howard Amendment" in the South. Michigan's other senator, Zachariah Chandler, had come out strongly against President Johnson and the amendment. Like New England Radicals, he felt that the proposal did not go far enough and claimed that Democrats would fail to pay the national debt without strong guarantees.[56] He nevertheless felt obligated to accept the amendment as the final condition for readmission if ratified.[57]

Democrats had countered on 6 September with their best efforts to dramatize the radical opposition by inserting the following immoderate language in their platform: "believing, as we do, that our country is threatened by an unscrupulous faction in Congress, who propose to hold power at all hazards, and in violation of all law, and who, unless arrested, will precipitate another war upon us...."[58]

After a brief consideration, the Michigan Senate passed a resolution of ratification by a vote of twenty-five to one on 15 January.[59] The following day this action was duly reported to the House. There, under suspended rules, it was read three times and passed by a seventy-seven to fifteen vote.[60] Obviously this legislature knew what it wanted to do and did it with almost unseemly haste.

At the same time that Michigan was passing on the proposal, the governor of the neighboring state of Minnesota was reviewing the results of the last election to support his assertion that the people had spoken clearly. Governor William R. Marshall claimed in his message to the legislature that the proposal was both reasonable and just. If the Southern states should fail to indicate their acceptance of the amendment, "it may become the duty of Congress to reorganize their civil governments on the basis of equal political rights to all men, without distinction of color, and thus to devolve upon the now disfranchised loyal people of the South the work of national reintegra-

---

[56]Wilmer C. Harris, *Public Life of Zachariah Chandler, 1851-1875* (Chicago: University of Chicago Press, 1917) 92.

[57]Benedict, *A Compromise of Principle*, 272; *Zachariah Chandler* published by *Detroit Post*, 1866.

[58]*Annual Cyclopedia* (1866) 508.

[59]*Michigan Senate Journal* (1867) 125.

[60]*Michigan House Journal* (1867) 180-82.

tion."[61] Such statements indicated what extremists desired and what they were paving the way for.

In Minnesota, the Republicans had expressed themselves in party convention by endorsing congressional proposals. Democrats both opposed and endorsed the actions and words emerging from the Philadelphia National Union Convention. Republicans won by a satisfying majority.[62] On 15 January, the legislature heard the reading of a ratification motion and, after refusing to table it in the House, speedily approved it unanimously.[63] The next day the Senate read it three times with great speed under suspended rules and also expressed its approval by a vote of sixteen to five.[64]

While these events were transpiring in the Northwest, the New England state of Rhode Island took action. Once again Republican control of the legislature was complete. Republican majorities were twenty-eight to five in the Senate and sixty-five to seven in the House.[65] General Ambrose E. Burnside, whose independent command before Fredricksburg has been much criticized, but who was a trained and experienced West Point graduate, had just been elected governor. His political experience was lacking, but his attitudes toward war issues were akin to those of his fellow Rhode Islanders.

When the legislature convened on 14 January, a resolution of ratification was introduced in the House the same day. It was referred to the Judiciary Committee.[66] Similar action took place in the Senate the following day, but in this instance, the committee retired to formulate its report immediately. Nevertheless, the matter was temporarily laid on the table.[67]

---

[61]*Annual Cyclopedia* (1866) 518.

[62]Ibid., 518-19.

[63]*Minnesota House Journal* (1867) 26; McPherson, *Political History of Reconstruction*, 194.

[64]*Minnesota Senate Journal* (1867) 22-23.

[65]*Annual Cyclopedia* (1866) 670.

[66]*Providence Daily Journal*, 15 January 1867; *Rhode Island House Journal* (1867) 228-29. Note: page numbers in *House Journal* MSS added by Archives; none in original.

[67]*Providence Daily Journal*, 16 January 1867; *Rhode Island Senate Journal* (1867).

The resolution of ratification was postponed until Thursday, 21 January, when it would become the special order of business. However, it was not taken up until 24 January, being yet again postponed until Wednesday, 30 January. Discussion was to be "resumed" 1 February. At that time, a final vote was postponed until the following Tuesday, 5 February. At long last it was voted upon and adopted by a roll-call vote of twenty-six to two.[68]

The House went through similar procedures of postponement. Notice that the amendment was to be reviewed had been given 15 January for the following week and again on 16 January for a week later. On 6 February the resolution to adopt was considered and referred to the Judiciary Committee (probably because of the prior Senate action). The Senate resolution, passed the previous Tuesday was voted on in the House on Thursday, 7 February, and passed by a roll-call vote of sixty to nine.[69]

In Maine the voters of 1866 had in September expressed their preference for the Republican candidates in no uncertain manner. That party gained unanimous control of the Senate and complete dominance of the House, 138 to 13. Republicans had backed the congressional plan centered on the Fourteenth Amendment, and the Democrats had severely indicted the Thirty-ninth Congress for vindictiveness, sectionalism, and fanaticism. They had also openly approved taxation of government bonds.[70]

Governor Joshua L. Chamberlain addressed the Maine legislature on 3 January 1867, having been elected within months of being mustered out of the military service. He termed the congressional proposal magnanimous "without parallel" and claimed that the demand of Southern states to be restored to their places in the federal government was "so little in the spirit of surrender as to seem like mockery of triumph."[71] His attitude is an excellent example of the general feeling in many parts of the North. It was not enough for the

---

[68]*Providence Daily Journal*, 6 February 1867; *Rhode Island Senate Journal*.

[69]*Providence Daily Journal*, 8 February 1867; *Rhode Island House Journal*, 271.

[70]*Annual Cyclopedia* (1866) 467-68.

[71]*Maine Senate Journal* (1867) 20-22.

South to surrender and accept the terms of that surrender, but a more apologetic mien and admission of wrong-doing was expected. Traditional Southern pride and feelings of personal honor stood in the way of Southerners further atonement; this refusal to bow their heads still further was encouraged by President Johnson and other less aggressive Northerners who wanted a smooth return to "normal" relations. On the other hand, mere restoration of Southern states deprived many Northern citizens of the feeling that they had really achieved something by their heroic efforts through four years of bloody battle; saving the Union did not seem enough. The "fruits of victory" needed to be more apparent. This was a thoroughly natural and human reaction though it led to difficulties of reconciliation and played into the hands of the Radicals.

Changes to be introduced into the Constitution by the Fourteenth Amendment were at least moving in the right direction even if they did not demand sufficient guarantees, said Governor Chamberlain. Because the proposal had been the declared issue in the recent campaign and elections, good faith required the victorious party to support it. Such ratification must not, however, be considered a complete settlement of the situation.[72] The implication throughout the address was that additional requirements must be demanded. That these should include suffrage for blacks was well understood by many, for that was the stated purpose of those who took such a position. Governor Chamberlain was not the typical politician, for he had been a college professor and was to become president of Bowdoin. His family roots were deep in Maine history, however, and he undoubtedly spoke for most of the voters in that state.

Senator W. P. Fessenden of Maine had been chairman of the Reconstruction Committee that framed the Fourteenth Amendment. He was more moderate than Stevens and Sumner, whom he greatly scorned. He naturally supported the proposal as being a moderate document.[73] Congressman Fred Pike was an early advocate of black suffrage and the exclusion of the South from the Union for as long

---

[72]Ibid., 23.

[73]Joseph B. James, *The Framing of the Fourteenth Amendment* (Urbana: University of Illinois Press, 1956) 155-56.

as possible. He demonstrated another reason for his stand when he wrote that Southerners should be kept out of Congress "till we can get our debts saddled off on the General Government." His brother, James Shepherd Pike, returning from a diplomatic post, was influenced by him and argued with Seward about the practical necessity of suffrage for blacks in the beginning (1866). Chief Justice Chase urged support for the amendment and also asked James Pike's help in gaining suffrage for the blacks.[74]

The Maine legislature first took up the Fourteenth Amendment in the House of Representatives. Its Committee on Federal Relations reported it favorably on 11 January. After compressing the two remaining readings into one day by suspending the rules, the House approved it 126 to 12.[75] The next day the Senate committee reported to that body, but its final reading on the resolution did not come until 16 January. Only one member was absent on that day, and the vote of those present was unanimous in favor of the amendment.[76]

Thus, by the Spring of 1867, thirty-four states had considered the Fourteenth Amendment in their respective legislatures. Of this number, twenty-one had formally registered their ratification although there were some questionable situations like those of Tennessee and Oregon and a possible doubt of the status of the act of West Virginia as a state. However, these points aside, it is true that thirteen state legislatures had either rejected the proposal outright or formally refused to take any action on it because they disapproved of it. Of these thirteen, two border states, Maryland and Delaware, had never been thought to be outside of the Union, and another, Kentucky, had been somewhat doubtful in its position despite its recognition by the Confederacy as one of its member-states. In summary, then, it can be said that less than three-fourths of the states that had considered the proposal had given assent. Certainly this figure was less than three-fourths of all the states. Of course, according to the Sumner "suicide theory," twenty-one states, or three-fourths of

---

[74]Robert Franklin Durden, *James Shepherd Pike: Republicanism and the American Negro, 1850-1882* (Durham: Duke University Press, 1957) 163, 166-67, 168.

[75]*Maine House Journal* (1867) 78.

[76]*Maine Senate Journal* (1867) 87, 101.

the loyal states, were sufficient to incorporate the amendment into law. There was no complete agreement about this statement, but opinion seemed to be that a full three-fourths of the thirty-six states was necessary—thirty-seven after the admission of Nebraska.

Most states of the North had ratified by February or March of 1867. These were not sufficient to make constitutional approval beyond question even if some did not believe Southern states had to be counted. They were expected to ratify to demonstrate their contriteness or to guarantee the future. In some instances, members of the same Northern state delegation in Congress held decidedly different views, as in Wisconsin and Indiana. Midwestern states were increasingly concerned with party realignment, which conceivably might unite them in a coalition with New England instead of the South.

Ratification in Massachusetts was remarkable in that the minority report of the legislative committee was the basis for approval. Its minority members were controlled by Republicans less radical than the leaders of the majority. Hoping to gain more extreme action including the black vote, the majority delayed a vote on the amendment until March. Popular opinion, more moderate than that of the legislative majority, caused action on the basis of the minority report. The legislature approved the Fourteenth Amendment.

Messages of governors and reports of majority committees of legislatures brought out points at times that were not merely repetition of those in other states. More than one governor mentioned the necessity of changing the organization of Southern states in order to secure equal rights for all if the amendment should be rejected. Others lamented that the Fourteenth Amendment did not go far enough, the principal deficiency being that it did not provide for suffrage for blacks. The black vote was deemed necessary not only to contribute to Republican control, but to enable blacks to protect themselves within their own states. Democrats at times criticized the debt section as a feature for capitalists. Some claimed that taxation to meet the war debt would be higher if interpretation of that section prohibited paper money to be substituted for gold. Change in the reconstruction picture was freely anticipated as the Fortieth Congress convened in March 1867. The outcome of national legislation would determine the fate of the Fourteenth Amendment.

Chapter Fourteen

Changing Course

Nebraska was admitted as the thirty-seventh state on 1 March, but before it could ratify the Fourteenth Amendment in June, much happened that changed the entire national situation. There was no question that on the eve of congressional reconstruction in March 1867, new states were proposed specifically to add voting strength to the dominant group. This policy seemed all the more important in view of the fact that a presidential veto of the proposed action was certain.

Both Nebraska and Colorado had been considered for some time as candidates for statehood. In fact, an enabling act had been passed in 1864 to permit citizens of Colorado, Nevada, and Nebraska to take steps preparatory to admission, but only Nevada was admitted at that time. Its votes figured in the reelection of Lincoln even though its sparse population raised a good many practical and theoretical questions concerning its eligibility.

As early as 14 December 1866, after the fall elections and after the convening of the Thirty-ninth Congress, the admission of Nebraska and Colorado was debated. Benjamin F. Wade of Ohio humorously stated that the counsel of two senators from each of these states was needed. Sumner of Massachusetts opposed their admission, partly because of limits on suffrage in the proposed Nebraska constitution but probably also because New England's influence would diminish with the admission of each new western state. Wade reprimanded him for standing in the way "when really he wants her aid to carry great measures in the direction that he and I advocate."[1] On 19 December, Jacob M. Howard of Michigan bluntly stated that "I do desire the admission of Colorado and Nebraska because their Senators here and their Representatives in the House would greatly increase the Republican loyal strength in Congress."[2]

The question of whether Congress could include binding conditions on a state prior to its admission, such as unlimited manhood suffrage, was discussed at length.[3] This kind of constitutional question involving the equality of all states in the Union was to be a live issue into the twentieth century. A bill to admit Nebraska on the condition of nonabridgement of suffrage because of race or color was passed in January but received the anticipated presidential veto because of its claimed unconstitutionality. In addition, Johnson charged that not only were there election irregularities, but that the sparse population of Nebraska did not meet the required unit of representation in Congress, which was then 127,000 residents. In his opinion, Nebraskans could afford to wait for statehood.[4]

The territorial governor of Nebraska addressed the council on 11 January, declaring that restoration of the Union must be achieved, but not by keeping out unrepresented states or by creating constitu-

---

[1]*Congressional Globe*, 39th Cong., 2d sess., 121-22.

[2]Ibid., 186.

[3]Ibid., 178, 216. Pre-conditions held not binding as early as 1845 in *Pollard v. Hagan*, 3 Howard 212 (1845).

[4]James D. Richardson, *A Compilation of the Messages and Papers of the Presidents, 1789-1897* (Washington DC: Bureau of National Literature and Art, 1898) 6:490-91.

tional amendments "containing what are considered impossible requirements by those most deeply interested." Restoration should, in his opinion, be achieved quickly.[5] His remarks pertained in no direct way to the issue of Nebraska's admission as a state and did represent views contrary to the majority in Congress.

Congress was nearing action on reconstruction and did not cause Nebraska to wait long for admission. It overrode the executive veto on 8 February in the Senate and the next day in the House.[6] The proclamation of Nebraska as a state was delayed until 1 March because of the necessity of clearing documents involved in the special conditions exacted. Colorado had also been approved for statehood, but its case did not stand up as well in Congress, and Johnson's veto was not overridden.[7] Before Nebraska could have an impact on the ratification of the Fourteenth Amendment, it was to have a voice through its representation in Congress on the proposed military reconstruction of the South.

It is worth remembering that the counterproposal for a Fourteenth Amendment sponsored by Johnson and some conservatives, both Northern and Southern, had been presented as a Southern concession to a reasonable settlement for restoration. It was being discussed in February at the same time that Nebraska was being acted upon for statehood. It is also pertinent to note that the last Southern states filed their rejections during this same period. Also in the public mind, and much discussed in some circles both in the North and in the South, was the decision in the Milligan case. It had only been announced on 17 December, although the fact of the decision was well known in advance. The press only gradually reported the majority opinion that declared that military tribunals could not try civilians when the regular courts were open and functioning. Though the case was based on Indiana facts, the implications of it were not lost on those discussing military supremacy in such matters in the South. It

---

[5] *Nebraska Territorial Council Journal* (1867) 17.

[6] *Congressional Globe*, 39th Cong., 2d sess., 122; *Annual Cyclopedia* (1867) 532.

[7] *Annual Cyclopedia*, 127.

was late December before the majority opinion was widely known and the minority opinion was not in print until January.[8]

All else having failed, the South was now tempted to look for relief to the Supreme Court. The *Little Rock Gazette* expressed a general view when it stated that it saw the Supreme Court as a "barrier to the sweeping progress of Northern fanaticism."[9] This function of the Supreme Court seemed especially true because military control, as proposed in Congress, involved provisions that would seem to have parallels in the Milligan case. After the new reconstruction acts had established army control in the South, this question was to come into sharp focus in the McCardle case in which the validity of the entire congressional program might well have been threatened. The Court caught the attention of the same people during January 1867, when it voided both state and federal laws requiring a test oath for certain officials.[10] All this gave members of Congress reason to think carefully, or at least to react emotionally against the Court because it was creating obstacles to Congress's complete control. Not until July did the legislative branch provide for a gradual reduction of the number of Supreme Court justices to seven, which effectively prevented possible Johnson appointments and might gradually swing the majority to a more radical orientation. It was not until the whole fabric of congressional methods of reconstruction was called into question by the sequel to *Ex Parte Milligan* in the McCardle case in 1868 that jurisdiction of the Supreme Court was altered by Congress to curtail interference. Without realizing its possible application, Congress had passed a bill in early 1867 to protect individuals from injustice in the South by giving them direct access to the Supreme Court through writs of habeas corpus.[11] This bill opened the way for the McCardle case, which was to pose such a threat to the congressional program.

---

[8]*New York Times*, reported in 27 December 1867, and the minority opinion on 1 January 1868.

[9]27 December 1867.

[10]See *Cummings v. Missouri*, 4 Wallace 277 (1867) and *Ex Parte Garland*, 4 Wallace 333 (1867).

[11]*United States Statutes at Large* 14 (1867) 285.

One of Elihu B. Washburne's correspondents summed up the concern of some supporters of congressional reconstruction when in January he wrote that, "The chief danger now is from the Supreme Court." Other problems seemed to the writer to be more manageable.[12] Even the *Nation* expressed the fear that the Court might consider legitimate the state governments in the South as instituted by the President.[13] Chief Justice Salmon P. Chase, who lamented the failure of Southern states to ratify the Fourteenth Amendment, freely predicted suffrage for blacks, and more stringent measures before matters could improve.[14] Justice David Davis, who had written the majority opinion in the Milligan case, confided that "I have no faith in the purposes and aims of the extreme men of the dominant party, and they control the legislature."[15] In 1867, Justice Samuel F. Miller, whose opinion in the Slaughter House Cases of 1873 was to set the pattern of narrow interpretation of the Fourteenth Amendment for a long time, wrote, "I am for universal amnesty and universal suffrage, not because any one of these are the best in themselves but because we are losing what is more valuable than any of these things in the struggle which is demoralizing us worse than the war did."[16] Horace Greeley in the *New York Tribune* expressed much the same feeling. He endorsed the amendment, but preferred general amnesty and universal suffrage.[17]

Thomas Ewing wrote Justice Davis to congratulate him on his published opinion in the Milligan case. It was "sound in every partic-

---

[12]J. L. Camp to Elihu B. Washburne, 27 January 1867, E. B. Washburne Papers, Library of Congress.

[13]*The Nation*, 7 February 1867.

[14]Salmon P. Chase to Robert A. Hill, 1 March 1867, S. P. Chase Papers, Library of Congress.

[15]David Davis to "Rockwell," his brother-in-law who was a Massachusetts judge. Quoted in Charles Fairman, *Reconstruction and Reunion, 1864-1888* in pt. 1, *History of the Supreme Court of the United States*, Paul A. Freund (New York: MacMillan Co., 1971) 4:233.

[16]Charles Fairman, *Mr. Justice Miller and the Supreme Court* (Cambridge: Harvard University Press, 1939) 190-93.

[17]Glendon G. Van Deusen, *Horace Greeley: Nineteenth Century Crusader* (Philadelphia: University of Pennsylvania Press, 1932) 345-50.

ular & [*sic*] the sound constitutional law is laid down in happily appropriate language."[18] The *Springfield Republican* praised the Court for upholding jury trials.[19] Apprehension of possible judicial action is shown in the *Newark Evening Courier* by a professed lack of confidence in the Court.[20] In the *Washington Daily Morning Chronicle* J. W. Forney charged that "Treason has at last found a secure shelter in the bosom of the Supreme Court."[21] Reverdy Johnson denounced him in the Senate for that statement.[22]

It was apparent early in the second session of the Thirty-ninth Congress that action on a congressional plan was probable. With support of the amendment demonstrated in recent elections and with continuing ratification of it by Northern legislatures and rejection of it by former Confederate states, even moderates felt the need to enact something.

> Nor does there seem to be too much reason to doubt that a large majority of Congress is fully determined to adopt some plan for the reorganization of the Southern governments as soon as the rejection of the Amendment is definitely settled.[23]

Congress should declare where it stands on the amendment, claimed the *New York Times*. Is it part of the Constitution or not? Bingham went so far as to introduce a resolution directing the secretary of state to report which states had ratified and which had not. Some criticized Seward for even submitting the amendment to all thirty-six states instead of only twenty-five.

It seemed altogether logical to many to declare void the presidential program under which the South at first had been governed provisionally and then governed by more permanent governments of regularly elected officials. The slate would be wiped clean for a new

---

[18]Thomas Ewing to David Davis, 20 January 1867, David Davis Papers, Illinois Historical Society, Springfield, IL.

[19]January 1867.

[20]January 1867.

[21]*Washington Daily Morning Chronicle*, 19 December 1866.

[22]*Congressional Globe*, 39th Cong., 2d sess., 210.

[23]*The Nation*, 3 January 1867.

beginning under the direction of Congress and, until new governments could be set up, the military would be supreme.[24]

When bills to accomplish this purpose were considered, the problem of timing became important. Democrats would have less influence and the dominant party would be stronger in the Fortieth
Congress, reflecting the results of the fall elections. It would meet on
the same day that the Thirty-ninth Congress passed into history.[25]
Unless compelling urgency caused the old Congress to pass drastic
legislation, extreme measures might have a better chance after 4
March. To many, that became the final date of leniency, before
stronger measures would be enacted upon the South if it obstinately
refused to cooperate.[26] There seemed to be consensus among the
majority that military control would be necessary, but beyond that
there was little agreement.

Stevens's bill would place blacks and Unionists in control, and
would be backed by military power. Others, led by Bingham of Ohio,
wished to include a firm commitment that when a state had ratified
the Fourteenth Amendment and had complied with other requirements, it would be admitted to representation. Bingham also declared that three-fourths of the loyal states would be sufficient to
meet constitutional requirements for ratification. Approval by reluctant Southern states would thus merely confirm their loyalty.

In the Senate, Howard took the same unequivocal position on 15
February when he solemnly declared, "I do believe most seriously
that it is the right of three-fourths of the loyal states remaining in the
Union at any time to amend the Constitution."[27]

In view of declarations that it was unnecessary to consider the disloyal states when approving the Fourteenth Amendment, and in
view of the difficulties in getting these Southern states to approve it,
there is a certain logic in the statement of *Harper's Weekly*: "They
[Congress] have not proclaimed the Amendment adopted by three-

---

[24]*New York Times*, 28 January 1867; See Eric L. McKitrick, *Andrew Johnson and Reconstruction* (Chicago: University of Chicago Press, 1960) 478-79.

[25]*United States Statutes at Large*, 14, 486-87.

[26]*Congressional Globe*, 39th Cong., 2d sess., 288.

[27]Ibid., 1365.

fourths of them as part of the Constitution and until that is done nobody is entitled to act upon it as if it were a part of the Constitution." In demanding Southern observance of parts of the amendment as if it were law, Congress was indeed leaving the situation blurred. In this connection, it should be noted that when Congress did proclaim the Fourteenth Amendment a part of the Constitution, it did so listing all states approving—even those required by military rule to do so in the unrepresented South. Others seemed to feel it important to provide an alternative to military rule.[28]

The Stevens bill, after bitter debate, was referred to the Joint Committee. A compromise was then suggested by George W. Julian that would place the South under military rule. Such an approach gave new hope and even gained support from Stevens when he saw that his original purpose could not be obtained at that time.[29] James G. Blaine had introduced an amendment to the Stevens measure on 12 February that would permit Southern representation when Southern state legislatures had ratified the amendment and had provided for black suffrage. Democrats joined Radicals to defeat that proposal.[30] Throughout the debates, Democrats tried to vote in such a way so as to divide or disrupt a Republican plan. This strategy eventually resulted in a more extreme program than the Democrats' proclaimed position would support[31] and caused Southern disillusionment over any future help from Democrats. Earlier, groups of Northern politicians might have advised cooperation with moderate Republicans.

When deadlock appeared to be in the offing, a special committee was selected by the Republican caucus to work out a program that could be accepted. John Sherman was made chairman, and what resulted was mostly due to him. The plan that evolved was reported on

----

[28]Ibid., 1080-83; *New York Times*, 17 January 1867.

[29]*Congressional Globe*, 39th Cong., 2d sess., 1182-84.

[30]Ibid., 1206-13.

[31]Ibid., 40th Congress, 1st session, 64. See analysis in McKitrick, *Andrew Johnson*, 479-85 and Michael L. Benedict, *A Compromise of Principle: Congressional Republicans and Reconstruction, 1863-1869* (New York: W. W. Norton Press, 1974) 232-39.

17 February.[32] Sherman later described his part in the process by saying, "I did nothing but reduce and group the ideas of others, carefully leaving open to the South the whole machinery of reconstruction." The intense pressure of this period is suggested by Senator James W. Grimes in a letter to his wife on 18 February. "On Friday we were in session until half-passed three o'clock, Saturday morning. Saturday in committee at 10 A.M. and in session from 12 P.M. to half-passed six o'clock Sunday morning. Our bill was the new reconstruction measure, which [the] House is now trying to defeat."[33]

Deadlock in the House was broken by an amendment offered by James Wilson of Iowa to exclude those disqualified by the Fourteenth Amendment from serving as delegates to constitutional conventions or from voting. Samuel Shellabarger of Ohio submitted the final amendment to solve the House dilemma when he proposed extending the disqualification of all officeholders under the new provisional governments.[34] With Senate approval, this was the bill sent to President Johnson on 20 February for his expected veto.[35] Johnson sent his written veto message on 2 March.[36] Both houses promptly overrode it by the necessary vote. The President had not needed to submit this document in order to veto the legislation, for at the end of the session a pocket veto would have sufficed. Such a passive negation might even have been an advantage, for there would have been no opportunity to override it, and there would have been a delay, at least, before new legislation could have been submitted to him. Why he chose to file the written message with the Thirty-ninth Congress is probably a reflection of Johnson's personality and perhaps his feeling that in this way his objections would be clearly shown to the coun-

[32]*Congressional Globe*, 39th Cong., 2d sess.

[33]William Salter, *The Life of James W. Grimes: Governor of Iowa, 1854-1858, Senator of the United States, 1859-1869* (New York: D. Appleton Co., 1876) 322.

[34]*Congressional Globe*, 39th Cong., 2d sess., 1399-1400.

[35]Ibid., 1645; *United States Statutes at Large*, 14, 478.

[36]*Congressional Globe*, 39th Cong., 2d sess., 1976; Richardson, *Messages and Papers*, 6:498-511.

try. It was an able paper drafted by Jeremiah S. Black with assistance from the attorney-general, Henry Stanbery.[37]

Two days later the galleries of the House of Representatives were filled with families and friends of representatives to witness the end of the Thirty-ninth Congress. It was a rainy, drab day that some may have taken as an omen. A little after twelve o'clock Speaker Colfax in his deep, strong voice made some remarks to conclude the session and pronounced the session adjourned. Almost immediately, Edward McPherson, clerk of the House, called the roll of members elected in 1866. Colfax was reelected Speaker, and the first session of the Fortieth Congress was begun.[38] New members were sworn in before the Senate, but there was no need of total reorganization there because of the nature of that house as a continuing body.

Republicans were even more solidly in control of both houses than they had been in the last Congress. Some questioned the special session set up by Congress; for it was not called by the President. Particularly was this emphasized since seventeen states were initially unrepresented. Brooks called it a "Rump of a Rump" and the minority party protested formally. Defenders reminded their colleagues that the first session of the Fortieth Congress had been called according to law.[39]

Before long it became obvious that the reconstruction statute would have little immediate effect. State governments in the South were still under the control of the same people, and nothing in the new law imposed any requirement that they take any particular action. The option was theirs. The army was present to guarantee order but usually got along well with those in positions of trust in state government. Johnson was still in the presidency. Representation in Congress was all that could be gained by following instructions to qualify. These would bring the vote to the blacks and probably turn over state

---

[37]Fairman, *Reconstruction and Reunion*, 307; Lawanda and John Cox, "Andrew Johnson and his Ghost Writers," *Mississippi Valley Historical Review* (December 1961) 48:460ff; William Norwood Brigance, *Jeremiah Sullivan Black: A Defender of the Constitution and the Ten Commandments* (Philadelphia: University of Pennsylvania Press, 1934) 161.

[38]*New York Times*, 5, 17 March 1867.

[39]*Congressional Globe*, 40th Cong., 1st sess., 204.

governments to others if not to the blacks. The natural instinct of a political leader would be to retain what power he had. For this purpose military power seemed preferable to Congressional reconstruction. Representation in Congress lost most of its attractiveness if, by following new suffrage rules, those presently exercising leadership would no longer do so and, therefore, not really be represented.[40] This, coupled with the narrow interpretation of the congressional act left things much as they had been in the South.[41]

It did not take Congress long to see that in their haste they had accomplished little except to produce a rather empty gesture. There was no new reconstruction in the South and no restoration of the Union. Guidelines had to be supplied and the initiative had to be taken by the national government if anything was to be accomplished. There were, at first, more questions than answers, but these began to be addressed by a supplementary act, largely drafted by Chief Justice Chase,[42] and passed on 23 March. Under the act, military commanders were instructed to begin the process described in the proposed amendment: voters were to be registered, and delegates to state constitutional conventions were to be selected by a modified suffrage that disqualified Confederate leaders and enrolled former slaves. The conventions must propose new constitutions, which must then be approved in a ratification process that used the new suffrage rules. Johnson's narrow interpretation of this act when it became law over his veto[43] continued to be a problem in its implementation. Thus, a third reconstruction act was passed on 19 July that spelled out intent and methods beyond the power of the attorney-general to modify through interpretation. Final authority was clearly placed with the military commanders who could remove any

---

[40]This line of thought is documented by Michael Perman, *Reunion Without Compromise: The South and Reconstruction, 1865-1868* (London: Cambridge University Press, 1973) 311.

[41]Martin E. Mantell, *Johnson, Grant and the Politics of Reconstruction* (New York: Columbia University Press, 1973) 30.

[42]Salmon P. Chase Papers, Library of Congress; *United States Statutes at Large*, 15, 2.

[43]Richardson, *Messages and Papers*, 6:533-34.

civil officer who failed to cooperate fully in carrying out the intent of Congress.[44] Some officials were removed, including the governors of four states—Georgia, Mississippi, Texas, and Virginia.

Despite a tangle of details dealing with many different opinions and problems of enforcement, congressional reconstruction at last began to move. The base procedures, except for the changed rules on suffrage, were much like that proposed by President Johnson in 1865. Such changes were subject to the kind of interpretation furnished by ex-President Buchanan who contended that "the radicals have determined that these states shall not vote for President in the next election. They have both the power and the will to prevent it and the detailed provisions of the Bill itself have been evidently framed to accomplish this very object."[45]

Perhaps he was right, but other purposes may be observed such as obtaining suffrage for blacks and even "the idealism that they inherited from the abolitionists."[46] In 1867 most states in the North did not permit the black vote, and some actually defeated such proposals that year in state election that were won by Democrats on this very issue.

In the South, bewilderment gave way to practical attempts to cope with the changed situation. Compliance with the acts was one approach advocated by leading newspapers.[47] Herschel V. Johnson urged such a policy of expediency.[48] Perhaps the former masters could control the black vote. Such was the position of Joseph E. Brown in Georgia, Wade Hampton in South Carolina, and James L. Alcorn in Mississippi.[49] Black groups were addressed in many parts

[44]*Congressional Globe*, 40th Cong., 2d sess., 582-83; *United States Statutes at Large*, 15, 14.

[45]James Buchanan to Minton Marble, 4 March 1867 in James Buchanan, *Works of James Buchanan*, ed., John Bassett Moore (Philadelphia, 1908-1911) 11:437.

[46]Lawanda and John H. Cox, "Negro Suffrage and Republican Politics," *Journal of Southern History* 33 (1 August 1967) 303.

[47]McKitrick, *Andrew Johnson*, 483.

[48]Herschel V. Johnson to Alexander H. Stephens, 28 March 1867, Alexander H. Stephens Papers, Duke University Library.

[49]*Atlanta Intelligencer*, 9 March 1867; *Charleston Courier*, 25 March 1867; *Coahoman*, 21 April 1867; Hampton M. Jarrell, *Wade Hampton and the Negro: The Road Not Taken* (Columbia SC: University of South Carolina Press, 1949) 18-19.

of the South by ex-Confederates. Their purpose was not merely to gain restoration for the states but to stabilize the economy in such a way that earning a living would once more be possible. Business influences in the North made their presence felt in this same direction.[50] Another fear was felt but unvoiced by many, "Nearly everybody was rampant for the convention and to get back into the Union, to secure their lands from confiscation by Congress."[51] Some hoped that compliance would cause Congress to remove the disabilities of the Fourteenth Amendment that were incorporated into the reconstruction acts as if that proposal were already law. By registering and voting, many hoped to influence black votes also. Cooperation might at least "place ourselves in a position that would cause our application for relief to be favorably considered."[52]

Opposition to compliance looked toward court intervention or new political developments in the North. Even if the worst had to be suffered, there were those who failed to see the merit of abandoning all principles and helping in their own destruction.[53]

Governor Patton of Alabama urged speedy action in accordance with the acts of Congress. He stated, "to contend against it now is simply to struggle against the inevitable."[54] Governor Frances H. Pierpoint of Virginia sent a message to the legislature on 4 March stating that "with liberal action, Virginia can get anything she wants."[55] Governor J. W. Throckmorton of Texas believed that cooperation alone

---

[50]Julian Selby to B. F. Perry, 29 July 1867, B. F. Perry Papers, University of North Carolina Library; William Cornell to Andrew Johnson, 25 February 1867, and A. McLean White to Andrew Johnson, 14 February 1867 in Andrew Johnson Papers, Library of Congress; A. E. Bass to Gideon Welles, 11 February 1867, Gideon Welles Papers, Library of Congress.

[51]J. B. Sutton to B. F. Perry, 13 July 1867, Perry Papers.

[52]David Swain to William A. Graham, 15 March 1867, W. A. Graham Papers, University of North Carolina Library; Walter H. Crenshaw to Robert M. Patton, 11 March 1867, Patton official correspondence, Alabama Archives.

[53]Rembert W. Patrick, *The Reconstruction of the Nation* (New York: Oxford University Press, 1967) 115.

[54]*New Orleans Times*, 8 March 1867.

[55]*Richmond Times*, 5 March 1867.

could save the South.[56] The realistic attitude of Alcorn in Mississippi was also voiced by John W. Robinson and others, "We will have to deal with things as they *are*—not as we would have them."[57] The recommended strategy for the Southern states seemed to be to get back into the Union, and then try to change those matters that were unfavorable to them.[58]

Threats of even harsher terms were uttered from time to time in the North.[59] Others, seemingly in growing numbers, agreed to admit the South if it would only cooperate.[60] Johnson was openly blamed for bringing about Southern rejection of the Fourteenth Amendment by "patronage and intrigue and false hope."[61] In administering the congressional act, fewer Southerners were eliminated from political activity than had been anticipated. The required loyalty oath accounted for some, but refusal on the part of the Southerner to participate was a greater cause of exclusion from the political process. In five of the ten unreconstructed states, black registrants outnumbered white, but the latter were in the majority of all states but South Carolina in the elected conventions.

Of course, these whites represented several different interests and did not work in harmony as a bloc. There were Southern Unionists prepared to seek an end to reconstruction by whatever means, some who sought personal gain, and some from the North who were constructive leaders and others who were greedy for power or financial gain. The voting had been not only on the question of a constitutional convention but on the election of delegates if the first vote should be affirmative. All but Texas held such elections in 1867.

---

[56]J. B. Throckmorton to Ashbell Smith, 5 April 1867, printed in *Arkansas Gazette*, 14 May 1867.

[57]*Jackson Clarion*, 16 March 1867.

[58]Mantell, *Johnson, Grant and the Politics of Reconstruction*, 40, 54.

[59]*New York Times*, 14 August 1867.

[60]Mantell, *Johnson, Grant and the Politics of Reconstruction*, 51.

[61]Jacob M. Howard in a Senate speech, 10 July 1867, *Congressional Globe*, 40th Cong., 1st sess., 549-50.

Out of these conventions came constitutions that met the requirements of Congress and that were surprisingly good as instruments of government. They all required universal manhood suffrage except for those persons disqualified specifically by Congress. When submitted to the voters, the flaw in the reconstruction acts that still remained was identified and exploited by conservative Southerners. By absenting themselves from the polls, though registered to vote, they attempted to defeat the constitution by preventing a favorable majority of the registered voters even if a majority of those voting was assured. This tactic worked in Alabama and Mississippi before Congress passed a fourth reconstruction act to remedy the defect in its earlier acts.[62]

In early 1867, the South had apparently defeated the ratification of the Fourteenth Amendment although Congress had not ruled on its status. Still not represented in Congress and facing the probability of military control under new acts being prepared, Southern states naturally turned toward the courts as their best hope. By 1867, Congress had already been lost, and the President had proved ineffective in protecting Southern interests. The courts were the only other possible source of aid.

Just at this time the Milligan case came to the forefront and caused some congressmen to fear further court action. Voiding of test oaths increased these fears and led to the reduction of the Supreme Court to seven members. This reduction effectively blocked presidential appointments and warned the Court to be careful. No jurisdictional changes were made at this time. They remained a part of the congressional arsenal in its competition with the judicial branch.

Congress was in control, but was not sure what it wanted to do. Only two things were agreed upon: to abolish executive reconstruction in the South and to install military power there. When nothing happened as a result of these measures, congressional leaders realized that something additional was necessary to accomplish their purposes. They drew up a reconstruction plan for reorganizing state governments in the South. It included suffrage for blacks, disqualification of leading Confederates, and election of conventions to

---

[62]Patrick, *Reconstruction of the Nation*, 104-14.

frame new constitutions. The President was bypassed in order to insure that the military would enforce congressional policies. Some Southern officials were removed, including several governors, and military orders began to cause action. Leaders in Southern states began to see the advantage of cooperation with the new plan. Spurred on by threats of further penalties, different groups of Southern leaders realized that their interests included representation by the only route now available.

The new rules demanded ratification of the Fourteenth Amendment by reconstructed governments as one price of readmission. In each state circumstances were different, but there was discernible movement in the South. In the North, new state elections began to demonstrate substantial changes in popular reaction.

Thus, the Fourteenth Amendment was finally submitted for approval to the new legislatures resulting from the reconstruction acts except in Texas, which had held no election, and in Virginia, where the constitution had not been submitted to the voters. What happened in each state during that period broadly described in the foregoing chapter and in the legislatures when they were considering the Fourteenth Amendment will receive closer examination. How the document was perceived by different groups in each state and how votes were marshalled for or against it are topics worthy of study. At the same time, political developments in the North and their effect in the South must be taken into account, as well as how court action played a part.

Chapter Fifteen

Which
Channel

The first attempt to impeach President Johnson began in January 1867.[1] It led to lengthy investigations by the House Judiciary Committee as many charges and rumors, including his gifts of pardons and other favors to "rebels" and even implication in the assassination of Lincoln, were sifted. Finally, a divided committee recommended action by the full House, but on no specific articles of impeachment. Although the motion to impeach was defeated in December, the thought of impeaching remained, especially in connection with the squabble that had developed on the removal of Stanton and the Tenure of Office Act. New proposals for impeachment would be filed and would result in an actual trial.

Would-be Republican presidents were maneuvering for position. Though Grant seemed the desirable choice of either party,

---

[1]*Congressional Globe*, 39th Cong., 2d sess., 320.

Chief Justice Salmon P. Chase, Ben Wade, B. F. Butler, Speaker Schuyler Colfax, and others still eyed their possibilities. Much competition developed for the vice-presidential nomination.

In the stormy activities of May and June 1867, action by Nebraska, the twenty-second state to ratify the Fourteenth Amendment, attracted little attention. Its admission as a state that March had produced much more comment, but not as much as the developing state election campaigns and numerous other political events, and especially the evolving congressional reconstruction program for the South.

The Nebraska legislature was strongly Republican. In the Senate, the majority was ten to three, and in the House, thirty to nine.[2] Republican Governor David Butler, in his 17 May message, urged that the amendment be approved in that session. It "represented the principles of freedom and national integrity" for which the war had been fought.[3]

The governor forwarded a copy of the proposed amendment to the legislature. It was referred to the Senate Committee on Federal Relations on 30 May,[4] but in the House the measure was already being acted upon. A joint resolution to ratify had been introduced on 22 May; immediately, a motion to reject was made and defeated. It was read a second time on the next day, referred to the Committee of the Whole House, and made the special order of business for 29 May. At that time it was duly discussed and ordered to a third reading for the following day, but was postponed until 8 June. The vote on final passage, 10 June, was twenty-six to eleven.[5]

The House resolution was received in the Senate the same day it was passed. It was referred the next day to the Senate Committee on Federal Relations, which had not yet made a report on the amendment. The committee reported the House resolution favorably, without change, on 12 June. Two days later a proposal to refer the

---

[2]*Annual Cyclopedia* (1867) 532.

[3]*Nebraska Senate Journal* (1867) 58.

[4]Ibid., 104-48.

[5]*Nebraska House Journal* (1867) 101-48.

Fourteenth Amendment to a referendum of the people of Nebraska was defeated. The third reading took place on 15 June and ratification passed by a close vote of eight to five.[6] Some Republicans obviously voted against approval.

Between March and November, twenty states in the North held elections for state officials. In most of them the Republican party lost at least some ground and suffered severe defeats in others. These results would seem to create a sobering effect on extremists and create support for more moderate congressmen. The *New York Times* interpreted the results as "a reaction against the extreme acts and measures of the Republican party," especially suffrage for blacks and confiscation; it should be a warning to advocates of such policies in Congress.[7]

Republicans, especially the more radical ones, were moving toward requiring Southern black suffrage as well as impeaching the President, who was still opposing what the people had apparently endorsed in 1866. Whether admission of Southern representatives would follow ratification of the Fourteenth Amendment by reconstructed legislatures and suffrage for blacks was not certain, and even confiscation of property held by leading "rebels" was debated. In conjunction with these differences was an attempt by Republicans to organize their party in the South around more pragmatic leaders such as Joseph E. Brown and General James W. Longstreet. This organization might avoid further polarization of blacks and whites in the South. Henry Wilson, senator from Massachusetts, and Horace Greeley were both vocal in support of this aim and appeared more conservative in the process. A split became increasingly apparent between the more radical and more conservative leaders of the Republican party. In such a division lay the principal danger for Republicans in 1867. Sumner attacked Fessenden as "the head of the obstructives," and Fessenden seemed amused by the antics of his opponent. "All the world is laughing at him for making such an ass of himself," he wrote.[8]

---

[6]*Nebraska Senate Journal*, 137-76.

[7]*New York Times*, 10 October 1867.

[8]Fessenden to Grimes, 20 September 1867, Fessenden Papers, Library of Congress.

Economic issues entered into the campaign with the administration's policy to contract the amount of greenbacks in circulation. The possibility of depression if too much money was retired from use too quickly bothered businessmen. Whatever the causes, business activity did slow in 1867, adding another element to the political races.

In March, Connecticut voters elected a Democratic governor and three Democratic representatives to Congress with only one Republican. Democrats in that state had earlier protested "the revolutionary acts and usurpations of the present Congress." In convention they complimented Johnson and praised the Supreme Court while Republicans justified the Fourteenth Amendment. The Republicans retained control, but by thin majorities of one in the Senate and ten in the House.[9] Coming so early in the campaigns that year, the news of Democratic resurgence was much publicized and had its effect elsewhere. It raised Southern hopes, which rested on Northern Democratic power.[10]

Republicans saw their majorities reduced in Maine.[11] In Connecticut and Maine as in others, many secondary issues entered into the situation; the trend disturbed Republicans.[12] Blaine wrote of the Maine election that the results would be a good discipline.[13] New Hampshire reelected Republicans, but by decreasing majorities. There, Democrats opposed tendencies toward centralization and favored states' rights. They opposed what was termed unconstitutional legislation. In neighboring Vermont, Republicans won overwhelmingly on issues that included equal rights and impartial suffrage, al-

---

[9]*Annual Cyclopedia* (1867) 472.

[10]Charles Fairman, *Reconstruction and Reunion, 1864-1888*, pt.1 in *History of the Supreme Court of the United States*, ed., Paul A. Freund (New York, MacMillan Co., 1971) 400.

[11]*Annual Cyclopedia* (1867) 472.

[12]Michael Les Benedict, *A Compromise of Principle: Congressional Republicans and Reconstruction, 1863-1869* (New York: W. W. Norton and Co., 1974) 273.

[13]Blaine to Israel Washburne, 12 September 1867, quoted in Gaillard Hunt, *Israel, Elihu and Cadwallader Washburne: A Chapter in American Biography* (New York: MacMillan Co., 1925) 122.

ready a part of that state's constitution.[14] Republicans were likewise successful in Rhode Island where their large majorities in the legislature were maintained: twenty-eight to six in the Senate and sixty-two to eight in the House. Despite this, the Republican percentage of the vote suffered.[15]

Massachusetts voters reelected Republicans, but also by reduced majorities. The election was "like a bucket of cold water on the head of a drunken man," commented the *Springfield Republican*.[16] Conservative Republicans should take a larger part in public affairs without driving Radicals out of the party, advised the *Boston Evening Journal*.[17] Even before the election, John A. Andrew had predicted that they "will scare us enough to wake up every honest heart" in preparing for the 1868 election.[18]

In New Jersey, Democrats made new gains with the main issue being the black vote and the right of a state to control rules for voting. In that state, Republicans lost control of the Senate by one vote but lost by a substantial margin in the House. They also lost in local elections.[19] The Democrats' gain of legislative control in New Jersey is of particular significance due to their later attempt to rescind the New Jersey ratification of the Fourteenth Amendment. Maryland Democrats retained control by even greater margins, which emphasized their opposition to black suffrage and the Fourteenth Amendment. The legislature was completely Democratic.[20]

Republican strength was still strong even though it was numerically reduced in Iowa where an amendment to the state constitution

---

[14]*Annual Cyclopedia* (1867) 540, 755-76.

[15]Ibid., 676; Benedict, *Compromise of Principle*, 272.

[16]6 October 1867; Benedict, *A Compromise of Principle*, 272.

[17]November 1867.

[18]Henry Greenleaf Pearson, *The Life of John A. Andrew, Governor of Massachusetts, 1861-1865* (Boston: Houghton Mifflin Co., 1904) 2:319.

[19]*Annual Cyclopedia* (1867) 540.

[20]Charles L. Wagandt, "Redemption or Reaction," in Richard O. Curry, ed., *Radicalism, Racism and Party Realignment: The Border States during Reconstruction* (Baltimore: Johns Hopkins University Press, 1969) 169; *Annual Cyclopedia* (1867) 480.

to strike the word "white" from the state constitution was adopted. The Fourteenth Amendment, not yet ratified in Iowa, was discussed, but principal interest centered on economic questions, especially currency and bond issues.[21] Although Republican, Iowa voters were not radical, which lead Senator Grimes to say, "There is not a man who fought against us in the rebellion in whom I have no more confidence and for whom I have not a greater respect than I have for Mr. B. F. Butler." "Thad Stevens is no better," he added.[22]

In Minnesota, the question of taxing federal bonds was an issue as was a proposal to enfranchise blacks by a state constitutional amendment. Here, too, the percentage of Republican votes dropped.[23] Wisconsin voters were even more closely divided. Republicans barely retained control of the Senate, though the majority was greater in the House. A Republican was also elected governor. Democrats accused them of invading states' rights. Republicans emphasized the importance of honoring the public debt and equality of treatment for blacks.[24]

In Michigan, Republican strength actually increased, although an amendment to the state constitution for impartial suffrage failed by a narrow margin.[25] The drift among leading Michigan citizens is shown in the gradual shift of position by Zachariah Chandler—until 1867, he was definitely among those labeled radical.[26]

Kentucky, whose legislature had rejected the Fourteenth Amendment earlier in 1867, proceeded to reelect Garret Davis to the United States Senate where he had consistently been the proverbial thorn in the Republican side.[27] Democrats, meeting in Frankfort that

---

[21]*Annual Cyclopedia* (1867) 408.

[22]Benedict, *A Compromise of Principle*, 276.

[23]Ibid., 273.

[24]*Annual Cyclopedia* (1867) 772.

[25]Ibid., 513; Benedict, *A Compromise of Principle*, 272.

[26]Leon Burr Richardson, *William E. Chandler, Republican* (New York: Dodd, Mead & Co., 1940) 78-81.

[27]E. M. Coulter, *Civil War and Readjustment in Kentucky* (Chapel Hill: University of North Carolina Press, 1926) 217.

February, criticized Congress for its efforts to establish a military despotism in the South and endorsed Johnson's veto messages.[28] Their party succeeded in congressional and state elections of that year, although Republican strength did increase.[29] There were eighty-five Democrats to ten Radicals and five Conservatives in the House and twenty-eight to seven Radicals and three Conservatives in the Senate.[30] These figures reflect the division of Republicans in the state into separate ideological fragments.

Ex-Confederates were so completely in control that the House Judiciary Committee of Congress sent a subcommittee to Lexington and Louisville to hold hearings. Out of this came the question of the qualification of some of those elected to Congress, and a continuing battle with Congress resulted.[31] James M. Bank, one of those not seated in Congress, wrote that "All that Congress wants is for us to give them a pretext to put our state down to the level of the other Southern States." Some regarded it as an effort to build Republican support,[32] especially since a congressional committee was also looking into Delaware and Maryland, the only other states outside the excluded South that had rejected the Fourteenth Amendment.[33]

The election of 1867 in the large state of New York attracted attention. When the Republican convention met on 25 September in Syracuse, a movement developed to purge the party of those who had supported President Johnson and the 1866 National Union Convention. Although an appearance of harmony was achieved, the purge was felt in the election. Conkling addressed the group and strongly supported human rights and the impeachment of Johnson. The

[28]Ross A. Webb, "Kentucky, Pariah Among the Elect," in Curry, *Radicalism, Racism and Party Realignment*, 128; *Annual Cyclopedia* (1867) 422.

[29]Benedict, *A Compromise of Principle*, 272.

[30]Coulter, *Civil War and Readjustment in Kentucky*, 325; *Annual Cyclopedia* (1867) 423.

[31]*Congressional Globe*, 40th Cong., 1st sess., 656; Coulter, *Civil War and Readjustment in Kentucky*, 337-38.

[32]Coulter, *Civil War and Readjustment in Kentucky*, 333.

[33]James M. Ogden to Joseph Holt, 22 October 1867, Joseph Holt Papers, Library of Congress; *Congressional Globe*, 40th Cong., 1st sess., 656.

platform included advocacy of impartial suffrage and congressional policies on reconstruction. It referred to the need of protecting the financial obligations of the nation, but left its position on this important issue somewhat ambiguous.[34]

Plans to tax bonds or to pay them with depreciated greenbacks were among the movements that were said to threaten the validity of the national debt guaranteed in the Fourteenth Amendment. *Harper's Weekly* eloquently and emotionally stated its position on this issue in October: "The blood of every soldier who fell in battle cries out from the ground against repudiation, no matter in what shape it comes; whether a wholesale wiping off of the slate, or the payment of gold obligations with paper."[35]

Democrats convention in Albany on 3 October denounced Republican policies concerning suffrage for blacks, especially that of improving black suffrage by force in the South. They believed that the issue should be submitted to the people in New York.[36] Here, as in most of the North, the suffrage issue hurt Republicans not just because of racial feelings, but because of a states' rights reaction to national control of state voting law.

After a vigorous campaign, the early November election resulted in a Democratic landslide.[37] Thomas Ewing commented that the New York election was a sensation: "Our Radical Congress will be on its last legs."[38] The legislature selected in the Democratic victory proved to be rather even in the Senate: fifteen Democrats and one Independent to sixteen Republicans. In the House there were seventy-three Democrats and fifty-five Republicans. Statewide election

---

[34]Homer Adolph Stebbins, *A Political History of the State of New York, 1865-1869* (New York: Columbia University Studies in Economics and Public Law, vol. 55, 1913) 150-67; *Annual Cyclopedia* (1867) 544.

[35]2 October 1867.

[36]Stebbins, *Political History of New York*, 171; *Annual Cyclopedia* (1867) 545.

[37]Stebbins, *Political History of New York*, 171; *Annual Cyclopedia* (1867) 545; Glendon G. Van Deusen, *Horace Greeley, Nineteenth Century Crusader* (Philadelphia: University of Pennsylvania Press, 1952) 306.

[38]Thomas Ewing to his son, Hugh, 7 November 1867, Thomas Ewing Papers, Library of Congress.

for secretary of state produced a Democratic majority of over forty-seven thousand.[39] What presidential patronage did to influence the election is not clear except that it was used in New York as elsewhere to support moderate Republicans rather than Democrats.[40]

The Pennsylvania election of 1867 attracted about as much attention as New York's. Democrats, meeting in convention on 11 June in Harrisburg, criticized Congress for requiring black suffrage in the South. They also opposed it in Pennsylvania. Democrats accused Republicans of disregarding the Constitution and trying to establish a congressional dictatorship.[41]

Republicans met at Williamsport on 26 June. They demanded the security offered by the Fourteenth Amendment against renewal of treason and endorsed congressional methods of reconstruction. They lost in a statewide election for a member of the Supreme Court by 922 votes out of 534,570 cast, but did manage to retain control of the legislature by a small margin. In the Senate, Republicans still held control by nineteen seats to fourteen; in the House, by fifty-four to forty-six.[42] Hard money and other economic issues had played a part in the campaign. Pendleton's Ohio Idea for repaying bonded indebtedness with paper money was charged by Republicans to be repudiation forbidden by the Fourteenth Amendment.[43] Stevens continued to advocate reparations from the South by means of confiscation.[44]

Increasingly, Republicans saw that the only hope of a presidential victory in 1868 lay with Grant. Andrew Curtin wrote in October after the election, Grant "is the only man living who can carry the

---

[39]Benedict, *A Compromise of Principle*, 273; *Annual Cyclopedia* (1867) 546.

[40]Martin E. Mantell, *Johnson, Grant and the Politics of Reconstruction* (New York: Columbia University Press, 1973) 65.

[41]*Annual Cyclopedia* (1867) 619.

[42]Ibid., 620; Fairman, *Reconstruction and Reunion* 400; Benedict, *A Compromise of Principle*, 213.

[43]Benedict, *A Compromise of Principle*, 275.

[44]*New York Times*, 27 May 1867.

State next year on present issues."[45] This was to become a more general Republican view in other states.[46] While the conservative ex-President Buchanan continued to grumble about violations of states' rights under the Constitution, the fall elections were causing new hope in the South for help from Northern Democrats.[47]

The election in Ohio was regarded by the *New York Times* as the key to the entire Midwest.[48] Here, more than in any Northern state, the racial issue became paramount although economic and reconstruction politics, as well as purely local issues, played a part. The important Radical leader, Senator Ben Wade, had his reelection and political career at stake in the contest to control the legislature. This contest would also effect the effort to rescind Ohio's earlier ratification of the Fourteenth Amendment. General W. T. Sherman, a native of Ohio and a possible candidate for president, considered the black vote more a question of prejudice than principle. He thought, however, that "a voter has as much right to his prejudice as to his vote."[49] Ben Wade claimed that "we went in on principle, and got whipped."[50] It is doubtful that practical political purpose was absent, but there was no doubt that Wade was right about the result.

Ohio Republicans endorsed the black vote with a constitutional amendment to accomplish that objective. Rutherford B. Hayes, then a member of Congress, accepted the nomination for governor on a

---

[45]Andrew Curtin to E. B. Washburne, 17 October 1867, E. B. Washburne Papers, Library of Congress.

[46]William B. Heseltine, *U. S. Grant, Politician* (New York: Dodd, Mead & Co., 1935) 99.

[47]Example is *Charleston Courier*, 20 November 1867; Buchanan to August Scheel, 9 November 1867 in Philip Shriver Klein, *President James Buchanan* (University Park PA: Pennsylvania State University Press, 1962) 422.

[48]7 May 1867.

[49]W. T. Sherman to John Sherman, October 1867, in John Sherman, *Recollections of Forty Years in the House, Senate and Cabinet: An Autobiography* (Chicago: Werner Co., 1895) 415.

[50]B. F. Wade to Zachariah Chandler, 10 October 1867, Zachariah Chandler Papers, Library of Congress.

platform that included impartial suffrage.[51] Democrats opposed extension of suffrage and charged that Republicans were trying to make white men inferior. They even suggested that interracial marriages would result. Girls were placed on a platform with a sign that begged "Fathers, save us from negro equality." Hayes won by a narrow margin, but the Democrats gained control of the legislature and the amendment was defeated by thirty-eight thousand votes.[52]

After the election, John Sherman was still convinced that the national dilemma could not be solved without universal suffrage and universal amnesty.[53] Senator Fessenden of Maine agreed with "most of our influential journals" that the Ohio defeat for Republicans was due to "a general disgust with the leadership of Stevens and his drove."[54] Among the interesting alterations of politicians' positions during the conflict in Ohio was that of James A. Garfield, who had argued the Milligan case before the Supreme Court but now was allied with the majority of his fellow congressmen on the side of military control over civilians in the new reconstruction acts.[55]

California, which had taken no action on the Fourteenth Amendment, was swept into the Democratic camp in state elections. Republican candidates were defeated for governor and lieutenant-governor as well as for a post on the Supreme Court. The new legislature turned out to be divided, with Republicans still in control of the Senate twenty-three to seventeen, and Democrats dominating the House fifty-one to twenty-nine.[56] This composition rather effec-

---

[51]Henry Barnard, *Rutherford B. Hayes and His America* (Indianapolis: Bobbs-Merrill Co., 1954) 238.

[52]Edgar A. Tappen, "The Negro Suffrage Issue in Ohio Politics," *Journal of Human Relations* (1863): 242-43; E. H. Roseboom and F. P. Weisenberger, *A History of Ohio* (New York: Prentiss Hall Co., 1934) 286; Edward L. Gambill, *Northern Democrats and Reconstruction, 1865-1868* (Ph.D. diss., University of Iowa, 1969) 46-50.

[53]John Sherman to W. T. Sherman, 11 November 1867, W. T. Sherman Papers, Library of Congress.

[54]Fessenden to James W. Grimes, 20 October 1867, Fessenden Papers at Bowdoin College.

[55]Robert Granville Caldwell, *James A. Garfield: Party Chieftan* (New York: Dodd, Mead & Co., 1931) 174.

[56]*Annual Cyclopedia* (1867) 96.

tively prevented cooperation with the congressional plan, including the amendment's ratification.

In reviewing the results of the 1867 fall elections in many Northern states, Ben Wade succinctly stated that "The nigger whipped us." He added in explanation that he "had no idea that there were so many Republicans in Ohio who were willing to see Negro suffrage in the South, but wouldn't let the few niggers in Ohio vote."[57] These results seemed to raise a question about the prediction made by Governor Oliver P. Morton of Indiana that March that within two years the South would be readmitted to Congress following the congressional plan. Speaker Colfax endorsed Wade's statement.[58] It long had been said that the Radicals' purpose for black suffrage, both North and South, was to "secure perpetual ascendancy to the party of the Union."[59] Congress was persuaded to grant suffrage to blacks in the District of Columbia over the veto of President Johnson on 8 January 1867.[60] Of course, voters there could not affect state or national matters, and it proved somewhat embarrassing to have the states of congressmen who had supported the measure voting against suffrage for blacks later in the year.

When Congress assembled for the second session of the Fortieth Congress in December after the Northern elections and after the initial step in Southern reorganization under the reconstruction acts of the first session, it was met by a presidential message calculated to consolidate the opposition that had appeared in the summer. In addition to charging the Congress with ignoring the Constitution, Johnson recommended the repeal of reconstruction acts. "It is manifestly and avowedly the object of these laws to confer upon negroes the privilege of voting and to disfranchise such a number of white citizens as will give the former a clear majority of all elections in the

[57]*New York World*, 9 November 1867.

[58]*New York Times*, 10 March 1867.

[59]*Congressional Globe*, 39th Cong., 1st sess., 878.

[60]Edward McPherson, *The Political History of the United States of America During the Period of Reconstruction* (Washington DC: Philip and Solomons, 1871) 160.

Southern States."[61] It was not the time for black suffrage, said the President, and there were congressmen who were beginning to be tempted to hesitate, if not to agree.

Radicals seemed to believe that there was a real danger of an attempted coup d'etat by Johnson.[62] Impeachment of the President was still a possibility despite the failure of the earlier attempt and seemed to some necessary if Congress were to "tie his hands."[63] To others it seemed even more necessary to establish Republican control in the South so as to offset growing Democratic strength in the North.[64] Representative James M. Ashley of Ohio expressed something of this feeling in a speech 10 December in which he restated his earlier fear that a restored South siding with others in the North would gain control of the nation in the 1868 election. "No man is more thankful than I that they rejected our proposition. Only by their rejection of the proposed Amendment were we saved from a doom as certain as the coming of November, 1868."[65]

Ashley introduced his version of a Fourteenth Amendment, which he wanted to substitute for the original. Many of its provisions he carried over intact as had the counterproposal endorsed by Johnson that January and February. In this act, the author proposed to make it more radical rather than less so. He included a strong section for universal suffrage that was stated in such a way as to enfranchise all "citizens," a term that presumably would include women although it is doubtful if that was his intent. Disqualification for engaging in rebellion was permitted. Civil rights guarantees were rearranged,

---

[61]James D. Richardson, *A Compilation of the Messages and Papers of the Presidents, 1789-1897* (Washington DC: Bureau of National Literature and Art, 1898) 6:560-68.

[62]Carl Schurz to his wife, 9 November 1867, in Carl Schurz, *Intimate Letters of Carl Schurz*, ed., Joseph Schafer (Madison WI: State Historical Society of Wisconsin, 1928). As early as July 1866 John Sherman had expressed a similar fear in a letter to W. T. Sherman, 8 July 1866, John Sherman Papers, Library of Congress.

[63]William Salter, *The Life of James W. Grimes, Governor of Iowa, 1854-1858, Senator of the United States, 1859-1869* (New York: D. Appleton Co., 1876) 323.

[64]Charles Fairman, *Mr. Justice Miller* (Cambridge: Harvard University Press, 1939) 139-41.

[65]*Congressional Globe*, 40th Cong., 2d sess., 118.

but were still included as was the same definition of citizenship. Aside from the suffrage innovation, the most striking change was the introduction of a provision requiring states to "establish and maintain by equitable taxation a thorough and efficient system of free public schools throughout the State sufficiently numerous for the accommodation of all the children of the State."⁶⁶ It is noteworthy that he recognized a logical connection between universal voting and universal education.

With full awareness of congressional attitudes that had produced military reconstruction acts and pushed them into mandated elections for or against constitutional conventions and with Northern elections making earlier interpretations of national sentiment based on 1866 elections at least questionable, Southern states faced an uncertain future. It seemed more than likely that they could not be represented in Congress or cast votes for presidential electors in 1868 unless they accepted a new political organization including suffrage for blacks, which would make reinstatement less desirable. The terms of the Fourteenth Amendment were being applied to them by statute, but the fate of the amendment was still in doubt. Congress had not proclaimed it to be a part of the Constitution, leaving an impression that the dictated ratification by the South would be necessary for final approval. To submit to the will of the conquerer was accepted without question, but to take positive steps under allowable options raised new questions for ex-Confederate states.

---

⁶⁶ Ibid., 117.

Chapter Sixteen

Full
Speed Ahead

While states of the South were reorganizing under the reconstruction acts of Congress, Iowa finally acted on the Fourteenth
Amendment. This seeming delay was due to the legislature's meeting
only every two years, but the more moderate attitude of its leaders
and considerable racial feelings added their influence as well.

It should be remembered that in 1865 the Iowa election largely
turned on the issue of the black vote for that state as the voters overwhelmingly repudiated extending the vote to blacks. As late as 1867,
the lieutenant governor asked the Republican state convention,
"How can you insist that loyal negroes shall vote in South Carolina,
when you refuse to allow colored soldiers of your own Iowa colored
regiment to vote here?" Few politicians had dared advocate black suf-

frage and as in some of the midwestern states, even the immigration of blacks was feared.[1]

In the election of 1867, the percentage of Republican support dwindled, but substantial majorities were retained in the legislature.[2] Other issues besides the Fourteenth Amendment influenced the race, including some German disaffection, debates on debt, and taxation of bonds, as well as the striking of the word "white" from the state constitution.

The home state of the moderate Republican Senator James W. Grimes, who helped frame the Fourteenth Amendment, finally ratified it in 1868. Governor Samuel Merrill, in his inaugural address on 16 January, seconded the recommendation of the retiring governor, William M. Stone[3] and expanded upon it:

> We have felt bound to insist that those States should concede whatever guarantees are essential to the future safety of the Union. We cannot permit the truths established by the war to relapse into a state of doubt, nor the fruits of victory to be swallowed up in a maganimity which neglects its own salvation.

In restoring the Southern people to rights within the Union, he added, "let no discrimination be made against the black man." He considered the ballot a necessity to blacks as he also favored doing away with racial distinctions in Iowa.[4]

The House responded by introducing and passing a resolution of ratification in one day, 27 January, by a vote of sixty-eight to twelve.[5] The Senate referred the House resolution to its Committee on Constitutional Amendments, which made a favorable report on 30 January. On 3 February, it was taken up and postponed until 26 February when it became the special order of business. However, it was 3 March before it was again called, at which point it was reset for

---

[1]G. Galen Berrier, "The Negro Suffrage Issue in Iowa, 1865-1868," *Annals of Iowa* 39 (Spring 1968): 241-61.

[2]*Annual Cyclopedia* (1867) 407-408.

[3]*Iowa Senate Journal* (1868) 33.

[4]Ibid., 46-48.

[5]*Iowa House Journal* (1868) 132.

special order of business on 9 March. After some debate, the chair ruled that a motion to vote on each section was out of order and was sustained. The amendment finally passed by a vote of thirty-four to nine.[6]

A Southern state that had not yet acted was Arkansas. The legislature as established under presidential reconstruction was in session when the first of the reconstruction acts became law in March 1867. Members had been debating what, if anything, should be done to bring about congressional representation of the state.[7] On 8 March, the House proposed a joint committee to report on the best policy for renewing relations with the federal government.[8] The legislature's position was that it was a proper republican government under the Constitution and was entitled to be represented in Congress.[9]

Under military reconstruction, Arkansas found itself grouped with Mississippi in a district commanded by General E. O. C. Ord who was instructed by the Act of 23 March to carry out registration and elections for a constitutional convention under the new statute. At first, calm continued to reign with acceptance of the new governmental controls. Even General Ord's order to cancel the session of the legislature scheduled for 8 July was not opposed until Attorney-General Stanberry on 24 May gave his opinion that the congressional acts of March were unconstitutional.[10]

Various military orders set aside instituted legislation, and vacant offices were filled by military appointment.[11] Governor Murphy cooperated with the military authorities and continued to function in a more limited way.[12] Military commissions now began to try criminal

---

[6]*Iowa Senate Journal*, 108, 112, 122, 141, 204-205.

[7]*Arkansas Senate Journal* (1866-1867) 561.

[8]*Arkansas House Journal* (1866-1867) 821.

[9]Ibid., 832; *Arkansas Senate Journal*, 743.

[10]*Reports of the United States Attorney-General*, 12:141-68.

[11]*Daily Republican*, 17 September 1867.

[12]*Van Buren Press*, 17 November 1867.

cases when Loyalists complained of treatment in civil courts.[13] This use of military courts raised questions that would be considered later when the McCardle case came to the forefront in the same military district in neighboring Mississippi.

Boards were set up to register qualified citizens to vote on the issue of a constitutional convention and to elect delegates at the same time in case the measure should be approved. These boards were instructed to register any male citizen of the United States who was twenty-one years old and a resident of Arkansas for one year and who had not been disfranchised by act of Congress or convicted of a felony. Each registrant was to take the prescribed oath. Registration began in May 1867 after questions of eligibility were temporarily solved by a ruling of the United States attorney-general that authorized registration, subject to review, of all those who could take the oath. General Grant objected, but registration continued as before till passage of the act of Congress of 19 July, which impowered registrars to decide questions of qualification. These rules were applied only after 2 August. The time limit was extended, finally ending in early September.[14] Radical Unionists organized quickly and held a state convention including only a few Negroes.[15] Ex-Confederate officials were specifically excluded.[16]

Issues presented on the eve of the election by friends of congressional reconstruction emphasized, in addition to suffrage for blacks and equal rights, such economic and social matters as good roads, free public education, and development of manufacturing. Confiscation of property or worse was implied if the convention failed.[17] Conservatives, leaderless and in disarray, claimed that the conven-

---

[13]*Daily Republican*, 17 September, 12 October 1867; *Van Buren Press*, 18 October 1867.

[14]*Annual Cyclopedia* (1867) 52; *New York Tribune*, 21 October 1867.

[15]*Van Buren Press*, 1 March 1867; *Arkansas Gazette*, 9 April 1867.

[16]James D. Richardson, *A Compilation of the Messages and Papers of the Presidents, 1889-1897* (Washington DC: Bureau of National Literature and Art, 1898) 6:552.

[17]*Daily Republican*, 29 October, 12 November 1867.

tion would mean a black regime that would be much worse than a military one.[18]

The election began on the first Tuesday in November; it had no termination date. Fraud was said to be widespread. General Ord announced results that favored a convention, one being scheduled to meet 7 January in Little Rock.[19] Many eligible whites had stayed away from the polls, with the result that 27,576 voted for the convention and 13,558 opposed it.[20] Republicans had elected over sixty of the seventy-five delegates.[21] When the convention assembled and organized on the designated date, 7 January 1868, all members were not yet present. Only three blacks secured appointed positions. The *Daily Republican* boasted that every one of the delegates "can write his name."[22] Of the nine native Arkansans, three were blacks.[23]

Conservatives challenged the constitutionality of the convention and urged economy while objecting to black suffrage.[24] They argued that because it was not a constituent assembly, it had no powers beyond those stipulated.[25] It was a common thing in the constitutional conventions of the reconstructed states to enact ordinary legislation while sitting to frame a fundamental document. In particular, they asked for and received permission to appropriate money from the state treasury for the expenses of the convention. In the case of Arkansas, the commanding general authorized the state treasurer to pay out amounts up to fifty thousand dollars raised through sale of United States bonds held by the state.[26]

---

[18]*Van Buren Press*, 29 October 1867.

[19]*Daily Republican*, 9, 19 November 1867; *Debates and Proceedings of the Arkansas Constitutional Convention of 1868*, 27, 41.

[20]Thomas S. Staples, *Reconstruction in Arkansas, 1862-1874* (New York: Columbia University Studies in History, Economics and Public Law, vol. 109, 1923) 178.

[21]*Daily Republican*, 8 January 1868.

[22]Ibid., 27 December 1867.

[23]*Debates and Proceedings*, 629.

[24]*Van Buren Press*, 10 January 1868.

[25]*Arkansas Gazette*, 22 January 1868.

[26]*Debates and Proceedings*, 686.

The first proposed constitution was the 1864 constitution, submitted to the people for approval. This occasioned several days of debate before it was defeated.[27] Though the discussions were heated, the constitution that was finally developed was not as radical as conservatives feared. It contained a bill of rights and a specific renunciation of secession. The right to vote was granted to all males born or naturalized in the United States or who had declared their intention of becoming a citizen. The age requirement was twenty-one and the residence qualification was six months in Arkansas and one month in the county. Disfranchized and disqualified from holding office were those who had violated an oath of allegiance to the United States, those disqualified in another state, or those who had violated the rules of civilized warfare. These provisions were in addition to those under the terms of the Fourteenth Amendment or reconstruction acts of Congress. Regardless of these restrictions, anyone who had openly supported congressional reconstruction was to be eligible. The legislature could remove disabilities by a two-thirds vote in each house. An oath was prerequisite to voting.[28]

Requirements set up for the office of governor made it possible for recent settlers to be selected. They specified five years as a citizen of the United States and one of Arkansas. The minimum age was twenty-five. A system of public schools and a university were required.[29] The convention finished its labors and adjourned on 14 February with a provision for reassembling should the proposed constitution fail to be approved.[30]

The election for adoption was scheduled to begin on 3 March, allowing about a month for the people to be informed and to decide on the issues. As in the election for the convention, there was no limit of how many days the election should last.[31]

---

[27]Ibid., 102.

[28]Ibid., 878-79.

[29]Ibid., 887.

[30]Ibid., 754.

[31]Staples, *Reconstruction in Arkansas*, 246.

Conservatives set out to organize their efforts to defeat the proposed constitution. These included a state convention at Little Rock on 27 January to coordinate their organization with the national Democratic party.[32] They passed a resolution for "a white man's government in a white man's country" while denouncing suffrage for blacks but supporting civil rights. They challenged the constitutionality of the constitutional convention and the refusal of Congress to admit representatives from Arkansas to that body under the constitution of 1864.[33] That document had been a product of early presidential reconstruction.

Republicans also called a state convention on 15 January. They nominated a slate of candidates and adopted a platform for restricting cooperation with the congressional plan.[34] It should be noted that both party conventions had been held while the constitutional convention was in session, making it possible for some members of the constitutional convention to take part in party assemblies. Thus, when the constitutional issue was placed before the people, both parties were girded for the fray. Republicans urged the adoption of the proposed document as being necessary for the economic prosperity of the state.[35] Democratic organs critically evaluated the new constitution in detail.[36]

The ratification of the proposed constitution was to be accomplished in a most complicated method adopted by General A. C. Gillem. The military closely controlled one set of polls for the vote on the constitution while civil authorities officiated at a different election for county and state officers as well as for members of Congress. No troops, however, were stationed near the polls.[37]

Congress had changed the original act that required the vote of a majority of all registered voters for approval. This change meant that

---

[32]*Van Buren Press*, 10 January 1868.

[33]*Arkansas Gazette*, 30 January 1868.

[34]*Daily Republican*, 15 January 1868.

[35]Ibid., 5, 15 February 1868.

[36]*Van Buren Press*, 28 February 1868.

[37]*Executive Documents*, 40th Cong., 2d sess., 9, 231.

only a majority of those voting would secure ratification; staying away from the polls would not defeat the constitution.[38] After the election, marred by many irregularities and possible fraud on both sides, commissioners announced official ratification. It became effective on that date, 1 April 1868. Officials elected would take office at the time specified in the document. Appeals claiming election fraud went to General Grant who turned them over to Congress, which meant that eventually the Joint Committee on Reconstruction received them.[39] From that body was to come a recommendation for the admission of Arkansas.

It was 3 April when Governor Murphy once again recommended the approval of the Fourteenth Amendment, but this time it was to the new legislature that had assembled without approval of Congress under the reconstruction statute. Governor Murphy reiterated his previous position that ratification was necessary for economic recovery in Arkansas as well for seating representatives in Congress. A joint resolution was called that same day in the House and approved without a dissenting vote, although twenty-five members were absent.[40]

The Senate took up the resolution "unanimously adopted" in the House on the same day. A motion to suspend the rules so as to permit three readings and a vote to take place immediately was defeated in a tie vote, eleven to eleven. The following Monday, 6 April, the resolution was read a second and third time and a vote was taken. Ratification was assured by unanimous support.[41]

Eventually, having considered the information from Arkansas in leisurely fashion after a report was sent by the President on 5 May,[42] the Reconstruction Committee reported a resolution for the admis-

---

[38]*Arkansas Gazette*, 8 March 1868.

[39]*Executive Documents*, 40th Cong., 2d sess., 5; *Debates and Proceedings*, 93-94.

[40]*Arkansas House Journal* (1868) 19-23; *Arkansas Senate Journal* (1868) 18-19.

[41]*Arkansas Senate Journal*, 20-23.

[42]Richardson, *Messages and Papers*, 6:632; Orville Hickman Browning, *Diary of Orville Hickman Browning, 1865-1881*, ed., Theodore C. Reese and J. G. Randall (Springfield IL: Collections of the Illinois State Historical Library, vols. 20, 22, 1933) 2:195.

sion of Arkansas. It did so after much debate on a proposal by Thaddeus Stevens that a permanent condition be inserted to prevent Arkansas from ever changing the state constitutional provisions on suffrage. Finally approval for admission of Arkansas that included the above provision passed the House by a vote of 110 to 32.[43]

All this was taking place while impeachment of the President was a major concern. The Senate took up the House resolution to admit Arkansas on 15 May, but was temporarily stalled by the problem involved in the transition from the old constitution of 1864 to the new one just declared ratified. To be legal, the new state constitution needed congressional approval, and yet that body had informally convened without opposition from the military and had ratified the Fourteenth Amendment. However, the Judiciary Committee proceeded to recommend the passage of the resolution of admission on 16 May; a slightly modified version passed the Senate on 6 June. It was immediately vetoed by the embattled president. Both House and Senate overrode this obstacle on 20 June and 22 June, respectively.[44]

These actions transpired before newly elected officials were installed according to the new constitution in Arkansas. Ratification of the Fourteenth Amendment was accomplished by the legislature on recommendation of the outgoing governor selected under the old constitution and before the legislature ordinarily would have met according to the new document. Duplicate salaries were paid in Arkansas to state officials during this chaotic transition.[45] Congress had overlooked all these problems as well as election irregularities in recognizing Arkansas for representation.

Florida had been assigned a place in the third military district with Georgia and Alabama under General Pope. The development of reconstruction legislation had been watched closely by Floridians in the first half of 1867. There had been some hope that the Supreme Court would overturn these acts. Talk of emigration was reflected in a press

---

[43]*Congressional Globe* (1901) 40th Cong., 2d sess., 2399; *Acts and Resolutions of the 40th Congress*, 2d sess., 43.

[44]*Congressional Globe* (1901) 40th Cong., 2d sess., 2399; Walter L. Fleming, *Documentary History of Reconstruction* (Cleveland: Arthur H. Clark Co., 1906) 1:416.

[45]Staples, *Reconstruction in Arkansas*, 274.

admonition not to "pack up your bags yet."[46] The legislature of Florida had rejected the Fourteenth Amendment with other Southern states and now waited for the inevitable, which some thought would be a return to territorial status.[47] Military rule was relatively mild under Colonel John Sprague, a soldier with Florida ties.[48]

Republicans were impatient with a Congress that to them seemed to be unduly hesitant about disfranchizing ex-Confederates and enfranchizing blacks. Many Floridians hoped that the new constitution would be framed and approved, the Fourteenth Amendment ratified, and the state readmitted to Congress.[49] Even the *Tallahassee Floridian* saw no "manifest advantage" in postponing what must be done eventually.[50] This, it realized, would include initiating suffrage for blacks and ratifying the Fourteenth Amendment. As in other Southern states, some Florida conservatives sought to turn this suffrage question to their advantage,[51] but, as elsewhere, had only moderate success. As reconstruction proceeded with military appointments filling civil vacancies in government, and military tribunals acting on occasion instead of regular courts, the full impact of Congressional reconstruction began to be felt. Some actually joined others from Georgia and Alabama in emigrating to Brazil.[52]

Splits in the Republican ranks did not prevent that party's victory in the election of the constitutional convention that was to assemble in Tallahassee in January 1868. Membership in this body was ideologically controlled by conservatives, and the new constitution re-

---

[46]*Tallahassee Semi-Weekly Floridian*, 6 November 1866.

[47]Jerrell H. Shofner, *Nor Is It Over Yet: Florida in the Era of Reconstruction, 1863-1877* (Gainesville: University Presses of Florida, 1974) 157.

[48]*St. Augustine Examiner*, 9 March 1867.

[49]*Gainesville New Era*, 5 March 1867.

[50]March 1867.

[51]*Gainesville New Era*, 20 April 1867; Joe M. Richardson, *The Negro in the Reconstruction of Florida, 1865-1877* (Tallahassee FL: Florida State University Studies, vol. 46, 1965) 150-51.

[52]Shofner, *Nor Is It Over Yet*, 120.

flected this.[53] After a temporary boycott by moderates had caused an attempt to operate without a quorum,[54] military intervention reached a point at which Colonel Sprague began presiding over the conflicting groups in full military uniform.[55] General Meade, who had succeeded Pope in command of the region, recommended the constitution adopted by the convention of 29 February. It was submitted to the people under the new suffrage rules. After a three-day election that May, the constitution was endorsed by a large majority.[56]

The new legislature met on 8 June and the next day received Governor Harrison Reed's message. As conservative as the legislature, he recommended that "no action be taken save such as dictated by the Acts of Congress as conditions precedent to admission, to wit: The passage of the proposed Amendment to the Constitution, known as the Fourteenth Article, and the election of United States Senators."[57] That same day, 9 February, the Senate suspended the rules and held all three readings and the vote on ratification. It passed ten to three.[58] The House immediately took up the Senate resolution and approved ratification of both the Thirteenth and Fourteenth Amendments by rushing through all three readings and the vote. The majority was twenty-three to six.[59]

Congressional approval of Florida's adopting an acceptable constitution and ratifying the Fourteenth Amendment involved much debate in Congress, ostensibly on the question of seating members. In the Senate, the power of the President to report the ratification in Florida was discussed. Additional light is shed on the actions of par-

---

[53]Richard L. Hume, "Membership of the Florida Constitutional Convention of 1868," *Florida Historical Quarterly* (1972): 101-21.

[54]*New York Times*, 7 February 1868.

[55]Shofner, *Nor Is It Over Yet*, 183-85.

[56]Ibid., 183; Edward McPherson, *The Political History of the United States during the Period of Reconstruction* (Washington DC: Philip and Solomons, 1871) 328-29.

[57]*Florida House Journal*, 1st sess. (1868) 7.

[58]*Florida Senate Journal*, 1st sess. (1868) 8-9.

[59]*Florida House Journal*, 9.

ticipants when it is remembered that the trial of Johnson on impeachment charges had ended only recently in a failure for his opponents. During the discussions, Jacob Howard of Michigan announced that he did "not think that ancient statute [the Constitution] applies to the seceding states."[60]

Admission of senators was the problem, but their individual qualifications were not the real point. Rather, discussion centered on whether the state had fulfilled conditions prescribed by Congress in adopting the new constitution and ratifying the Fourteenth Amendment. Once again the problem was aired as to whether a permanent commitment on suffrage could be required in a state constitution as a condition of recognition by Congress. The perpetual conditions had been required of Arkansas, the first state to be readmitted since Tennessee, though questioned then and later. Other acts to follow affecting North Carolina, South Carolina, Louisiana, Alabama, and Florida also included such a questionable requirement.[61]

In answer to Fessenden's insistent question about proof of ratification if the secretary of state had not formally certified ratification based on official documents, Trumbull of Illinois replied that this lack "would not alter its validity." He added that there was no real doubt as to ratification, and its promulgation was not really necessary for its adoption. The secretary merely was obliged to publish that fact.[62] This statement by the distinguished member of the Judiciary Committee will be worth remembering when studying the clamor for official proclamation of the amendment's adoption only a month later.

Technical questions in addition to the necessity of a report from the secretary of state included reported variations in the text of the approved amendment. Senator Charles D. Drake of Missouri pointed out that such errors were numerous. Others minimized the importance of such mistakes and declared that the intent to ratify the Fourteenth Amendment was clear. Senator Frederick T. Freling-

---

[60]*Congressional Globe*, 40th Cong., 2d sess., 3598.

[61]*United States Statutes at Large* (1867) 15:72-74.

[62]*Congressional Globe*, 40th Cong., 2d sess., 3602.

huysen of New Jersey showed that similar errors had occurred in ratification by New York, Pennsylvania, Wisconsin, and Michigan.[63]

In such an atmosphere and with increasing pressure to admit Southern states to Congress as well as to declare the Fourteenth Amendment ratified, Florida was approved. It was the second of the seceded states to have successfully completed the congressional requirements for reinstatement that included ratification of the amendment, the fundamental issue of the elections of 1866. Now all eyes were looking toward the elections of 1868, which would include not only congressional seats but the presidency.

In North Carolina, indecision continued. Like other states in the South, it found itself under military control as required by reconstruction acts of Congress. The two Carolinas were grouped into a single district commanded by General Daniel Sickles. The Act of 25 June, which included Florida, also spelled out conditions necessary for North Carolina to meet if it wished to be readmitted to congressional representation. This general list included, in addition to the ratification of the Fourteenth Amendment, the condition of a perpetual guarantee of suffrage for blacks in its revised constitution. Though disregarded many times and generally thought to be unenforceable, such conditions exacted at the time of a state's admission continued to be a practice well into the twentieth century.

The last instance was in the case of Arizona and involved removing the recall of judges from the constitution as the price of admission. After becoming a state, Arizona promptly placed the measure back in its constitution by amendment. This was its right as interpreted in 1911 by the Supreme Court as it ruled in the first case involving this particular aspect of the principle of equality of states, *Coyle v. Smith*.[64] In this case, restrictions on congressional power to prescribe permanent provisions in a new state constitution, certainly a problem in reconstruction, were validated in the twentieth century both in practice and law. During March 1867 in the House of Representatives, Bingham of Ohio stated the argument of equality as clearly as anyone when he said: "The American system of govern-

---

[63]Ibid., 3598-3607.

[64]U.S. 559 (1911).

ment is total failure if the people cannot be intrusted with the right of altering and amending their constitution of government at their pleasure, subject to the general limitations of the Federal Constitution."[65]

Elections for delegates to a constitutional convention in North Carolina were ordered by General Edward R. S. Canby. It was to assemble in Raleigh on 14 January. The election used new rules of suffrage required by Congress and resulted in the selection of 107 Republicans and only 13 conservatives of all types. Conservative people in North Carolina called the assembly "the convention (so called)."[66] The election was full of the usual irregularities with additional pressures from the Freedman's Bureau and the Ku Klux Klan and their various forms of intimidation or persuasion.

The result of the convention's work was, on the whole, not a bad constitution, in spite of the fact that some features borrowed from the midwest, such as townships for local government, were not popular. Regardless of its good qualities, the 1868 constitution was distasteful to North Carolinians due to the circumstances of its construction. They believed that it had been forced upon them. However, they submitted to it and to the ratification of the Fourteenth Amendment that followed with resignation to a fate over which they had lost control. "They were worn down to the earth by the degradation imposed upon them by the negro-equality of the Civil Rights Bill and all the racking evils of the times," was the remark of a contemporary.[67]

The vote on the new constitution and election of state officers under its provisions took place over a three-day period, 21-23 April. The new constitution was adopted by an unusually close vote of 93,086 to 74,016. William W. Holden, who would be impeached and removed from office in 1870, was elected governor. Congressmen were elected at the same time. The new legislature seated eighty Republicans and forty conservatives in the House, with thirty-eight to twelve, respectively, in the Senate. Many elected Republicans were

---

[65]*Congressional Globe*, 40th Cong., 2d sess., 2211.

[66]Hugh T. Lefler, ed., *North Carolina Told by Contemporaries* (Chapel Hill: University of North Carolina Press, 1965) 334.

[67]Ibid., 350.

North Carolina white men though some were from the North, and a few were black.[68]

On 1 July, the new government was installed in Raleigh. On the eve of this event, Governor Jonathan Worth wrote the newly elected William W. Holden in these words: "You have no evidence of your election save the certificate of a major-general of the United States Army. I regard all of you as in effect appointees of the military power of the United States, and not as deriving your powers from the consent of those you claim to govern."[69]

Despite the existence of such strong feelings among the people of North Carolina, a resolution to ratify the "Howard Amendment" was promptly introduced in the House. A motion to form a joint committee to consider it was defeated by tabling. When the vote was taken, the ratification resolution was passed eighty-two to nineteen. All this was accomplished on the same day.[70]

The Senate immediately took up the House resolution and in a four o'clock session approved it by a vote of thirty-four to two. This also was accomplished on that same 2 July legislative day.[71] Senators were elected and were sworn in at Washington on 13 July. Representatives elected earlier in the popular vote were recognized in the United States House of Representatives on 20 July.[72] At last North Carolina had completed it restoration and added its ratification of the Fourteenth Amendment as a condition precedent.

---

[68]Robert Selph Henry, *The Story of Reconstruction* (Indianapolis: Bobbs-Merrill Co., 1938) 317.

[69]Ibid.

[70]*North Carolina House Journal* (1868) 11-12.

[71]*North Carolina Senate Journal* (1868) 12-15.

[72]Henry, *Story of Reconstruction*, 318.

Chapter Seventeen

Running
Before the Wind

North Carolina's sister state, South Carolina, finally conformed to all the terms of Congress and registered its ratification of the Fourteenth Amendment on 9 July 1868. Needless to say, much had changed since its earlier rejection, and all was not due to military control declared by Congress.

In the ten Southern states that had rejected the proposed amendment, suffrage had continued to be strictly limited to whites, although all whites were not eligible to vote. These states' leaders had leaned heavily on President Johnson and his advice against the mounting evidence of disapproval in Congress and in the North of 1866 that it represented. Attempts had been made to break the grip of the military as it checked and overruled civil acts of states. An example had been the removal of a judge by General Canby for not carrying out congressional policy.[1]

Supreme Court cases that had influence here will be considered later, but suffice it to say that nationally, much interest had centered on a possible judicial check of congressional reconstruction. In the same way and with even more interest, it also focused on impeachment as a means of removing presidential opposition to Congress. This scene had prompted the *Nation* to observe in September 1867 that "The Supreme Court is simply, when the destiny of the nation is at stake, nine old men." Judge Lyman Trumbull, senator from Illinois, had continued to insist that reconstruction was a political matter that should not concern the Court.[2] Just as strongly, he and some others who would sit in the Senate as a court of impeachment continued to regard that function as judicial rather than political. As in Florida, there were some South Carolinians so discouraged by the prospect of developing chaos that they were willing to leave their native land to settle in Honduras. Only a few did so. At one point that March, there were even some comments about a possible renewal of hostilities between North and South. A South Carolinian dismissed this notion in these words: "Gentlemen, it may do very well for you to talk of revolution, but we have had enough of it." Political apathy, coupled with the feeling that military rule could not last forever, more succinctly describes the average state of mind.[3] The *Charleston Courier* urged tranquility and expressed no hope of rescue by the Supreme Court.[4]

Wade Hampton represented a type of leader among conservative white men who at first believed that it would be possible to work with blacks and achieve a harmonious restoration of prosperity. From March to July he cultivated black votes with barbecues and per-

---

[1]Charles Fairman, *Reconstruction and Reunion, 1864-1888*, pt. 1 in *History of the Supreme Court of the United States* ed., Paul A. Freund (New York: MacMillan Co., 1971) 6:502.

[2]*The Nation*, 10 September 1867, 20 February 1868.

[3]*The Juhl Letters to the Charleston Courier: A View of the South, 1865-1877*, ed., John Hammond Moore (Athens GA: University of Georgia Press, 1974) 160-64, 173.

[4]March 1867.

suasion.[5] B. F. Perry typified a different kind of attitude. He urged acceptance, and active registration and voting to defeat the proposed new state constitutional convention, and later, its product. Military control seemed to him and to many a preferable state of affairs compared to what could follow under a state reconstructed according to the congressional formula.[6]

Most newspapers urged compliance and peace. The *Camden Journal* stated that "It behooves us in the State to be wise as serpents and harmless as doves."[7] "Do your duty and leave the consequences to God," was the advice of the *Columbia Phoenix*.[8]

The Freedmen's Bureau was brought into greater disrepute and aroused new hostility by its attempts to aid blacks under military rule. Schools were being used to indoctrinate blacks to vote Republican. Troops had to be called out to protect an agent of the Bureau in Kingstree, but most attacks stopped with words.[9] The Union League aroused strong support from blacks and animosity from whites.[10]

After military reconstruction was initiated, President Johnson issued a new proclamation of amnesty on 7 September 1867. In it, pardon was granted to all who participated "in the rebellion" except those who had held high positions in the Confederacy, military or civil, or any who had any part in the assassination of President Lincoln.[11] Again, on 4 July 1868, Johnson issued an even broader pro-

---

[5]Hampton M. Jarrell, *Wade Hampton and the Negro: The Road not Taken* (Columbia SC: University of South Carolina Press, 1949) 18.

[6]Lillian Adele Kibler, *Benjamin F. Perry: South Carolina Unionist* (Durham NC: Duke University Press, 1946) 450ff.

[7]April 1867.

[8]May 1867.

[9]Martin Abbot, *The Freedmen's Bureau in South Carolina* (Chapel Hill: University of North Carolina Press, 1967) 122-25; Peggy Lamson, *The Glorious Failure: Black Congressman Robert Brown Elliott and the Reconstruction of South Carolina* (New York: W. W. Norton and Co., 1973) 43.

[10]Francis Butler Simkins and Robert Hilliard Woody, *South Carolina During Reconstruction* (Chapel Hill: University of North Carolina Press, 1932) 74-75.

[11]James D. Richardson, *A Compilation of the Messages and Papers of the Presidents, 1789-1897* (Washington DC: Bureau of National Literature and Art, 1898) 547-49.

clamation granting pardon to all who were not under indictment for a felony.[12] This last was issued after his acquittal on impeachment charges before the Senate. According to the Fourteenth Amendment, which was to be proclaimed law in a few weeks by a resolution of Congress, that body retained power over forgiveness of leading ex-Confederates.[13]

Those eligible to vote under the new rules of Congress were urged to register and take part in an election to decide whether or not to have a state constitutional convention. The voters would at the same time elect delegates in case the measure passed. There were 80,832 blacks who registered as compared to 46,929 whites.[14]

The *Columbia Phoenix* reacted like other newspapers to what seemed to them the sad spectacle of leading South Carolinians like General Wade Hampton pleading with blacks for their votes.[15] Governor Orr hoped that blacks might be convinced to cooperate with conservative whites[16] who preferred military rule to the kind of society they feared would result from victory of congressional plans. "It is my honest and firm belief," said General Hampton, "that the voluntary acceptance of these measures by our people would surely bring, not only to the South, but to the whole country, evils far greater than any we have suffered."[17] Others, impatient with opponents of reconstruction who were holding back economic recovery, asked "Do they desire to see the present agitation indefinitely prolonged, industry clogged, commerce checked, credit and confidence altogether destroyed?"[18] Most local papers endorsed the convention.[19]

---

[12]Ibid., 655-56; John S. Reynolds, *Reconstruction in South Carolina* (Columbia SC: State Company, 1905) 37.

[13]*Congressional Globe*, 40th Cong., 2d sess., 4266, 4295-96.

[14]Avery Craven, *Reconstruction: The Ending of the Civil War* (New York: Holt, Rinehart and Winston, 1969) 241.

[15]1 July 1867.

[16]Simkins and Woody, *South Carolina During Reconstruction*, 83.

[17]Manly Wade Wellman, *Giant in Gray* (New York: Charles Scribner's Sons, 1949) 216.

[18]*Charlotte News*, quoted in *Columbia Phoenix*, 6 August 1867.

[19]Kibler, *Benjamin F. Perry*, 457-58.

In late October, conservative whites met in Columbia and, too late, decided to urge nonparticipation in the election. The results of the balloting could have been anticipated: 4,628 whites voted as did 66,468 blacks, and although there were votes cast without regard to color, the result was victory for the convention.[20]

The constitutional convention assembled in Charleston 14 January. Of the 124 delegates, 76 were black. Fifty-seven were former slaves.[21] The *Charleston Daily News* voiced a common apprehension when it declared, "the demagogue is to rule the mass, and vice and ignorance control the vast interests at stake."[22] Stability was needed even by would-be exploiters from the North and certainly by native Southerners in their efforts to make a living.[23]

The result of the convention's efforts, like other new Southern constitutions, was a surprisingly good organic document and was far from radical.[24] It did include, as mandated by Congress, suffrage for blacks, which by itself would have won white opposition. B. F. Perry and others urged the defeat of the constitution,[25] but the final vote was in favor of ratification 70,758 to 27,228.[26] Democrats won only 6 of the 31 Senate seats and 14 of the 124 in the House.[27]

General Canby ordered Governor Orr replaced by the newly elected executive, Robert K. Scott. He assumed his position on 9 July after the new legislature met on 6 July in Janney's Hall on the campus of the University of South Carolina in Columbia, not far from the roofless capitol.[28] General Hampton had appealed to Congress not to approve the new constitution, "the result of ignorant Negroes,

---

[20]Simkins and Woody, *South Carolina During Reconstruction*, 87-91.

[21]Ibid., 91.

[22]20 January 1868.

[23]Craven, *Reconstruction*, 256.

[24]Ernest McPherson Lander, Jr., *A History of South Carolina, 1865-1960* (Chapel Hill: University of North Carolina Press, 1960) 11-12.

[25]Kibler, *Benjamin F. Perry*, 469; *Greenville Southern Enterprise*, 15 April 1868.

[26]Simkins and Woody, *South Carolina During Reconstruction*, 188.

[27]Kibler, *Benjamin F. Perry*, 471; *Greenville Southern Enterprise*, 22 April 1868.

[28]Lamson, *Glorious Failure*, 71; Kibler, *Benjamin F. Perry*, 470.

Northern adventurers and a few renegades." The state, he said, "would never submit to Negro rule."[29]

The *Charleston Daily Courier* announced the new legislature in these words: "Today the Legislature, created by the Reconstruction Act, and who owe their origin not to the votes of the accustomed voters of our State, but the Radical Majority in Congress, and the presence of arms, will convene."[30] General Order No. 120, covering the inauguration of the new government, had been published the previous week.[31] Governor Orr, who was stepping down for the inauguration of Governor Scott, gave his address on 7 July.[32] The new executive was not installed until after the Fourteenth Amendment was ratified on 9 July. His opening speech was published in full by the press as was the valedictory of Governor Orr.[33]

The Senate completed its approval of a ratifying resolution on the second day of the special session, 7 July, by a vote of 23 to 5.[34] According to the *Charleston Courier*, only Democrats opposed the measure. "Some colored Republicans spoke against the proscriptive tendency of the Amendment" but approved it as a necessity.[35] The House took up the resolution that same day but made it the special order of business for the next day, 8 July.[36]

On 9 July, before the inauguration of Governor Scott, the House took up the business of ratification and approved it by a vote of 108 to 12.[37] The twelve were all Democrats according to the *Charleston Courier*.[38] Having met all standards set forth by Congress, members

---

[29]Jarrell, *Wade Hampton and the Negro*, 25.

[30]July 1868.

[31]July 1868.

[32]*Charleston Courier*, 8 July 1868.

[33]Ibid., 10 July 1868.

[34]*South Carolina Senate Journal*, special session (1868) 10-12.

[35]*Charleston Courier*, 8 July 1868.

[36]*South Carolina House Journal*, special session (1868) 46.

[37]Ibid., 49-50.

[38]1 July 1868.

elected at the time of the selection of the legislature, and the senators selected by the legislature were now ready to be seated. Reconstruction was complete in South Carolina, and the Fourteenth Amendment had been ratified. General Canby ordered the authority to govern to be returned to the civil authority.[39]

From the second year of the Civil War, parts of Louisiana had come under control of Union military forces. The emancipation proclamation had specifically excluded portions of the state from its application.[40] Such civil government as existed was reestablished under presidential authority during the actual war period. These efforts merged with Lincoln's more formal plans that had collided with the Wade-Davis Bill in 1864. The organization under the presidential plan elected congressmen, but they were not seated by Congress, for it was dominated by the organization's opponents under the new Johnson regime.

Presidential efforts toward rejection of the Fourteenth Amendment in 1866 and in early 1867, including solicitation of state legislatures, have already been suggested. March brought the first of the Reconstruction Acts as well as reactions of citizens of Louisiana. The *New Orleans Times* counseled "prudence, circumspection and the most careful and wise deliberation."[41] Opinions of ex-Confederate generals such as James Longstreet, Hood, and Beauregard, were solicited and had influence when they urged moderation and submission.[42] Longstreet reminded his fellow citizens that they were a "conquered people." In his mind this naturally led to acceptance of the terms of the conquerer, which in turn meant compliance with congressional legislation. General Beauregard expressed his sentiment that "a futile resistance would only cause our rivets to be driven closer."[43]

---

[39]*South Carolina House Journal*, special session (1868) 81.

[40]Abraham Lincoln, *The Collected Works of Abraham Lincoln*, ed., Roy P. Basler (Princeton NJ: Rutgers University Press, 1953-1955) 6:468.

[41]1 March 1868.

[42]*New York Herald*, 30 November 1866.

[43]*New Orleans Times*, 18, 26 March 1867.

Longstreet followed up his first published statement with a public letter in April that went further in support of congressional reconstruction. He joined the ranks of nonmilitary advocates of cooperation like Joseph E. Brown of Georgia and James L. Alcorn of Mississippi in urging an early conclusion to reconstruction by following the demands of Congress. Others like former Justice of the United States Supreme Court John A. Campbell were willing to sacrifice much to restore civil authority.[44]

Local Republicans were enthusiastic about support from these people.[45] All this combined with a visit to New Orleans by Senator Henry Wilson of Massachusetts, who was touring the South and addressing possible new bases of Republican strength. The movement to cooperate developed rapidly in July, but opposition was still voiced in all sections by some elements in the press.[46]

Conservatives in Louisiana and across the South tried to appeal to blacks. However, they did not work with Republicans and had little success. Leaders of this group had sent delegates to talk with President Johnson and were bolstered in their opposition to the movement for a constitutional convention.[47] Southern whites resented the use of the blacks by Northern Radicals.[48] The Freedmen's Bureau played a part in efforts to integrate schools and public places including public transportation, most notably street cars in New Orleans.[49]

The question of whether or not a constitutional convention would be held was voted on 27-28 September 1867 in Louisiana, earlier than in other states. The result was overwhelmingly in favor of the framing of a new constitution. The convention assembled in the

---

[44]Ibid., 6 April 1868.

[45]Thomas Robson Hay, *James Longstreet: Politician, Officeholder, and Writer* (Baton Rouge: Louisiana State University Press 1952) 332.

[46]Michael Perman, *Reunion Without Compromise: The South and Reconstruction, 1865-1868* (London: Cambridge University Press, 1973) 209, 291.

[47]Joe Gray Taylor, *Louisiana Reconstructed, 1863-1877* (Baton Rouge: Louisiana State University Press, 1974) 166.

[48]*New Orleans Crescent*, quoted in *New York Times*, 9 March 1867.

[49]Howard R. White, *The Freedmen's Bureau in Louisiana* (Baton Rouge: Louisiana State University Press, 1970) 156-57.

Mechanics Institute in New Orleans, 23 November, and remained in official session until 9 March 1868. Only two members were not Republicans and, like South Carolina, the majority of the delegates were blacks.[50] The convention levied a tax for its expenses as was done in other Southern states.[51]

The new constitution framed by the convention was approved 51,737 to 39,096 in the election of 16-17 April. It was a document that declared strong support for civil rights and the black vote but stopped short of many extremes urged upon it. The result was a good constitution as compared with other Louisiana organic documents.[52]

In the election that ratified the constitution, new state officials were elected as well as congressmen. It was an election with much racial tension. Henry Clay Warmouth of Illinois was elected governor although he was only twenty-six years old. He did not take office until after the ratification of the Fourteenth Amendment by the legislature that had been elected at the same time.[53]

In the new House of Representatives, which assembled on 29 June 1868, the Fourteenth Amendment was approved by a vote of fifty-seven to three on 1 July.[54] The Senate took up the resolution the next day, but postponed further action temporarily because its organization was still incomplete. Returning to the amendment later in the day, the legislature had it read for the first time. The next day it was read a second time but was then tabled. On 6 July, it was made the special order of business and tabled again. After various motions to adjourn, refer to committee, and table, it was finally called up on 8 July. When the amendment was considered for passage, a sharp de-

[50]E. M. Coulter, *The South During Reconstruction, 1865-1877* (Baton Rouge: Louisiana State University Press, 1947) 134.

[51]*Journal of the Louisiana Constitutional Convention, 1867-1868*, 355, 201-202.

[52]Taylor, *Louisiana Reconstructed*, 150-153, 158; Francis Norton Thorpe, ed., *The Federal and State Constitutions: Colonial Charters and Other Organizations of the States Now or Hereafter Forming the United States of America* (Washington DC: Government Printing Office, 1909) 3:1449-71; Robert A. Fischer, *The Segregation Struggle in Louisiana, 1862-1877* (Urbana: University of Illinois Press, 1974) 59.

[53]Ralph Selph Henry, *Story of Reconstruction* (Indianapolis: Bobbs-Merrill Co., 1938) 515; *Alexandria Democrat*, 8 April 1868.

[54]*Louisiana House Journal* (1868) 8.

bate ensued with arguments that it was not proper to consider the amendment because it had been rejected in the last session, that it was proposed to make the states act under duress, and that it violated the original principles of the founders of the republic. Nevertheless, it was passed on 9 July by a majority of twenty-two to eleven.[55]

Alabama had been even more divided on the proper course to pursue than some other Southern states. It had been involved in the counterproposal for a different Fourteenth Amendment and had to work through a long, uncertain period of delay before rejecting the congressional proposal. Leaders had been in close contact not only with the President, but with Radical leaders and others through correspondence and meetings in Washington.

As the reconstruction acts of March 1867 were being passed, Chief Justice Chase continued to urge a speedy settlement. To Governor Patton he wrote: "Had the Constitutional Amendment been adopted as you recommended, there is little room for doubt that the ratifying States would have been promptly allowed representation in Congress and the disability clauses would have been so modified as to relieve very many—all, indeed, who should manifest sincere and hearty good will to the Union and to the National Government." He asked if it still would not be best to follow Joseph E. Brown's advice and conclude the matter swiftly.[56]

About the same time, Patton was sending a telegram to Senator John Sherman: "I think Alabama will readily conform to the reconstruction bill. . . ."[57] By August, the Ohio senator expressed the opinion that "The suffrage and reconstruction questions will be settled before the election, and in such a way as to secure the Republican party an even chance in every Southern State except Kentucky." He felt sure that Grant could have the presidency if he wanted it.[58]

---

[55]*Louisiana Senate Journal* (1868) 8-21.

[56]S. P. Chase to Patton, 11 March 1867, Salmon P. Chase Letter Book, Chase Papers, Library of Congress.

[57]Patton to John Sherman, 10 March 1867, John Sherman Papers, Library of Congress.

[58]John Sherman to W. T. Sherman, 9 August 1867, W. T. Sherman Papers, Library of Congress.

On 14 November, the *Nation* published a detailed analysis of the electoral vote if it were cast on the basis of recent 1867 elections. Republicans would have won handily in the North, but with no change in the suffrage laws in the South, Republicans would lose there by some eight votes, though the vote in Georgia and Virginia might be very close. That December, Justice Samuel F. Miller voiced his belief that many Republicans were now sorry that suffrage for blacks had been insisted upon in the reconstruction acts but that party leaders believed that now there was no alternative but to push on. It seemed fatal to turn back. Such a policy offered the only chance of carrying the South or any part of it.[59]

An election was called in Alabama at the end of August to take place over a three-day period beginning 1 October 1867. The balloting was to determine whether or not a constitutional convention should be called. Delegates to such a convention were also to be elected to avoid another election should the convention be approved.[60] Johnson's September amnesty proclamation raised the question of the eligibility of many ex-Confederates. Grant's order to the general-in-command refused to permit those disqualified by act of Congress to register.[61]

The election results were proclaimed as favoring the convention. The date for its convening was set for 5 November 1867. Governor Patton had recommended speedy compliance with congressional reconstruction, since "to contend against it now is simply a struggle against the inevitable."[62] His recommendation was only one sign of the realism that seemed to sweep over the South in the summer and fall of 1867.[63] The convention did convene on schedule and took

---

[59]Charles Fairman, *Mr. Justice Miller and the Supreme Court* (Cambridge: Harvard University Press, 1939) 138.

[60]Edward McPherson, *Political History of the United States of America during the Period of Reconstruction* (Washington DC: Philip and Solomans, 1871) 319.

[61]Martin G. Mantell, *Johnson, Grant and the Politics of Reconstruction* (New York: Columbia University Press, 1978) 37.

[62]*New Orleans Times*, 8 November 1867.

[63]Eric L. McKitrick, *Andrew Johnson and Reconstruction* (Chicago: University of Chicago Press, 1973) 483.

about a month to write the proposed new state constitution. On 20 December, the document was ordered to be approved or rejected in a four-day election beginning 4 February 1868. Twenty-six delegates did not vote at all when the final draft of the constitution was approved sixty-six to eight.[64]

The campaign to defeat the constitution by registering and then not voting succeeded when less than the required majority of qualified voters approved it, although a majority of the actual voters did voice approval. In this way the constitution seemed to be defeated and the strategy threatened congressional reconstruction with failure in other states. Congress, however, passed an additional act permitting approval by a majority of those voting, which nullified the apparent victory for conservatives in Alabama.[65]

On 26 June 1868, Governor-elect William H. Scott proclaimed that the new legislature elected at the time of ratification of the constitution should convene 13 July.[66] It did so under General Mead's orders of 9 July to "purge itself of all members who may be disqualified for holding office under the provisions of Section 3 of the Amendment to the Constitution known as Article 14." In such a manner, the proposed Fourteenth Amendment was enforced as law before it was proclaimed ratified later that month. No other business was to be transacted until ratification of the Fourteenth Amendment was completed.[67]

After organizing, the Senate proceeded to consider a joint resolution to ratify the Fourteenth Amendment. Under suspended rules, it was read three times and passed twenty-six to none. The Senate then received the House resolution ratifying the Thirteenth Amendment, which was also duly approved by a unanimous vote.[68]

---

[64]McPherson, *Political History of Reconstruction*, 319; Henry, *Story of Reconstruction*, 280.

[65]Coulter, *The South During Reconstruction*, 137; *United States Statutes at Large*, 15:41.

[66]*Alabama House Journal* (1868) 4; *Alabama Senate Journal* (1868) 8.

[67]General Orders, no. 100, 3d military district, quoted in Walter L. Fleming, *Documentary History of Reconstruction* (Cleveland: Arthur H. Clark Co., 1906) 1:447.

[68]*Alabama Senate Journal*, 9.

In the meantime the House had considered its own joint resolution to ratify the Fourteenth Amendment and had approved it after defeating a motion to table. The first vote to approve it was sixty-seven to four. The negative vote had not been expected.[69] This House joint resolution was sent to the Senate, which had correspondingly sent its joint resolution to the House. In the end, the Senate approved the House joint resolution unanimously.[70] The governor, who had been sworn in on 14 July before the new session of the legislature, signed the resolution.[71] It is interesting to note that the copy of the Fourteenth Amendment published in the House journal as part of the joint resolution of ratification is incomplete, containing only the first two sections.[72]

The new governor was a native of Alabama, but the two new senators were recent settlers in the state: one from Ohio and one from New England. These and previously elected congressmen were seated in Congress 21 July[73] after considerable congressional argument. In the congressional debates of March, which preceded the passage of the 25 June act authorizing the admission of Alabama and five other states, a challenge was registered against the power of Congress to exact permanent pledges that were not subject to amendment in the future. In this case the restriction was in the form of a promise never to amend its state constitution "as to deprive any citizen of any class of citizens of the United States of the vote who are entitled to vote by the constitution herein recognized, nor so amended or changed as to allow any person to vote who is excluded from office by the third section of the Fourteenth Amendment to the Constitution of the United States, until the disabilities imposed by said section shall have been removed in the manner therein pro-

---

[69]*Alabama House Journal*, 10; J. W. DuBose, *Alabama's Tragic Decade, 1865-1874* (Birmingham AL: Webb Book Co., 1940) 225.

[70]*Alabama Senate Journal*, 10.

[71]*Alabama House Journal*, 15.

[72]Ibid., 1868, 9.

[73]Henry, *Story of Reconstruction*, 320.

vided."[74] This was part of the act under which Alabama was permitted admission after meeting all congressional requirements.[75]

Once again the Fourteenth Amendment is referred to as if it were already ratified, and once again a permanent condition beyond the power of the state to change by amendment was insisted upon. As has already been mentioned, this and other attempts to bind particular states in ways not applied to other states as a precondition to admission have not been found enforceable. In this case no attempt to change the provision appeared.

---

[74]*Congressional Globe*, 40th Cong., 2d sess., 2138.

[75]*United States Statutes at Large*, 15:73-74.

Chapter Eighteen

Dangerous Passage

The last of the six states authorized to be readmitted by the act of 25 June 1868 was Georgia. Even after Congress recognized it, that state was to experience a second period of military reconstruction, and when finally readmitted to Congress, Georgia had ratified the Fourteenth Amendment twice after rejecting it initially in 1866.

During the period in early 1867 when Johnson attempted to put forward a counterproposal for a Fourteenth Amendment in an effort to reconcile differences, the state had not roused from its apathy as much as had some other Southern states. An Augusta newspaper reflected this attitude in its comment that "The mountain had been in labor; behold the mouse." The whole idea was dismissed as "futile and foolish" and "absolutely unworthy of consideration."[1] On the other hand, "The New Plan" was supported by the *Georgia Weekly Re-*

[1]*Tri-Weekly Constitutionalist*, 8 February 1867.

publican as answering every question against the restoration of Southern states except the loss of power to the Republican party.[2]

Georgia's wartime governor, Joseph E. Brown, like many other Southern politicians, went to Washington to try to analyze events at close range to see "on which side of the bread was the butter."[3] With few illusions and with very practical purposes including his own pardon, he agreed with Judge Joseph Henry Lumpkin that "we are a ruined people."[4] Brown's realistic approach is expressed in his report to Lumpkin in February 1867 stating that they were not dealing with an abstract problem but should look at facts "as they exist and not as we would have them."[5] In an interview with the *New York Herald*, however, he tried to defend Southern conservatives by predicting a kind of anarchy if freedmen should gain control and the Fourteenth Amendment should disqualify the most intelligent people.[6] He presented no hopeful picture for fellow Georgians when he reported that the Radical party "is sustained by the majority of the people of the North" and that the "reconstruction policy of the President is not sustained by the popular sentiment of the Northern People."[7] Failure to ratify the Fourteenth Amendment, Brown feared, would cause white citizens of the South to lose their votes and bring about confiscation of property. An everpresent fear throughout the South was confiscation and Brown believed "We shall never get better terms." Georgia should quickly accept them and get back into Congress.[8]

Controversy followed Brown's expression of opinion, and he was vilified by many, though some voices were raised in support of such

---

[2]*Georgia Weekly Republican*, 15 February 1867.

[3]Joseph H. Parks, *Joseph E. Brown of Georgia* (Baton Rouge: Louisiana State University Press, 1977) 364.

[4]Lumpkin to Brown, 29 January 1867, McLeod Collection, University of Georgia Library.

[5]Brown to Joseph Henry Lumpkin, February 1867, McLeod Collection.

[6]Quoted in *Atlanta Intelligencer*, 27 February 1867.

[7]Letter of February 7 quoted in *Milledgeville Federal Union*, 5 March 1867.

[8]*Atlanta Intelligencer*, 8 April 1867.

ideas, particularly after the first of the military reconstruction acts in March.[9] Benjamin H. Hill took the lead in excoriating Brown and his approach to problems of reconstruction.[10]

Governor Charles J. Jenkins, in an address to the citizens of Georgia from Washington on 10 April, held out hope that the Supreme Court would rule favorably in Georgia's suit to prevent enforcement of the reconstruction acts. He advised the people of his state to remain temperate and firm in opposing Congressional policies.[11]

Benjamin H. Hill delivered an address in Atlanta's Davis Hall after being warned by General John Pope about his controversial provocation, calling on Georgians to continue to oppose radical reconstruction.[12] Governor Jenkins was also warned by General Pope, commander of the third military district, that he could not continue to freely oppose the policy of military reconstruction. The governor replied by saying "I suppose I was exercising such freedom in the public expression of opinion relative to public matters as seems still to be accorded to citizens of the Republic, not imagining that it was abridged by the accident of the speaker or writer holding public office."[13]

General P. G. T. Beauregard, like General Longstreet, was writing words of advice to accept the verdict of war and reconcile the Southern states with Congress.[14] The *Georgia Weekly Telegraph* argued that "We have a Congress of fanatics, who know nothing about

---

[9]*Augusta Daily Constitutionalist*, 2 March 1867; *Milledgeville Federal Union*, 5 March 1867; *Atlanta Intelligencer*, 13 March 1867; *Atlanta New Era*, 8 April 1867; *Augusta Daily Press*, 25 April 1867.

[10]"Notes on the Situation," in *Augusta Chronicle and Sentinel*, beginning 19 June 1867.

[11]*The Confederate Records of the State of Georgia*, 6 vols.(Atlanta, 1909-1911) 6:71-76.

[12]Louise Biles Hill, *Joseph E. Brown and the Confederacy* (Chapel Hill: University of North Carolina Press, 1939) 271.

[13]Charles J. Jenkins Papers, Georgia State Archives; *Milledgeville Federal Union*, 30 April 1867.

[14]*Georgia Weekly Telegraph*, 7 January 1867.

the negro and are animated by no other sentiment but hatred of the South and their love of power."[15]

Other moves in the first part of 1867 included conservative attempts to organize the Ku Klux Klan as the answer to the Radical-inspired Union League. General John B. Gordon was reputed to be the Grand Dragon of the Klan in Georgia.[16] The *New York Times* declared that the greatest obstacle to restoration was the failure of those in power to "state definitely the terms on which the excluded States can be readmitted into the Union." Expressions of divergent views by individuals was confusing and insufficient. The North, that paper explained, looked upon the rebellion as a heinous crime while the South regarded it as a "lost cause." Stability was needed to attract Northern capital that was greatly needed to restore the South.[17]

Some, like the *Georgia Weekly Telegraph*, supported the counterproposal for a fourteenth amendment as a means of reassuring moderates of the North concerning the policy of the South after it had been restored. The vital part of the problem was black suffrage, it claimed. A qualified suffrage for blacks would not interfere with the power and the prosperity of the section.[18] Admittedly, the terms of the counterproposal were prepared and presented some months too late. The Fourteenth Amendment, with its disqualification of able leaders, would prevent a viable government in the South, the weekly claimed. The inconsistency of Northern states in defeating the black vote for themselves and demanding it for the South was presented with voting statistics from these states of the North. It pointed out also how the proposed military control bill flaunted the Supreme Court[19] decision in the Milligan case.

Northern papers were quoted to support the conclusion that the counterproposal could not possibly be approved and that it was too

---

[15] 1 January 1867.

[16] Stanley F. Horn, *The Invisible Empire: The Story of the Ku Klux Klan, 1866-1871*, enl. ed. (Cos Cob CT: J. E. Edwards, 1969).

[17] *New York Times*, 12, 28 January 1867.

[18] 5 February 1867.

[19] *Georgia Weekly Telegraph*, 22 February, 1 March 1867.

late.[20] The *Georgia Journal and Messenger* had already quoted the *New York Herald* about military occupation in the South and the *New York Post* on the obligation of Congress to admit every Southern state that ratified the Fourteenth Amendment.[21]

Scathing comments appeared in the *Federal Union* about Southern delegations constantly visiting Washington to find out how they could be readmitted, "but what is surprising to many and mortifying to some, [is] the fact that many of the Southerners seem really anxious to eat dirt." "What responsible Southern man," it asked, "would wish to be a member of such a Congress and what good can it do them?"[22]

The full letter of Joseph E. Brown containing his findings on reconstruction was published throughout the state in late February and March. After presenting this and other analyses from the press in other sections, the *Federal Union* cut through to what was considered the heart of the matter: what could be done? Its answer was echoed in many attitudes of the time, "we must all go to work and make a living." Little dependence could be placed on Washington decisions, even concerning the status of blacks. Worrying about governmental matters including Radicals and military controls would not solve their basic problems.[23]

As April began with the establishment of military controls in Georgia, Democratic victories in some Northern elections gave some renewed hope. Though the *Savannah Republican* warned against unfounded anticipations, the *Federal Union* wrote "God bless them" about the voters' stand in Connecticut.[24] Governor Jenkins sent a message from Washington to the people of his state urging them to remain firm and to continue to look to the courts for relief.[25]

---

[20]Ibid., quoted 15 February 1867 from the *Philadelphia Evening Bulletin, Washington Chronicle, Worcester Spy, Newark Advertiser,* and *New York Times.*

[21]*New York Times,* 8, 9 January 1867.

[22]*Milledgeville Federal Union,* 15 January 1867.

[23]Ibid., 19 March 1867.

[24]April 1867.

[25]*Federal Union,* 16 April 1867.

Senator Henry Wilson of Massachusetts was initiating his Southern tour by trying to attract whites and blacks to the Republican party. He especially appealed to old-time Whigs and crowds of blacks. When he appeared in Virginia, his progress was noted in Georgia. As May wore on, congressman William D. ("Pig Iron") Kelley of Pennsylvania was also launching his personal travels through the South with dubious political results. Meanwhile, the Kentucky victory for Democrats improved the morale of some Southerners.[26]

Publicity was given to the biracial meeting of conservatives on 17 April in Nashville, Tennessee. Resolutions were passed approving the Fourteenth Amendment but opposing the disfranchisement of some voters and disapproving the use of armies in time of peace. Those at the meeting supported the rights of blacks and the efforts of President Johnson. A black made a principal speech against Radicals and emphasized the friendship of Southern whites and freedmen.[27]

The press also published a letter of ex-Governor B. F. Perry of South Carolina, describing the efforts of Mississippi and Georgia to win support in the courts. He recounted the general thought that while the South awaited a reaction in the North to congressional reconstruction, it must remain under military rule. "If we are to wear manacles," said Perry, "let them be put on by our tyrants, not by ourselves."[28] Herschel V. Johnson of Georgia paralleled Perry's statement when he wrote, "Our oppressors can put chains upon us, if they will, seeing us impotent and prostrate at their feet; but let us consent to it never."[29]

Joseph E. Brown continued to address crowds in Georgia urging approval of the Fourteenth Amendment and acceptance of other congressional terms. He looked for long delays in the test cases brought against reconstruction legislation. The judicial approach promised nothing in his view. He contended that the practical needs

---

[26]Ibid., 30 April 1867.

[27]Ibid., 30 April 1867.

[28]Ibid., 7 May 1867.

[29]Herschel V. Johnson to John W. Westmoreland, James F. Alexander, and others, 4 July 1867, H. V. Johnson Papers, Duke University Library.

of capital and peace justified compliance with congressional demands. Prosperity, said he, depends on it.[30] Their economic plight seemed more important than other considerations to many Southerners.

In May, the Georgia case was presented before the Supreme Court by a team led by Jeremiah S. Black and opposed by Attorney General Henry Stanberry and others. While the *Journal of Commerce* questioned the law and court as guarantees of constitutional government, the highest tribunal denied the writ of injunction on 13 May because of lack of jurisdiction.[31] It had already ruled similarly on much the same ground in the case brought by Mississippi against President Johnson.[32] Georgia had asked for an injunction against Secretary of War Edwin M. Stanton and General U. S. Grant, but the Court still considered it a political question. It would appear even today that the Court was unduly hesitant to take a position; there were precedents that the Court could have followed. The apparent challenge to Congress, which was then at odds with the President, and whose members had made threats against the Court,[33] seems to have been reason enough for caution. The McCardle case was still to follow as legal minds in the South sought to attain their objectives in court when all else seemed to fail.

Military reconstruction had brought black and white Republicans together in Georgia. In all of these developments, the leadership of Joseph E. Brown was quite significant, but it must be noted that several black leaders emerged at this time. One such leader, Henry M. Turner, received considerable respect from whites, more so than did Aaron A. Bradley.[34] The latter was expelled from the con-

---

[30]*Federal Union*, 7 May 1867; *Athens Southern Watchman*, 6 May 1867.

[31]*Federal Union*, 7 May 1867; *Georgia v. Stanton*, 6 Wallace 50 (1867); Charles Fairman, *Reconstruction and Reunion, 1864-1888*, pt.1 in *History of the Supreme Court*, ed., Paul A. Freund (New York: MacMillan Co., 1971) 386-90.

[32]*Mississippi v. Johnson*, 4 Wallace 475 (1867).

[33]Alfred H. Kelley and Winfred A. Harbison, *The American Constitution*, 5th ed. (New York: W. W. Norton and Co., 1976) 452; J. G. Randall and David Donald, *The Civil War and Reconstruction* (Lexington MA: D. C. Heath and Co., 1969) 644-45.

[34]Elizabeth Studley Nathans, *Losing the Peace: Georgia Republicans and Reconstruction, 1865-1871* (Baton Rouge: Louisiana State University Press, 1968) 28ff.

stitutional convention for gross insults to that body and to its members.[35]

Delegates to the constitutional convention had been elected by all registered voters regardless of color or race (except those disfranchised for participation in rebellion).[36] The election was finally held for three days beginning 29 October after much debate about military control and whether to vote or not. Joseph E. Brown had changed from his position in March when he said he would rather have "ten military governors than one Brownlow."[37] The spectacle of violence and misrule in Tennessee did little to encourage Georgians to accept the new order of affairs because of the consequences they feared would develop with military rule. Brown seemed converted by April when he advised that a new constitution should be framed and adopted "without appealing to the Supreme Court."[38]

Various leading Georgians opposed Brown's position. Alexander H. Stephens wrote, "If Governor Brown and others see fit to take to the lifeboats in our stranded position, I have no quarrel to make with him or them for pursuing this course." He thought, however, that they would be "swamped in the surf."[39] In another letter, he concluded that power was what Radicals wanted and that they would "do anything to secure that."[40]

Registration for voting on the issue of a constitutional convention under the Reconstruction Acts began in April. It resulted in almost twice as many registrants as October voters. The convention was approved and included a varied selection of representatives of all groups: whites, blacks, Democrats, Republicans, carpetbaggers, and

---

[35]*Journal of the Constitutional Convention of the People of Georgia, 1867-1868*, 294-97.

[36]Hill, *Joseph E. Brown*, 268.

[37]C. Mildred Thompson, *Reconstruction in Georgia* (New York: Colonel Press, 1915) 157.

[38]*Atlanta New Era*, 14 April 1867.

[39]Alexander H. Stephens to J. Barrat Cohen, 27 May 1867, Alexander H. Stephens Papers, Emory University Library.

[40]Ibid., 15 July 1867.

scalawags.[41] Although there were men of ability among blacks as well as whites, the *New York Herald* described the assembly as a "seedy looking body of men."[42] The *Federal Union* observed that both white and black representatives were of extremely low quality.[43] Governor Brown was not a delegate, but he was a close observer and wielded much influence.[44]

The Georgia constitutional convention met in Atlanta on 13 December. After organizing, it adjourned on 24 December to reassemble in January 1868.[45] In these initial stages, it was referred to as "The Negro Convention" and the "Sword and Bayonet Convention."[46]

Prior to the convention, on 5-6 December, the Conservatives had met in Macon. After much debate about the proper course, those at the convention produced a resolution addressed to the white men of Georgia. Among other observations, it stated that "We regret the efforts of the present ruling power to change the fundamental institutions of the United States Government as false in principle, impolitic in action, injurious in result, unjust to the South and detrimental to the General Government." It protested acts of Congress and urged that every county organize to defeat the work of the constitutional convention. Such leaders as Herschel V. Johnson and Benjamin H. Hill served on the resolutions committee.[47]

Similar Conservative actions as were being urged in Georgia were being advocated in an Alabama meeting 7 December.[48] Even earlier in South Carolina, a comparable address to the people had resulted from a Conservative convention.[49] Democratic victories that were

---

[41]Parks, *Joseph E. Brown*, 393.

[42]Quoted in the *Augusta Daily Constitutionalist*, 20 December 1867.

[43]1 December 1867.

[44]Nathans, *Losing the Peace*, 67.

[45]Parks, *Joseph E. Brown*, 395.

[46]*Atlanta Intelligencer*, 24 December 1867; *Richmond Journal*, 27 December 1867.

[47]*Federal Union*, 10 December 1867.

[48]Ibid., 17 December 1867.

[49]Ibid.

taking place in a number of Northern states helped to stimulate such action.[50]

General Pope was replaced by General George C. Meade in January 1868. He quickly became unpopular because of his action in removing uncooperative state officials. By far the most dramatic of such events followed the refusal of the Georgia state treasurer, John Jones, to pay out $40,000 to meet the expenses of the constitutional convention that was then meeting in Atlanta. Governor Jenkins refused to authorize this payment, which had not been appropriated by the legislature. This incident had begun in December before the departure of General Pope.[51] Meade removed Jones and, on 13 January, the governor himself.[52]

Jenkins, with the Georgia state seal and four hundred thousand dollars of state funds in his possession, departed for New York where he deposited the money in a bank with the expressed purpose of applying it to the state debt.[53] Meade appointed General Thomas H. Ruger to be governor and Captain Charles F. Rockwell as state treasurer. From such funds as they could assemble, the expenses of the convention were to be paid. Jenkins had filed a complaint with the Supreme Court against both Grant and Meade asking for an injunction.[54]

The Georgia convention issued a resolution asking that the court suit begun by the deposed Governor Jenkins be dismissed on the ground that it was not really an action by the state of Georgia.[55] It is interesting to note that the case of *Texas v. White* was already on the docket of the Supreme Court when the Georgia case was filed,

---

[50]Ibid., 24 September, 29 October, 26 November 1867.

[51]John Jones to General John Pope, 21 December 1867, Johnson Papers, Library of Congress.

[52]Parks, *Joseph E. Brown*, 395.

[53]Albert B. Saye, *A Constitutional History of Georgia, 1732-1845* (Athens GA: University of Georgia Press, 1948) 266.

[54]Alan Conway, *The Reconstruction of Georgia* (Minneapolis: University of Minnesota Press, 1966) 156.

[55]*Journal of the Constitutional Convention of the People of Georgia, 1867-1868*, 314-16.

though a decision in the Texas case was not to be handed down before 1869.[56] That case also dealt with money and the right of the state to sue while unrepresented in Congress. When the case was finally decided, the Court strongly affirmed the doctrine that the state had never been out of the Union and took jurisdiction in the controversy.[57] In the case filed by Jenkins, the Court denied jurisdiction as it had in other cases challenging action of federal officials under the reconstruction acts. The McCardle case, never decided because of congressional action removing appeals for habeas corpus in reconstruction matters from its jurisdiction, was the closest the Court ever came to considering the constitutionality of congressional reconstruction acts.

In *ex parte* McCardle, an appeal was taken from Mississippi on a writ of habeas corpus when an editor was arrested and tried by the military authority for his editorials, which were critical of the reconstruction program. McCardle tried to have his case taken to a federal court by means of a writ of habeas corpus. The United States Circuit Court in Mississippi sustained the military officer when he refused to produce his prisoner. His appeal to the Supreme Court to obtain his rights had the Milligan case as a precedent. The Court was actually in the process of hearing arguments when Congress intervened in March of 1868. An act was passed to change the appellate jurisdiction of the Supreme Court by excluding the power to hear appeals from lower federal courts involving habeas corpus. The inevitable presidential veto was overridden, and the Court meekly allowed the matter to drop for lack of jurisdiction. Members of the Supreme Court seemed to feel that they were in no position to take any action in opposition to Congress. McCardle had a strong case, and it was quite probable that the decision would have declared invalid much of military reconstruction.

The Conservative's address was carried to the people of Georgia by the state's newspapers. It attacked the constitutional convention, which was declared to be "run by Negroes." It severely criticized the North for refusing to give the vote to blacks in that section while seek-

---

[56]Fairman, *Reconstruction and Reunion, 1864-1888*, 433ff.

[57]*Texas v. White*, 7 Wallace 700 (1869).

ing to impose it in the South.[58] Joseph E. Brown, while not a member of the convention, addressed that body formally on 9 January. Trying to moderate forces then at work, he urged the convention to exclude the section disfranchising whites and the section making blacks eligible to hold office and serve on juries; if the convention excluded those sections there was a good possibility that the new constitution would be accepted.[59] General Meade had ordered the voting on the ratification of the new constitution to be held 20-24 April.[60] Democrats had not been very active, and many felt the necessity of accepting it[61] however objectionable they considered it.

News from Alabama reported the defeat of that state's new constitution by opposition voters staying away from the polls, thus preventing a favorable majority of all registered voters.[62] (It will be remembered that this apparent victory for conservatives was soon set aside by Congress.) But when the vote was counted in Georgia, not only had the voters approved their proposed constitution, they had elected new officials to serve under it. The governor was to be Rufus Bulloch, who won by defeating General John B. Gordon after two conservative candidates had been declared ineligible by the military authorities. The results were not entirely favorable for the Radicals, however. The constitution was much less radical than many pictured it. Although it did give the franchise to blacks, it did not disfranchise the white man. In fact, the new legislature was controlled by whites,[63] a result that was to lead to new problems in the state later that year.

Governor Bulloch informed General Meade that a number of those elected to the new legislature were ineligible under the terms

---

[58]*Federal Union*, 17 January 1868; P. S. Flippen, *Herschel V. Johnson of Georgia: State Rights Unionist* (Richmond VA: Deite Press, 1931) 285-86.

[59]*Federal Union*, 17 January 1868; *New Era*, 11 January 1868; Hill, *Joseph E. Brown*, 1939, 276; Conway, *Reconstruction of Georgia*, 154.

[60]Allen P. Tankersley, *John B. Gordon: A Study in Gallantry* (Atlanta: Whitehall Press, 1955) 238.

[61]Nathans, *Losing the Peace*, 88.

[62]*Federal Union*, 25 February 1868.

[63]Tankersley, *John B. Gordon*, 238; Conway, *Reconstruction of Georgia*, 162-63.

of the Fourteenth Amendment (not yet declared adopted).[64] He requested instructions. Grant ruled that each house must judge the qualifications of its members, an attitude he was to reverse later when he was president. Committees of both houses considered the issue, but after much controversy, no one was excluded.[65]

One of the functions of the new legislature was to elect United States senators who could be acceptable to Congress and still reflect political currents in Georgia. In a confusing situation, both Joseph E. Brown and Alexander H. Stephens were defeated, the former by Joshua Hill as a compromise candidate who had not strongly supported the reconstruction acts. Robert Toombs summed up the attitude of many when he wrote that "it could only be done by a Radical and there was political justice in making the earliest traitor defeat the worst one and break down his party."[66]

The new legislature met at noon on 4 July in the city hall of Atlanta,[67] the new site of the state capitol having been moved from Milledgeville. Because of disputes about seating members, it did not get down to business until much later in that month. On 21 July, Governor Bulloch delivered his message, which contained General Meade's authorization. He told the assembled legislators that by act of Congress "you are required to duly ratify the amendment to the Constitution proposed by the 39th Congress, and known as article 14 before the State shall be entitled and admitted to representation in Congress as a State of the Union." The amendment, he said, was applicable to all the states and "therefore no one state can reasonably object to it on the ground of inequality." It was right, he said, for the nation to define who was a citizen. Bulloch also defended the disqualification section, though he thought it harsh. In his opinion, it

---

[64]*Annual Report of the Secretary of War* (1868) pt. 1, 78-79.

[65]*Georgia Senate Journal* (1868) 18-19; 33-34; *Georgia House Journal* (1868) 31-45.

[66]Robert Toombs, Alexander H. Stephens, and Howell Cobb, *Correspondence of Robert Toombs, Alexander H. Stephens and Howell Cobb*, ed., U. B. Phillips, Annual Report of the American Historical Association (Washington DC: Government Printing Office, 1911) 2:703.

[67]*Federal Union*, 7 July 1868.

would be removed before long. The representation section he claimed to be just, and hence acceptable.[68]

Immediately a joint resolution was introduced in the House and passed by a vote of eighty-nine to seventy-one.[69] The Senate also approved ratification by a vote of twenty-seven to fourteen.[70] Though ratification was accepted and Georgia restored, much more was to occur before final restoration was complete in 1870. Mississippi, Texas, and Virginia did not ratify, and their representatives were not seated in Congress until 1870. The final approval by Congress of the ratification process and the final pronouncement of the adoption of the Fourteenth Amendment, partly based on Georgia's action that 21 July, was to be the last chapter in the ratification struggle.

After ratification was complete, Mississippi, Texas, and Virginia remained unrepresented and under military control. The only state to reject its new reconstruction constitution was Mississippi. Good organization and some support from black voters enabled conservatives to achieve that result. In Virginia, the work of the constitutional convention was not submitted immediately to the voters, and an understanding was worked out with congressional leaders. The new Grant administration was inclined to be lenient, and some tenseness had disappeared with the lapse of time. According to the agreement, which was applied also to Mississippi and Texas, the main issues were separated from the body of the constitution and voted upon by themselves. In this way, the disqualification of ex-Confederate leaders and a test oath requirement were defeated in all three states and the new constitutions approved. The new legislatures then approved the Fourteenth Amendment[71] and the Fifteenth Amendment also. These ratifications had no bearing on the adoption of the Fourteenth Amendment, but merely satisfied Congress of the good faith of these three states.

---

[68]*Georgia House Journal*, 48; *Georgia Senate Journal*, 67.

[69]*Georgia House Journal*, 50-51.

[70]*Georgia Senate Journal*, 46.

[71]*Mississippi House Journal* (1870) 20; *Mississippi Senate Journal* (1870) 19; *Texas House Journal* (1870) 33; *Texas Senate Journal* (1870) 29; *Virginia House Journal (1870)* 37; *Virginia Senate Journal* (1870) 27.

The last state to ratify the Fourteenth Amendment before it was declared adopted was Georgia. Like other Southern states, it had gone through the agonizing decisions leading to rejection in 1866. Under military reconstruction, it was still pondering its proper course. Georgians had watched national events and were cheered by Democratic victories in 1866. Instead of the mild wording of the Fourteenth Amendment and its vague warning of reduced representation if they should continue to oppose black voting (one of their chief worries), they now had to experience it whether or not they ratified. The counterproposal for a Southern version of a Fourteenth Amendment had aroused little interest.

Georgians' principal concern had always been accepting involuntarily what changes they must in order to "make a living." Several action programs developed to ward off the worst features of their situation. The Ku Klux Klan was one that involved a number of leading Georgians. Another was the organization of Conservatives into a statewide network of clubs for political action. Some participated in a biracial meeting of Conservatives in Nashville, Tennessee. The example of a reconstructed state presented by Tennessee under the leadership of "Parson" Brownlow did not appeal to them.

Governor Charles J. Jenkins and other leaders of Georgia were among those who looked to the courts for relief. In *Georgia v. Stanton*, they made an attempt to get a Supreme Court hearing on the validity of congressional reconstruction. They failed when the Court refused jurisdiction on the grounds that the question was exclusively a political one. In *Texas v. White*, decided in 1869, the Court declared that seceded states had never been out of the Union.

A curious coalition developed after war-time Governor Joseph E. Brown advised his fellow Georgians to ratify the amendment and gain restoration as rapidly as possible. To discouraged people faced with the necessity of rebuilding their society and personal fortunes, such a course seemed the only logical thing to do. This pragmatism was not the primary motivation of Radicals, but they advocated the same action. White and black Radicals moved closer together, giving Republicans on the national scene increased hope of help in the presidential elections of November.

Chapter Nineteen

Making
for Port

In order to understand the national situation in regard to the Fourteenth Amendment at the time of Georgia's ratification, it is necessary to look back to the first part of 1868. Ratification in the North had progressed to the point where only Iowa and California had failed to act. All states outside the South that had considered the proposal had ratified it with the exception of the border states of Delaware, Maryland, and Kentucky. These three had registered their rejection as had all of the Southern states. Only Tennessee had approved it, but in a highly irregular fashion almost immediately after the proposal had been sent to all states for their action.

What to do about this situation had been one of the factors in the decision to implement military reconstruction under congressional policies. The old question of whether or not it was necessary to count states of the defeated Confederacy, whose representatives had not been seated in Congress, still had no definitive answer. A new question was whether the restoration of Southern states with black voters could be completed in time to influence the presidential election of 1868 and the membership of the Congress that would meet the following year. Also, movements to rescind the ratification of some Northern states whose legislatures had been captured by Democrats in 1867 created new problems.

Until January 1868, the secretary of state had been receiving statements from states certifying official action on the amendment. He had not summed up the results nor notified Congress about what these records indicated, although obviously many would have kept a careful tally for themselves. On 8 January, Congressman George W. Schofield of Pennsylvania submitted a resolution "that the Secretary of State is hereby requested to inform the House how many and what State Legislatures have ratified the proposed Amendment to the Constitution of the United States known as the fourteenth article."[1]

Secretary William H. Seward sent his report, dated 7 January, a day before the House resolution was introduced. It was received 10 January[2] and listed twenty-one ratifying states made up entirely of Northern states and two border states, Tennessee and Missouri. It included the affirmative action of West Virginia, which had been admitted during the war with the approval of a legislature said to represent the fictional loyal state of Virginia. The new state of Nevada also had its ratification reported. On the day that Seward's report was received, Senator Charles Sumner of Massachusetts, true to his earlier concept of which states should be counted, introduced a joint resolution declaring the adoption of the amendment on the basis of approval by twenty-two states. He included Maine, which had been omitted from the Seward list. The resolution was referred to the Judiciary Committee.[3]

Three days later Congressman Bingham of Ohio introduced a similar resolution in the House declaring that the amendment had been duly ratified and was now a part of the Constitution. The reso-

---

[1]*Congressional Globe*, 40th Cong., 2d sess., 340.

[2]Ibid., 447.

[3]Ibid., 453.

lution was referred to the House Judiciary Committee.[4] In remarks the following day, 14 January, Bingham proclaimed that "We say to those states: 'Before you send Representatives to this Hall you must accept the decree which twenty-three states of the Union have already solemnly ratified, declaring that no state of this Union shall make or enforce any law which shall abridge the privileges and immunities of citizens of the United States, nor shall any State deny to any person the equal protection of the laws.'" His broader concept of the amendment, which he had helped frame, is shown in his statement that the spirit and intent of the Constitution in this regard "was most flagrantly violated long anterior to the rebellion and that the Government was powerless to remedy it by law."[5] There is no indication of which state he considered the twenty-third to ratify the Fourteenth Amendment. Bingham might have claimed only twenty-two because of Seward's report; certainly no other state ratified at this time. The basic error seems to have been Seward's, but there was additional confusion.

Discussions that January saw Representative Hamilton Ward of New York blaming the lack of cooperation from President Johnson for failure of Southern ratification. The McCardle case had not yet been terminated, and a move was begun to require a two-thirds vote of the Supreme Court to declare an act of Congress unconstitutional. The *Nation* commented that "there is no denying the fact that the majority in Congress does not possess the confidence of the party now as it did a year ago." That publication denounced Radicals for being frightened into changing positions.[6]

Additional confusion is shown late in January concerning the exact status of the Fourteenth Amendment. An example is the resolution to relieve Robert M. Patton of Alabama of political disabilities. According to whether or not the Fourteenth Amendment was already ratified, Congress could or could not remove these political dis-

---

[4]Ibid., 475.

[5]Ibid., 514.

[6]27 January 1868.

abilities by a two-thirds vote.[7] It will be remembered that Patton was pardoned by the President and had become provisional governor of Alabama.

Senator Charles F. Buckalew of Pennsylvania charged that the majority in Congress at that time wanted to organize "State governments of the South and to obtain from them Senators for introduction here and members for introduction in the House." It is proposed, said Buckalew, "to so mold and shape the political institutions in one third of the United States that their present power shall be increased in both Houses, or at all events, if disaster should befall them in other sections, that their power in both Houses shall be retained in future."[8] This is probably the clearest statement of charges against Radicals by their opponents in January of 1868.

There was a good deal of discussion at that time about not only suffrage for blacks but what was called repudiation—anything to reduce the value of government bonds. The *Nation* charged that Radicals had been frightened into supporting payment of bonds in greenbacks after denouncing this policy as repudiation earlier.[9] Taxing bonds would "break the faith" as would paying interest or principal in greenbacks, claimed *Harper's Weekly*.[10] The implication is that such "repudiation" was what was forbidden in the proposed Fourteenth Amendment.

The *Nation* continued to criticize political moves calculated to cheat "the public creditors in some shape or other" but admitted that most was talk "intended for campaign purposes." Such discussion had little effect on the money market.[11] Senator John Sherman of Ohio was especially lambasted for his urging substitution of long-term bonds for short-term ones and paying interest in greenbacks. He was accused of saying in substance, "Here is something which is not what was promised you, but which is nearly as good, and which

---

[7]*Congressional Globe*, 40th Cong., 2d sess., 765.

[8]Ibid., 823.

[9]January 1868.

[10]February 1868.

[11]2 March 1868.

we, the chiefs of the Republican party, advise you to accept, inasmuch as we may be compelled, by the growing feeling of hostility to you in the West, to sacrifice you altogether unless you make some compromise at once."[12]

In mid-March, Bingham was still asserting that the Fourteenth Amendment had already been ratified and that it should be proclaimed a part of the Constitution. "Yet every man in America knows," he asserted, "that that Amendment is not operative, and never will be operative as part of the Constitution until it is by the law-making power, in some form, so proclaimed, which has not been done." There was no consensus on the conclusion drawn by Bingham. As Speaker Colfax stated, in his opinion the amendment had already been adopted, and he regretted that he could not so rule because it was a political matter. Thaddeus Stevens also believed that the Fourteenth Amendment was law and that it had given Congress additional power "to regulate the franchise, so far as it regards the whole nation, in every state of the Union. . . ."[13]

In an 18 March comment on these statements of majority members, Congressman Michael C. Kerr of Indiana charged:

> It is their deliberate purpose, tomorrow or next week or a month hence, or as soon as they can, to make the Federal Constitution a different instrument from what it now is, and then, under the somewhat latitudinarian expressions contained in this proposed fourteenth article of amendment to the Constitution, not only will the bill but almost any other kind of law that the party majority here can desire be introduced into the House and enacted into law.[14]

State election results from New Hampshire, which favored Republicans, created a calmer atmosphere in which there was less talk of black suffrage, disfranchisement of ex-Confederates, and possible withdrawal of troops from the South. The principal fear that remained seemed to center around financial affairs affecting bonds and greenbacks.[15]

---

[12]*The Nation*, 5 March 1868.

[13]*Congressional Globe*, 40th Cong., 2d sess., 1808-67.

[14]Ibid., 1973.

[15]*The Nation*, 19 March 1868; *Harper's Weekly*, 28 March 1868.

While disagreements continued in Congress as to whether the Fourteenth Amendment had been ratified without Southern support, the state of Ohio acted to rescind its earlier ratification of January 1867. A highly emotional election later that year had swept Republicans from control of the state legislature although Republican Congressman Rutherford B. Hayes was elected governor by a narrow margin. Control of the Senate by the Democrats rested on a thin majority of nineteen to eighteen though they dominated the House of Representatives by fifty-six to forty-nine.[16] A Democrat who had opposed ratification in 1867 was elected Speaker.[17]

One of the first items of business introduced on 6 January was a resolution to rescind ratification of the Fourteenth Amendment. Echoes of the recent election campaign can be noted in the wording of the resolution, the statement that "one of the objects to be accomplished by said proposed amendment was to enforce negro suffrage and negro political equality in the states." Ratification of the amendment by the legislature had been "a misrepresentation of the public sentiment of the people of Ohio and contrary to the best interests of the white race, endangering the perpetuity of our free institutions."[18]

The House took up the measure on 11 January when a movement was just getting under way in Congress to proclaim the amendment ratified. In fact, Sumner introduced his motion in the Senate that same day. The rescinding resolution was approved that very afternoon in the Ohio House by a vote of fifty-two to thirty-seven with an amendment requesting the return of documents filed the previous year certifying ratification.[19] Obviously some Republicans failed to vote as did some Democrats.

The Ohio Senate, having introduced its rescinding resolution at the same time, had laid it on the table.[20] In what was described as a

---

[16]*Annual Cyclopedia* (1867) 605.

[17]*Cincinnati Commercial.* 7 January 1868.

[18]*Ohio House Journal* (1868) 12.

[19]Ibid., 33; *Cincinnati Commercial*, 12 January 1868.

[20]*Ohio Senate Journal* (1868) 7.

race between Congress and the Ohio legislature,[21] the House resolution was taken up in the Senate, 13 January. It was referred to the Committee on Federal Relations together with the Senate resolution on the same subject.[22] The committee reported the House resolution with amendments that same day. Each part was voted on separately, but each passed by the identical majority, nineteen to seventeen. Between each vote, a motion to adjourn had to be defeated.[23] On that very day, Bingham was introducing his resolution in Congress to declare the amendment ratified and in force. The president of the Ohio Senate and the Speaker of the House signed the rescinding resolution as soon as the House could approve Senate changes.[24] The certified copy forwarded to Washington bears the date of adoption as 15 January.

In the race with Congress, the Republican governor of Ohio entered the scene by not sending the rescinding resolution to the secretary of state in Washington as quickly as the legislature desired. The state senate inquired if the document had been sent and if not, why. Hayes replied he had just that day seen the document. The Ohio secretary of state had not sent it on to him because the vague instruction in the resolution made it unclear as to whom it should be sent and by whom it should be forwarded.[25]

It was, therefore, not until 31 January that the President pro tempore of the United States Senate presented the Ohio resolution and had it read. Senator John Sherman of Ohio at once rose to declare that the "resolutions do not speak the voice of the people of Ohio." Issues in the 1867 election of the legislature, he said, did not include that of rescinding ratification. He claimed that the matter had been dealt with only in the party caucus of Democrats and rushed to passage without debate.[26]

---

[21]*Cincinnati Commercial*, 12 January 1868.

[22]*Ohio Senate Journal*, 28.

[23]Ibid., 37-39.

[24]*Ohio House Journal*, 44-51.

[25]*Congressional Globe*, 40th Cong., 2d sess., 898.

[26]*Ohio Senate Journal*, 68.

Sumner immediately asserted that "the assent of the State once given is final." He added that as his resolution declared, the amendment was already in force even without Ohio, counting twenty states ratifying. Reverdy Johnson of Maryland, who had earned respect as a constitutional lawyer, argued that before final adoption, a ratification could be withdrawn. The entire matter was then referred to the Senate Committee on the Judiciary.[27] In the House of Representatives, the Ohio joint resolution to rescind was introduced by Benjamin Eggleston. It was read in full and referred to the Judiciary Committee. Stevens rose to object to the introduction, but the Speaker ruled that he was too late.[28]

The state of New Jersey also acted to rescind its earlier ratification of September 1866. Democrats had captured the legislature in elections of 1867 and now proceeded to use their advantage to embarrass Republicans in control of Congress and their Republican governor. The logical argument that they advanced was that the proposal was still pending thus opening the way for withdrawing the New Jersey approval before ratification should become a fact.

On 22 January a resolution was introduced in the New Jersey Senate "That the Judiciary Committee be, and they are hereby instructed to report a joint resolution withdrawing the consent of New Jersey to the proposed 14th Amendment to the Constitution of the United States." The resolution passed nine to six. Later that same day the Committee on Federal Relations reported Joint Resolution 1 "Rescinding the Joint Resolution approved September 11, 1866 relative to amending the Constitution of the United States and withdrawing the assent of the State of New Jersey to the proposed 14th Constitutional Amendment." After it was read, it was ordered printed.[29]

On 4 February, it was recalled for consideration. A week later it was again brought up but postponed for a week when a substitute was offered. The matter was once more postponed. On 19 February, a motion for further postponement was defeated. After disposing of

---

[27]Ibid., 296.

[28]Ibid., 876-78.

[29]Ibid., 890-98.

several arguments over points of order, the resolution was put to a vote and passed by a vote of eleven to eight.[30] The Senate action was reported to the House which suspended the rules and passed the joint resolution of 20 February by a vote of forty-four to eleven.[31]

The resolution to rescind was accompanied by arguments to support the action. These began with the straightforward assertion that because the proposed amendment had not yet received the approval of three-fourths of the state legislatures, "the constitutional right of the State to withdraw its assent is undeniable." The document then summed up charges that were commonly made against Radical congressional policies: (1) unwarranted exclusion of eighty representatives of eleven states; (2) expulsion of a member of the Senate from New Jersey without justification; (3) use of the power thus acquired to pass unconstitutional acts; (4) use of the cabinet against the President; (5) limitation of the power of the judiciary; (6) interference with the exercise of the pardoning power of the executive; (7) imposition of "new prohibitions upon the power of the States to pass laws and interdicts the execution of such parts of the common law as the national judiciary might deem inconsistant with the vague provisions of the said Amendment," deliberately vague in order to "facilitate encroachment" upon the life, liberty, and property of the people; (8) new apportionment of representation to secure votes of "a servile and ignorant race" to outweigh intelligent voices in Congress; and (9) demand that New Jersey adopt impartial suffrage to support the transfer of total power over suffrage to Congress.[32]

Governor Marcus L. Ward sent his veto message to the Senate on 25 February. He reasoned that the legislature's action had no validity because its earlier ratification completed the transaction, thus making it a contract. This was the same argument used by Congress and later sanctioned by the Supreme Court in refusing to overturn the decision of Congress. Governor Ward did not support the position of the legislature that while the proposal was pending rescinding was legal, though he denied it only on the ground of rules of contract as

---

[30]*New Jersey Senate Journal* (1868) 31.

[31]Ibid., 74-198.

[32]*New Jersey House Journal* (1868) 309.

presented above. The idea that there was no contract until a sufficient number had approved to make it a valid amendment was not
examined. He did not specifically deny it, however, for he declared:

> The ratification by three-fourths of the States must be deemed already to
> have been made, unless the Legislature shall assume to decide that when
> more than one fourth of the States have by rebellion and war, withdrawn
> from their duties and functions as States and rendered Constitutional
> Amendments essential to the welfare of the nation, such States can by their
> action, prevent the adoption of those amendments, thus occasion, indirectly
> and partially the results which rebellion and war were waged openly and
> thoroughly to produce.

He concluded that three-fourths of the loyal states had ratified and
such action was conclusive.[33]

The governor who had urged the passage of the amendment in
1866 now added to his legal arguments his belief that the resolution
to rescind was "repugnant to the convictions of the majority of the
people, and of the voters of the State." He claimed that the Fourteenth Amendment had not been considered in the election of 1867
by which the current legislature had been selected. He ended his message with his own analysis of the proposal, which convinced him that
it was a wise constitutional change.[34]

The New Jersey Senate promptly passed the resolution again by
a recorded vote of eleven to nine on the same day that the governor's
message arrived, 5 March.[35] In the House, the message was taken up
on 17 March and made the special order of business for 19 March. At
that time it was postponed until the next week when the veto was
overridden by a vote of forty-four to thirteen.[36]

On 30 March, New Jersey's Congressman Charles Haight presented in the House of Representatives the joint resolution from the
legislature of his state. After its reading, Washburne of Illinois objected to its being read and expressed the hope that it would be withdrawn. Speaker Colfax ruled that the objection was too late. The

---

[33]*New Jersey Legislature Documents* (1868) 951-54.

[34]*New Jersey Senate Journal*, 249-52.

[35]Ibid., 355.

[36]*New Jersey House Journal*, 645.

ensuing argument was interrupted by Colfax when he reminded the House that the impeachment trial of President Johnson was about to begin for the day in the Senate.[37]

Washburne continued to press for an opportunity to present a resolution, which he finally did:

> That the resolution of the Legislature of the State of New Jersey, presented by the gentleman from New Jersey Mr. Haight purporting to withdraw the assent of the said State to the Constitutional amendment known as the fourteenth article, be returned by the Speaker of the House to the gentleman who presented it, and that its title only shall be referred to in the Journal of the House, and in the *Congressional Globe*, and further that this House denies the Constitutional right of any State Legislature to withdraw such assent.

Amid exclamations that the attempt to rescind was "scandalous," with its extreme language critical of the Republican-dominated Congress that had submitted it, the motion to refuse to accept the New Jersey document was passed.[38]

How many ratifying states were necessary to declare the Fourteenth Amendment a part of the Constitution? That question had bothered Congress from the beginning and was still unsettled in 1868. Was the amendment already adopted by the ratification of all but three represented states? That would be more than three-fourths of the loyal states and was adequate according to some who had never considered Southern ratification necessary for adoption. It was asserted that ex-Confederate states never should have been asked to ratify except to show their pledge of good faith. A few congressmen were openly claiming that the amendment was already in effect. No questions were asked about the legitimacy of the ratification of West Virginia or Tennessee.

Another question that had never had a definitive answer was raised. Could a state withdraw its ratification during the time the amendment was pending and before adoption had been proclaimed? Ohio and New Jersey passed rescinding resolutions that were presented to Congress but not acted upon. Members of Congress stated that, once a ratification had been filed, it became a con-

---

[37]*Congressional Globe*, 40th Cong., 2d sess., 2225.

[38]Ibid., 953-54.

tract and could not be broken. Other leading lawyers in Congress disputed this claim. The Supreme Court has accepted the ruling of Congress on attempts to withdraw approval and has never claimed jurisdiction to decide the question. There was fear in 1868 that the Court might rule in favor of rescinding actions. Threats of congressional moves to limit the Supreme Court were made because of the possibility.

Much discussion in and out of Congress concerned the meaning of the debt guarantee in the Fourteenth Amendment. Movements to tax bonds, or to reduce their value by paying interest or principal in "greenbacks," were labeled repudiation. The public at that time seemed more concerned about the debt guarantee than about any other section of the amendment.

In these ways the stage was set for the final and dramatic events that would soon end the long ratification struggle in a strange and inconclusive way. Even after it was over, Oregon was to attempt to rescind its ratification and Georgia, which had ratified, was to be thrown back into the status of military control without congressional representation. This latter action resulted from Georgia's constitution ejecting black legislators as unqualified to hold office although they had the franchise. When later recognized and readmitted in 1870, Georgia ratified the Fourteenth Amendment a second time.

Chapter Twenty

An Uncertain Anchorage

As events affecting the adoption of the Fourteenth Amendment moved toward a July climax, political maneuvering included national conventions of both major parties. Republicans assembled in Chicago that May and, after some rivalry among several aspirants including Chief Justice Salmon P. Chase of Ohio and Schuyler Colfax of Indiana, General Grant was nominated with little difficulty. It is generally thought that he could just as easily have received the Democratic endorsement, but he had been gradually drifting into the Republican camp for some time, partly due to his difficulties with President Johnson and the cabinet crisis involving the Tenure of Office act and the eventual impeachment charges.

Colfax, as vice-presidential nominee, lent a more solid party appearance to the ticket. After the Chicago convention had done its work, Chase continued to make overtures to the Democrats for his nomination by them. He kept his options open for as long as possible and expressed himself in vague terms that would avoid uselessly antagonizing Democrats. His presiding over the impeachment trial in the Senate had antagonized many Republicans. On the ticklish issue of universal or impartial suffrage, he managed to leave the impression that, though he personally advocated it, he favored leaving the whole problem to the states.[1] He also managed to give supporters a basis for claiming his opposition to congressional reconstruction despite his advocacy of approval of the Fourteenth Amendment as a condition of readmission.[2]

The platform on which Republicans would campaign "congratulated the country" on the success of reconstruction. The President was declared guilty of impeachment charges despite his acquittal. Suffrage for blacks in the South was presented as a necessary guarantee, but elsewhere it was to be considered distinctly a state matter. The language of the platform ignored the mild pressure in the terms of the Fourteenth Amendment, which would be applied equally in all states. Republicans also sharply attacked any attempt to repudiate valid debts of the United States. The focus of their attack was the attempt made to pay bond interests and debts in paper currency.[3]

The Democrats did not meet in New York before July. Chase was still available and eager, but another Ohioan, George H. Pendleton, captured the support of many delegates because of his advocacy of paying United States debts in depreciated greenbacks as well as of taxing bonds. President Johnson captured substantial support. After much balloting, the chairman of the convention, Horatio Seymour, war-time governor of New York, was nominated. Francis P. Blair of Missouri, who had supported Lincoln and opposed Chase in 1864, was selected as his running mate. He had also been close to Johnson during his presidency.[4]

---

[1]James Lyons to S. P. Chase, 16 June 1868, Salmon P. Chase Papers, Library of Congress.

[2]H. S. Bundy to S. P. Chase, 22 May 1868, Chase Papers.

[3]Charles H. Coleman, *The Election of 1868: The Democratic Effort to Regain Control* (New York: Columbia University Press, 1933) 80-91.

[4]Ibid., 239-44; *Annual Cyclopedia* (1868) 744-49.

Completion of restoration of Southern states had become an important part of election considerations. Republicans in 1868 were in a hurry to readmit these reconstructed states with their black voters and disqualified ex-Confederate leaders. In May, Congressman Burton C. Cook of Illinois claimed that Johnson's opposition was all that had prevented restoration a long time before. He further urged early acceptance of representatives in Congress and recognition of state governments in the South as being truly republican in form. These reconstructed governments could enable freedmen to protect themselves and "secure the adoption of the constitutional amendment by a sufficient number of states to satisfy the scruples of Andrew Johnson himself."[5] None of the rebellious states should be readmitted until the Fourteenth Amendment was ratified and its purpose made secure for all time, said Senator George F. Edmunds of Vermont on 29 May.[6]

As the *Nation* analyzed the political situation in early June, a restored South "cannot fail to vote for Grant unless the Democratic Party should adopt a candidate and platform which should divide the colored votes—an improbable event."[7] The black ballot, Andrew Sherman Hill wrote in the *North American Review*, would enable the freedmen to protect life, liberty, and property. Many would not be able to vote intelligently, he realized, but "they will learn to swim by going into the water."[8] Hill gave full credit to Illinois delegates for the strong financial statement of the Republican platform. These included Horace White of the *Chicago Tribune* and C. H. Ray of the *Chicago Post*. *Harper's Weekly* compared both parties on the national debt and liked the Republican position that denounced "all forms of repudiation as a national crime."[9] As May and June gave way to July, the issue of "repudiation" was still the liveliest of topics. The *Nation*

---

[5]*Congressional Globe*, 40th Cong., 2d sess., 2405.

[6]Ibid., 2662.

[7]June 1868.

[8]July 1868, 167-86.

[9]July 1868.

pronounced the Democratic platform advocating taxing the interest of national bonds "repudiation in the meanest of ways."[10]

With his usual lack of moderation, Stevens called the Democratic party "the slave party" and claimed that "it will be a slave party until we grind them to powder under our heels and Freedom, with the flapping of her wings, shall blow the dust out of existence and consign them to everlasting oblivion."[11] Right down to the first proclamation on the Fourteenth Amendment, Republicans continued to denounce Democrats for the attempts of Ohio and New Jersey to rescind their ratifications.[12]

Individual Southern states were being readmitted to representation in June and July as soon as they were reorganized and had ratified the amendment. There was always the fundamental condition that the new constitution "shall never be amended or changed as to deprive any citizen or class of citizens of the United States of the right to vote who are entitled to vote by the constitution herein recognized."[13]

Here again the Congress continued to lay down conditions that forbade later changes in a constitution, a method of permanent control that was not to be recognized as binding in the future. Even at the time, the Radical Oliver P. Morton of Indiana argued that "when these states are admitted, when they have complied with all our conditions and come back and are received, then they stand upon the same platform with every other State in the Union; they have every right and power that belongs to every other state."[14] Georges Clemenceau, as a foreign journalist, duly reported these things as he saw them, including the requirement that the restored state must have

---

[10]July 1868.

[11]*Congressional Globe*, 40th Cong., 2d sess., 3777.

[12]Example is a speech by Robert Van Horn of Missouri, 16 July 1868. See *Congressional Globe*, 40th Cong., 2d sess., 4142.

[13]*United States Statutes at Large* (1868) 15:72.

[14]*Congressional Globe*, 40th Cong., 2d sess., 2603.

ratified the Fourteenth Amendment "which establishes absolute equality in civil rights between the blacks and the whites."[15]

Members of the dominant Republican party in Congress were trying busily to maneuver the President into accepting congressional reconstruction, at least by ceasing to refer to "purported state governments" or a "so-called government" of a state. Senator Jacob Howard of Michigan, who was one of the amendment's framers, propounded the problem on June 9 when he said that "Unless he shall issue this proclamation after all the States shall have ratified the fourteenth amendment, these States cannot be admitted into the Union; they are not entitled to their rights as States at all, they are still kept out; they are not admitted, as I say even to the right of representation." Howard predicted that Johnson would withhold such a proclamation and dare Congress to impeach him again. He urged Congress not to insist on a presidential proclamation because Johnson would never issue one and thus keep states out "as long as practicable."

The Michigan senator wanted the restoration act to go into effect upon ratification of the Fourteenth Amendment by the states.[16] It is interesting to observe the changing political roles of president and Congress in the reconstruction process. With blacks now able to vote in the South, it had become important to Republicans to bring about early restoration in order that Southern states could cast electoral votes in the approaching election. On the other hand, it was recognized that under such changed conditions, it was to Johnson's interest to prevent early participation of altered Southern states in the political process.

Senator George Edmunds of Vermont proposed that the President be compelled as a ministerial act to say officially that these states had now ratified the Fourteenth Amendment. He wished to commit the executive in that way to the congressional policy by "making him

---

[15]Georges Clemenceau, *American Reconstruction, 1865-1870, and the Impeachment of President Johnson*, trans., Margaret McVeagh, ed., Fernand Baldensperger (New York: Dial Press, 1928) 195.

[16]*Congressional Globe*, 40th Cong., 2d sess., 2967.

do the last official act that shall restore these States to their proper relations." Others were satisfied to leave it as it was in the alternate proposal that "it is hereby made the duty of the President within ten days after receiving official information on the ratification of said Amendment by the Legislature of either of said States, to issue a proclamation announcing that fact."[17]

The latter plan prevailed,[18] and Johnson did follow the prescribed pattern although he continued to refer to Southern governors and states in a manner calculated to avoid giving indirect recognition to the congressional program. An example is his report on 18 July of ratification in South Carolina:

> Whereas on the 18th day of July, 1868, a letter was received by the President, which letter being addressed to the President, bearing the date of July 15, 1868, and was transmitted under the name of R. K. Scott, who therein writes himself governor of South Carolina, in which letter was enclosed and received at the same time by the President a paper purporting to be a resolution of the senate and house of representatives of the general assembly of the State of South Carolina ratifying the proposed Amendment and also purporting to have passed the two said houses, respectively, on the 7th and the 9th of July, 1868, and to have been approved by the said R. K. Scott as governor of said State, on the 15th of July, 1868, which circumstances are attested by the signature of D. T. Corbin, as president pro-tempore of the senate and F. J. Moses, Jr., as speaker of the house of representatives of said State and of said R. K. Scott as governor.

Documents such as the above were received in the Senate and referred to its Judiciary Committee.[19] Representatives from Southern states whose ratification was reported in this fashion were seated.[20]

Senator Edmunds of Vermont, seeking to bring matters to a satisfactory conclusion in another way, introduced a resolution on 9 July requesting Secretary of State Seward to furnish a list "without delay" of Southern states whose legislatures had ratified the Fourteenth Amendment. He requested that Seward send a copy of its cer-

---

[17]Ibid.

[18]*United States Statutes at Large*, 15:73-74.

[19]James D. Richardson, *A Compilation of the Messages and Papers of the Presidents, 1789-1898* (Washington DC: Bureau of National Literature and Art, 1898) 6:657.

[20]*Congressional Globe*, 40th Cong., 2d sess., 4276.

tificate of ratification to any state whose ratification had been reported in such a manner. Seward was also to send copies to any state that ratified at a later date. The Senate approved.[21]

Not waiting for Secretary Seward's reply, Senator Sherman of Ohio introduced a joint resolution on 18 July declaring the Fourteenth Amendment to be duly ratified and in force. After the Judiciary Committee had reviewed the proposal, it was made a concurrent resolution on 21 July.[22] This action was taken immediately after the secretary had issued his proclamation of 20 July.

In a long statement, the secretary of state had reviewed his power under the act of 1818 that required him to "cause any amendment to the Constitution of the United States which has been adopted according to the provisions of the said Constitution, to be published in the newspapers authorized to promulgate the laws, with his certificate specifying the States by which the same may have been adopted, and that the same has become valid, to all intents and purposes, as a part of the Constitution of the United States." His problem under the act was that he had no power by law "to determine and decide doubtful questions as to the authenticity of the organization of State legislatures, or as to the power of any State legislature to recall a previous act or resolution of ratification of any amendment proposed to the Constitution."

Having said this, Seward laid out the facts as indicated in documents on file in his office. He first presented a list of those states with little or no question about their validity. These included Northern and Western states as well as Tennessee and the new states, West Virginia and Nebraska. Next he listed the states with "newly constituted and newly established bodies avowing themselves to be and acting as the legislatures, respectively, of the states of Arkansas, Florida, North Carolina, Louisiana, South Carolina, and Alabama." Finally, he stated that official documents from Ohio and New Jersey, states that were included in his first list as having ratified, now indicated that they "have since passed resolutions respectively withdrawing

---

[21]Example is South Carolina in House on 18 July; See *Congressional Globe*, 40th Cong., 2d sess., 4215.

[22]Ibid., 3857.

the consent of each of said States to the aforesaid Amendment." To him it was a "matter of doubt and uncertainty whether such resolutions are not irregular, invalid and therefore ineffectual for withdrawing the consent of the said two States."

Seward presented the first lists of twenty-three states as having ratified. Next he stated that "it further appears from the documents on file in this Department that the Amendment to the constitution proposed as aforesaid, has also been ratified by the newly instituted and newly established bodies avowing themselves to be and acting as the legislature" of the six Southern states recognized by Congress. Despite his doubts, he still counted Ohio and New Jersey among those having ratified the proposal.

Seward's final compilation counted the total states in the Union as thirty-seven, which included other Southern states not yet reinstated by Congress. The twenty-nine states in his first two lists being counted for ratification, he found that they "constituted three-fourths of the whole number of States in the United States." Thus he certified that "if the resolutions of the legislatures of Ohio and New Jersey ratifying the aforesaid Amendment are to be deemed as remaining in full force and effect, notwithstanding the subsequent resolutions of the legislatures of those States, which purport to withdraw the consent of said States from such ratification, then the aforesaid Amendment has been ratified in the manner hereinbefore mentioned, and so has become valid, to all intents and purposes, as a part of the Constitution of the United States."[23]

Georges Clemenceau summed up Seward's proclamation for his readers on 22 July by saying that the amendment had been ratified by twenty-nine of the thirty-seven states and was now a part of the Constitution if the action of the legislatures of Ohio and New Jersey to rescind were "null and void."[24]

In Congress, the reaction to the proclamation was strong. Dominant Republicans judged it to be completely unsatisfactory and took swift and angry action. The concurrent Senate resolution was

---

[23]Ibid., 4230.

[24]*United Statutes at Large*, 15:706-707.

adopted without debate or recorded vote.[25] In the House, there was some discussion about the ratification of Georgia; it had come too late to be included in Seward's list and had not been listed in the concurrent resolution. Boutwell sought to have it included as the last of the ratifying states on the basis of a telegram from Governor Bulloch of Georgia. The House finally passed the senate resolution to clarify the status of the Fourteenth Amendment by a vote of 127 to 33, with 55 abstaining.[26]

This resolution by which Congress sought to set the record straight and bring the Fourteenth Amendment into force declared that the proposal had been duly ratified by the legislatures of states that were listed. New Jersey and Ohio were included as were the six states of the reconstructed South. It also proclaimed that the Fourteenth Amendment was now a part of the Constitution and "it shall be duly promulgated as such by the Secretary of State."[27]

This statement seemed to satisfy the press, which now referred to the amendment as a part of the Constitution. Congress seemed to take the same attitude and considered proposed legislation to enforce parts of it. All this transpired before Seward could respond to instructions with his second proclamation of 28 July. Also during this time, President Johnson continued his habit of following the request of Congress by reporting on 27 July the ratification of Georgia on 21 July.[28]

The secretary of state issued a most peculiar proclamation on 28 July. He took no responsibility for its content, but quoted in detail the congressional resolution proclaiming the Fourteenth Amendment to be ratified by the twenty-nine states listed in that document "being three-fourths and more of the several States of the Union."[29] He directly quoted the statement of Congress declaring the "said fourteenth article of amendment to be a part of the Constitution of the

────────────

[25]Clemenceau, *American Reconstruction*, 208.

[26]*Congressional Globe*, 40th Cong., 2d sess., 4266.

[27]Ibid., 4296.

[28]Ibid., 4295-96.

[29]Richardson, *Messages and Papers*, 660.

United States and shall be duly promulgated as such by the Secretary of State." Seward then listed all states ratifying according to the records in his office together with other states that had acted by rejecting the proposal. He indicated dates for all such actions including not only Maryland, Kentucky, and Delaware as rejecting, but all those states of the South who had rejected in 1866. The latter were listed again when they later ratified, as had seven including Georgia. A note was inserted after the ratification report of Ohio and New Jersey indicating the passage of resolutions withdrawing assent with the date of this action. Counting Georgia, Seward's list totaled thirty of thirty-seven states as having ratified at some time.

The conclusion of the secretary's proclamation is unique in constitutional history. Assuming no part of the responsibility for the decision Seward proclaimed:

> Now therefor, be it known that I, William H. Seward, Secretary of State of the United States, in execution of the aforesaid act, and of the aforesaid concurrent resolution of the 21st of July, 1868, and in conformity thereto, do hereby direct the said proposed amendment to the Constitution of the United States to be published in the newspapers authorized to promulgate the laws of the United States, and I do hereby certify that the proposed amendment has been adopted in the manner hereinbefore mentioned by the States thus specified being more than three-fourths of the States of the United States.
>
> And I do further certify that the said amendment has become valid to all intents and purposes as a part of the Constitution of the United States.[30]

Even after the formal proclamation of the adoption of the Fourteenth Amendment, the story of its ratification is not quite complete. Three states under military reconstruction in the South eventually were to add their ratifications as part of the price of readmission to complete acceptance as a state. Mississippi, Virginia, and Texas went through much the same experiences as had other ex-Confederate states, but delayed completing the process until 1870. Mississippi was somewhat different in that it had voted against acceptance of the new

---

[30]*United States Statutes at Large*, 15:708-11.

state constitution in 1868 when seven of her sister states accepted Northern terms.[31]

As mentioned earlier, while Georgia's ratification was included in the thirty listed on 28 July, citizens of that state were again to experience another period of reconstruction under military control before final recognition as a state in 1870. Restoration in 1868 was hardly accomplished when the legislature expelled twenty-nine black members who had been elected under the new constitution so recently approved by Congress.

Provision for the right of blacks to vote had been required of all readmitted states, but there had been no mention in the Georgia constitution of their new right to hold office. Perhaps most assumed this to be true by implication, but legalistic legislative leadership seized on this point to rid the General Assembly of black members. A House resolution of 26 August led to action 3 September to expel.[32] Two black senators were also expelled on 16 September.[33] Another black senator, Aaron A. Bradley, was expelled because he held a criminal record in New York. Four members who were almost white were allowed to keep their seats. Significantly, forty-six Republicans voted with Democrats to remove the blacks in the House where the total vote was eighty-three to twenty-three.

Governor Bulloch protested their removal and appealed to Congress to intervene. He considered the Georgia action to be an indication that the state was not fully qualified for readmission. He apparently felt the need of support from the military and Radicals in Congress at that time.[34] Georgia had also ignored the provisions of the reconstruction acts by seating some former Confederate leaders. General Meade, under congressional authority, eventually removed

[31]J. G. Randall and David Donald, *Civil War and Reconstruction* (Lexington MA: D. C. Heath and Co., 1969) 619.

[32]*Georgia House Journal* (1868) 242-43.

[33]*Georgia Senate Journal* (1868) 277-78.

[34]*Milledgeville Federal Union*, 22 December 1868; Harold M. Hyman, ed., *Radical Republicans and Reconstruction, 1861-1870* (Indianapolis: Bobbs-Merrill Co., 1967) 447; Elizabeth Studley Nathans, *Losing the Peace: Georgia Republicans and Reconstruction, 1865-1871* (Baton Rouge: Louisiana State University Press, 1968) 147.

these members and caused the blacks to be brought back into the legislature.[35]

Georgia had voted in the 1868 election before Congress was ready to do anything about its status. Timidity about the election and the growing lack of interest in the North about reconstruction may partly explain the slow reaction. The third session of the Fortieth Congress did nothing, and in fact had difficulty deciding whether or not to count the Georgia electoral vote that had been cast for the Democratic candidate. Finally, after Grant and the Forty-first Congress had delayed still longer, the Georgia matter was taken up. When the legislature had reseated its black members and removed its disqualified whites, the state was readmitted. This was not permitted, however before it once more ratified the Fourteenth Amendment and, additionally, the new proposal for a Fifteenth Amendment. All this was finally accomplished on 15 July 1870.[36]

In the state of Oregon another kind of problem about rescinding ratification developed. Long after the 28 July proclamation, the legislature assembled that September. A resolution was introduced in the Senate 17 September to withdraw Oregon's approval of the amendment. It was passed two days later. Writers of the resolution advanced a broad constitutional argument that the legislatures of Southern states that had been counted as ratifying had been under the dictation of the military and the reconstruction acts "which were unsurpations, unconstitutional, revolutionary and void...." "Action by such bodies cannot legally ratify" for the states they "pretend to represent" and thus influence the rights of other states, even in the North. The Senate voted to rescind 5 October by a vote of thirteen to nine.[37] The House received the Senate document on 7 October and approved it on 15 October by a vote of twenty-six to eighteen.[38]

---

[35]Rembert W. Patrick, *Reconstruction of the Nation* (New York: Oxford University Press 1967) 142.

[36]Alan Conway, *The Reconstruction of Georgia* (Minneapolis: University of Minnesota Press, 1966) 166; *Federal Union*, 22 March 1870; C. Mildred Thompson, *Reconstruction in Georgia* (New York: Columbia University Press, 1915) 246; Walter L. Fleming, *Documentary History of Reconstruction* (Cleveland: Arthur H. Clark Co., 1906) 490-92.

[37]*Oregon Senate Journal* (1868) 273.

[38]*Oregon House Journal* (1868) 176-77, 256, 273.

It is true that a protest had been lodged at the time of the original Oregon ratification, which objected to procedures and the illegal seating of two members of the House who supported approval. These two members were later judged illegally elected and were expelled. They were replaced by two members who declared that they would have voted against ratification had they been properly seated.[39] The two votes subtracted from one side and added to the other would have prevented affirmative action. After all the publicized furor that July in Congress and in the executive branch concerning the final proclamation of the Fourteenth Amendment as law, it is surprising to find the Oregon rescinding resolution, penned that September, calmly referring to the addition to the Constitution as "the proposed 14th constitutional amendment."[40] The Oregon action was part of the resurgent Democratic movement that was national in scope; it furnished motive enough. There is no evidence that copies were ever forwarded or received in Washington. Newspapers ridiculed it in Oregon and made jests about how it would be received in Congress and by the secretary of state.[41]

The problem of possible rescinding action, even during the period when an amendment is still pending, has never been settled in the minds of many. In practice, these actions have never been recognized as valid despite a certain logic that the actions of states on a proposal to amend do not constitute a contract before a sufficient number have approved to make it law. The reverse has been sanctioned not only by the judgment of Congress in 1868, but in other instances when the question has been raised.

As early as 1891, Herman V. Ames concluded that precedent and usage had decided "that a State having once given its consent, the question is closed and it cannot recall its action, but on the other hand, that a State that has rejected an amendment can reconsider its acts at

---

[39]See Robert W. Johannsen, "The Oregon Legislature of 1868 and the Fourteenth Amendment," *Oregon Historical Quarterly* (March 1950): 6:3-12.

[40]*Oregon Senate Journal*, 57.

[41]Johannsen, "The Oregon Legislature of 1868," 12.

any time previous to the incorporation of the amendment into the Constitution."[42]

In addition to the efforts of those states that sought to rescind their endorsement of the Fourteenth Amendment, New York tried to withdraw its approval of the Fifteenth Amendment, and Tennessee made such an attempt regarding its action on the Nineteenth Amendment. In *Fairchild v. Hughes*, the Supreme Court refused to consider the possibility of the unconstitutionality of the Nineteenth Amendment and used the comparable example of recognition of the Fifteenth Amendment by long usage, regardless of arguments about its validity.[43] As late as the 1970s, several states sought to claim the right to rescind while the proposal for a twenty-seventh amendment was being considered.

The same argument could well be advanced against any modern claims concerning the highly irregular and questionable procedures as well as the terrific impact of the Fourteenth Amendment on the nature of the Union and the rights of individuals and corporations. In *Coleman v. Miller* in 1939, the Court did review questions pertaining to ratification. It specifically used the facts of ratification and attempts to rescind action by two states in the case of the Fourteenth Amendment as an example that the decision by the "political departments of the government as to validity of the adoption of the Fourteenth Amendment has been accepted."[44]

Purposes and motivations are never easy to assess accurately. Evidence seems clear, however, that no single objective animated those who proposed and ratified the Fourteenth Amendment. The motive of any one individual concerning any single act is usually a mixture of many elements in varied proportions, with some of them scarcely recognized in any conscious way. Such individuals and organized groups who took part in the ratification struggle either for or against

---

[42]Herman V. Ames, "The Proposed Amendments to the Constitution of the United States During the First Century of its History," *Annual Report of the American Historical Association*, 1891 (Washington DC) 2:300.

[43]*Fairchild v. Hughes*, 258 U.S. 126 (1922).

[44]*Coleman v. Miller*, 307 U.S. 433 (1939).

were obviously prompted by many genuine as well as affected reasons.

For over a century the Fourteenth Amendment has been in force as law. Its validity was questioned during the reconstruction period because it was ratified amidst improper procedures and highly irregular actions; it cannot be said to have given cause to question its status today. Long usage and general acceptance by all branches of government has made any theoretical objection impractical. The Fourteenth Amendment has altered too many relationships in a highly complex society ever to be reversed. Despite the questionable history and theory of its ratification, it is now firmly and irrevocably established in the organic law of the United States. The history of its introduction and passage into this body of fundamental law can only serve to illustrate that the American Constitution has grown and continues to develop in many and sometimes unique ways. Special circumstances and the resulting unusual methods of meeting problems must be recognized as one of the characteristics of its growth.

The entire spectrum of possible aims included unselfish and sincere patriotic, religious, or idealistic convictions. They included theoretical and closely reasoned positions. They involved political plans for retaining or achieving power and practical ways to bring those plans into effect. They expressed economic self-interest of a respectable and justifiable nature as well as that which could only be called greed, and at times was related to actual corruption and fraud.

Traditional values and outlooks, including prejudices, were a major influence in positions taken on the Fourteenth Amendment. Thus, states' rights and racial feelings exercised a large and restraining influence, even on persons in the North. They, in turn, influenced their leaders. Nevertheless, there was widespread feeling that states in the South must not be reinstated in the Union without some action indicating "guarantees for the future" that would go beyond acceptance of defeat. Contrition for the agonies of the recent war was an emotional expectation; one not easily given by the South.

Approval by that region finally hinged on accepting a different system than that which had prevailed before the war in order to stabilize society and enable an economic system to function again. Southerners responded unhappily to the application of force and the desire for peace rather than to any real support for the amendment.

Ratification was reluctantly accepted as the price required for other developments deemed absolutely necessary. Earlier acceptance might easily have resulted if the President and Congress had presented a united front and if restoration had been specifically promised in return for ratification. The initial Southern rejection, inspired in part by the President, merely hardened the Northern attitude and made the problem more difficult.

As always, power was a part of all these aims either as a means or as an end. One might expect these many facets of human personality to find expression in interpretations of the Fourteenth Amendment as a whole or in part. To some, the entire proposal was either acceptable or unacceptable, but to others, only a single part stood out as being absolutely necessary or utterly impossible.

This situation also has been true of the later history and development of the amendment as the nineteenth-century issues changed to those of the present. With modern times, new meanings emerged and old significances disappeared or lessened. Interpretations, not only by the judiciary, but by the legislative and executive branches, modified or gave new meaning to this influential part of organic law. Such developments continue to appear and in all likelihood will do so in the future, given current relevance to this vital part of the Constitution.

Appendix

The Fourteenth Amendment

Section 1. All persons born or naturalized in the United States, and subject to the jurisdiction thereof, are citizens of the United States and of the State wherein they reside. No State shall make or enforce any law which shall abridge the privileges or immunities of citizens of the United States; nor shall any State deprive any person of life, liberty, or property, without due process of law; nor deny to any person within its jurisdiction the equal protection of the laws.

Section 2. Representatives shall be apportioned among the several States according to their respective numbers, counting the whole number of persons in each State, excluding Indians not taxed. But when the right to vote at any election for the choice of Electors for President and Vice-President of the United States, Representatives in Congress, the executive and judicial officers of a State, or the members of the Legislature thereof, is denied to any of the male inhabitants of such State, being twenty-one years of age and citizens of the United States, or in any way abridged, except for participation in rebellion, or other crime, the basis of representation therein shall be reduced in the proportion which the number of such male citizens shall bear to the whole number of male citizens twenty-one years of age in such State.

Section 3. No person shall be a Senator or Representative in Congress, or Elector of President and Vice-President, or hold any office, civil or military, under the United States, or under any State, who, having previously taken an oath, as a member of Congress, or as an officer of the United States, or as a member of any State legislature, or as an executive or judicial officer of any State, to support the Constitution of the United States, shall have engaged in insurrection or rebellion against the same, or given aid or comfort to the enemies thereof. But Congress may, by a vote of two-thirds of each house, remove such disability.

Section 4. The validity of the public debt of the United States, authorized by law, including debts incurred for payment of pensions and bounties for services in suppressing insurrection or rebellion, shall not be questioned. But neither the United States nor any State shall assume or pay any debt or obligation incurred in aid of insurrection or rebellion against the United States, or any claim for the loss or emancipation of any slave; but all such debts, obligations, and claims shall be held illegal and void.

Section 5. The Congress shall have power to enforce, by appropriate legislation, the provisions of this article.

Bibliography

MANUSCRIPTS

Alcorn, James L. Papers. University of North Carolina Library, Chapel Hill.

Blair, Gist. Papers. Library of Congress, Washington DC.

Chandler, W. E. Papers. New Hampshire Historical Society, Concord.

Chandler, W. E. Papers. Library of Congress, Washington DC.

Chandler, Zachariah. Papers. Library of Congress, Washington DC.

Chase, Salmon P. Papers. Library of Congress, Washington DC.

Doolittle, J. R. Papers. Library of Congress, Washington DC.

Ewing, Thomas. Papers. Library of Congress, Washington DC.

Fessenden, William P. Papers. Library of Congress, Washington DC.

Fish, Hamilton. Papers. Library of Congress, Washington DC.

Graham, W. A. Papers. University of North Carolina Library, Chapel Hill.

Hedrick, Benjamin S. Papers. Duke University Library, Durham NC.

Holt, Joseph. Papers. Library of Congress, Washington DC.

Janney, John. Papers. University of North Carolina Library, Chapel Hill.

Jenkins, Charles J. Papers. Georgia State Archives, Atlanta GA.

Johnson, Andrew. Papers. Library of Congress, Washington DC.

Johnson, Herschel V. Papers. Duke University Library, Durham NC.

Johnson, Reverdy. Papers. Library of Congress, Washington DC.

McLeod Collection. University of Georgia Library, Athens GA.

Massachusetts Senate Journal, 1867, Massachusetts State Archives, Boston.

Moore, Colonel W. G. Stenographic Notes and Transcript. Library of Congress, Washington DC.

Morrill, Justin. Papers. Cornell University Library, Ithaca NY.

——————. Papers. Library of Congress, Washington DC.

Orr, James L. Papers. Duke University Library, Durham NC.

——————. Papers. South Carolina Archives, Columbia.

Patton, R. M. Official Papers. Alabama State Archives, Montgomery.

Perry, Benjamin F. Papers. Alabama State Archives, Montgomery.

——————. Papers. University of North Carolina Library, Chapel Hill.

Rhode Island House Journal, 1867. Rhode Island State Archives, Providence.

Rhode Island Senate Journal, 1867. Rhode Island State Archives, Providence.

Seward, William H. Papers. Library of Congress, Washington DC.

Sherman, John. Papers. Library of Congress, Washington DC.

Sherman, William T. Papers. Library of Congress, Washington DC.

Stanton, Edwin M. Papers. Library of Congress, Washington DC.

Stephens, Alexander H. Papers. Duke University Library, Durham NC.

——————. Papers. Emory University Library, Atlanta GA.

——————. Papers. Library of Congress, Washington DC.

Stevens, Thaddeus. Papers. Library of Congress, Washington DC.

Sumner, Charles. Papers. Harvard University Library, Cambridge MA.

——————. Papers. Library of Congress, Washington DC.

Trumbull, Lyman B. Papers. Library of Congress, Washington DC.

Washburne, Elihu B. Papers. Library of Congress, Washington DC.

Welles, Gideon. Papers and Diary. Library of Congress, Washington DC.

NEWSPAPERS AND PERIODICALS

Atlanta Intelligencer.

Atlanta New Era.

Atlantic Monthly.

Arkansas Daily Republican.

Arkansas Gazette.

Athens Southern Watchmen (Georgia).

Augusta Chronicle and Sentinel (Georgia).

Augusta Daily Press (Georgia).

Augusta Tri-Weekly Constitutionalist (Georgia).

Boston Advertiser.

Boston Daily Transcript.

Carolina Watchman (North Carolina).

Charleston Daily Courier.

Charleston Daily News.

Charlotte Observer (North Carolina).

Chicago Tribune.

Cincinnati Commercial.

Cincinnati Gazette.

Cleveland Herald (Ohio).

Federal Union (Milledgeville, Georgia).

Frank Leslie's Illustrated Newspaper.

Frederick Republican Citizen (Maryland).

Gainesville New Era (Florida).

Georgia Weekly Telegraph.

Georgia Journal and Messenger.

Georgia Weekly Republican.

Greenville Southern Enterprise (South Carolina).

Harper's Weekly.

Illinois Daily State Journal.

Jackson Clarion (Mississippi).

Knoxville Whig.

Lynchburg Republican (Virginia).

Macon Daily Telegraph (Georgia).

Mansfield Herald (Ohio).

Memphis Avalanche.

Mississippi Coahoman.

Mississippi Index.

Missouri Republican.

Montgomery Weekly Advertiser.

Natchez Daily Courier.

The Nation.

National Intelligencer.

Newark Advertiser.

New Orleans Bee.

New Orleans Crescent.

New Orleans Picayune.

The Ratification of the Fourteenth Amendment

New Orleans Times.

New York Evening Post.

New York Herald.

New York Independent.

New York Times.

New York World.

North American Review.

North Carolina Argus.

The Old North State (North Carolina).

Philadelphia Evening Bulletin.

Providence Daily Journal.

Tri-Weekly Standard (North Carolina).

The Reporter.

Richmond Daily Examiner.

Richmond Enquirer.

Richmond Examiner.

Richmond Journal.

Richmond Times.

Richmond Whig.

St. Augustine Examiner (Florida).

Savannah Daily Republican.

The Sentinel (Raleigh, North Carolina).

The Sentinel (Salisbury, North Carolina).

Southern Sentinel (Mississippi).

Tallahassee Semi-Weekly Floridian.

Toledo Blade.

Van Buren Press (Arkansas).

Vicksburg Herald.

Washington Daily Morning Chronicle.

Washington Gazette (Georgia).

Wilmington Journal (North Carolina).

Weekly Progress (North Carolina).

Worcester Spy (Massachusetts).

PRINTED PRIMARY SOURCES

Alabama House Journal. 1866, 1867, 1868.

Alabama Senate Journal. 1866, 1867, 1868.

American Annual Cyclopedia and Register of Important Events of the Year. 1865, 1866, 1867, 1868. New York: D. Appleton Co.

Ames, Blanche B., ed. *Chronicle of the Nineteenth Century: Family Letter of Blanche and Adelbert Ames*. 2 vols. Clinton MA: Colonel Press, 1957.

Annual Report of the Secretary of War. Washington DC, 1868.

Appleton Annual Cyclopedia. Appleton WI.

Arkansas House Journal, 1866-1867, 1868-1869.

Arkansas Senate Journal, 1866-1867, 1868-1869.

Avary, Myorta Lockett, ed. *Recollections of Alexander H. Stephens*. New York: Doubleday, Page and Company, 1910.

Barnes, Thurlow Weed. *Memoirs of Thurlow Weed*. Boston: Houghton Mifflin Co., 1884.

Bates, Edward. *The Diary of Edward Bates, 1859-1866*. Edited by Howard K. Beale. Vol. 4 of *Annual Report of the American Historical Association for the Year 1930*. Washington DC: Government Printing Office, 1933.

Blaine, James G. *Twenty Years of Congress: From Lincoln to Garfield with a Review of the Events Which Led to the Political Revolution of 1860*. 2 vols. Norwich CT: Henry Bill Publishing Co., 1884-1886.

Boutwell, George S. *Reminiscences of Sixty Years in Public Affairs*. 2 vols. New York: McClure, Phillips Co., 1902.

Browning, Orville Hickman. *The Diary of Orville Hickman Browning*. 1865-1881. Edited by Theodore C. Pease, and J. G. Randall. 2 vols. Collections of the Illinois State Historical Library, vols. 20, 22, Springfield IL, 1933, 1938.

Buchanan, James. *The Works of James Buchanan*. Edited by John Hammond Moore. 12 vols. New York: Reprints of New York Press, 1960.

Butler, Benjamin F. *Butler's Book: Autobiography and Personal Reminiscences of Major-General Benjamin F. Butler*. Boston: A. M. Thayer, 1892.

Candler, Allen D., ed. *The Confederate Records of the State of Georgia*. 6 vols. Atlanta, 1909.

Chandler, Zachariah. *An Outline Sketch of his Life and Public Services*. Detroit: Detroit Post, 1880.

Clemenceau, Georges Eugene Benjamin. *American Reconstruction*. Translated by Margaret MacVeagh. Edited by Fernand Baldensperger. New York: Dial Press, 1926.

Congressional Globe. 46 vols. Washington DC, 1834-1873.

Connecticut House Journal. 1866.

Connecticut Senate Journal. 1866.

Cox, Samuel Sullivan. *Union-Disunion-Reunion: Three Decades of Federal Legislation, 1855-1885*. Providence RI: J. A. and R. A. Reid, 1886.

Debates and Proceedings of the Arkansas Constitutional Convention of 1868.

Delaware House Journal. 1867.

Delaware Senate Journal. 1867.

312
The Ratification of the Fourteenth Amendment

Documents of the Second Session of the Second Legislature of the State of Louisiana. New Orleans, 1867.

Eppes, Susan Bradford. *Through Eventful Years: Reproductions of 1860 editing of Starter Printing Co.* Gainesville FL: University Presses of Florida, 1968.

Fleming, Walter L. *Documentary History of Reconstruction.* 2 vols. Cleveland: Arthur H. Clark Co., 1906-1907.

Florida House Journal, 1866, 1868.

Florida Senate Journal, 1866, 1868.

Georgia House Journal, 1866, 1868.

Georgia Senate Journal, 1866, 1868.

Grant, U. S. *Personal Memoirs of U. S. Grant.* 2 vols. New York: C. L. Webster and Co., 1885-1886.

Hampton, Wade. *Family Letters of the Three Wade Hamptons.* Edited by Charles E. Cauthen. Columbia: University of South Carolina, 1953.

Hayes, Rutherford Birchard. *Diary and Letters of Rutherford Birchard Hayes.* Edited by Charles Richard Williams. 5 vols. Columbus OH: Ohio State Archaeological and Historical Society, 1922-1926.

House Executive Documents, Thirty-ninth and Fortieth Congresses, 1867-1869. Washington DC.

Howerton, W. H. *Legislative Manual and Political Register of the State of North Carolina.* Raleigh: State of North Carolina, 1874.

Illinois House Journal, 1867.

Illinois Reports, 1867.

Illinois Senate Journal, 1867.

Indiana House Journal, 1867.

Iowa House Journal, 1868.

Iowa Senate Journal, 1868.

"Is the South Ready for Reconstruction?" Campaign pamphlet, Library of Congress.

Journal of the Constitutional Convention of the People of Georgia, 1867-1868.

Journal of the Louisiana Constitutional Convention, 1867-1868.

The Juhl Letters to the Charleston Courier: A View of the South, 1865-1877. Edited by John Hammond Moore. Athens: University of Georgia Press, 1974.

Kansas House Journal, 1867.

Kansas Senate Journal, 1867.

Kentucky House Journal, 1867.

Kentucky Senate Journal, 1867.

Krout, John A. "Henry J. Raymond on the Republican Caucuses of July 1866." *American Historical Review* 23 (July 1928): 835-42.

Lefler, Hugh Talmage, ed. *North Carolina History Told by Contemporaries.* Chapel Hill: University of North Carolina Press, 1965.

Lincoln, Abraham. *The Collected Works of Abraham Lincoln* Edited by Roy P. Basler. 9 vols. New Brunswick NJ: Rutgers University Press, 1953-1955.

Louisiana House Journal, 1867, 1868.

Louisiana Senate Journal, 1867, 1868.

McPherson, Edward, ed. *The Political History of the United States of America during the Period of Reconstruction.* Washington DC: Philip and Solomons, 1871.

Maine House Journal, 1867.

Maine Senate Journal, 1867.

Maryland House Journal, 1867.

Maryland Senate Journal, 1867.

Massachusetts House Journal, 1867.

Massachusetts Legislative Documents of 1867.

Michigan House Journal, 1867.

Michigan Senate Journal, 1867.

Minnesota House Journal, 1867.

Minnesota Senate Journal, 1867.

Mississippi House Journal, 1866, 1870.

Mississippi Senate Journal, 1866, 1870.

Missouri House Journal, 1867.

Missouri Senate Journal, 1867.

Moore, W. G. "Notes of Colonel W. G. Moore, Private Secretary to President Johnson, 1866-1868." *American Historical Review* 19 (October 1913): 98-132.

Nebraska House Journal, 1867.

Nebraska Senate Journal, 1867.

Nebraska Territorial Council Journal, 1867.

Nevada House Journal, 1867.

Nevada Senate Journal, 1867.

New Hampshire House Journal, 1866.

New Hampshire Senate Journal, 1866.

New Jersey House Journal, 1868.

New Jersey Senate Journal, 1868.

New York House Journal, 1867.

New York Senate Journal, 1867.

North Carolina Executive and Legislative Documents.

North Carolina House Journal, 1866, 1867, 1868.

North Carolina Senate Journal, 1866, 1867, 1868.

Ohio Executive Documents, 1867.

Ohio House Journal, 1867, 1868.

314

The Ratification of the Fourteenth Amendment

Ohio Senate Journal, 1867, 1868.

Oregon House Journal, 1866, 1868.

Oregon Senate Journal, 1866, 1868.

Pennsylvania House Journal, 1867.

Pennsylvania Senate Journal, 1867.

Prentiss, Georgia L. "The Political Crisis." *American Presbyterian and Theological Review* (October 1866).

Proceedings of the National Union Convention, 1866. Philadelphia.

Reid, Whitelaw. *After the War; A Southern Tour, May 1, 1865 to May 1, 1866*. Cincinnati: Moore, Wilstark and Baldwin, 1866.

Report of the Joint Committee on Reconstruction. Reports of the House of Representatives, 39th Cong. 1st sess. 2, no. 30.

Reports of the U. S. Attorney-General. Vol. 12. Washington DC.

Richardson, James D. *A Compilation of the Messages and Papers of the Presidents, 1789-1897*. 20 vols. Washington DC: Bureau of National Literature and Art, 1896-1899.

Schurz, Carl, *Reminiscences of Carl Schurz*. 3 vols. New York: Doubleday, Page and Co., 1908-1909.

Schurz, Carl. *Intimate Letters of Carl Schurz*. Edited by Joseph Schafer. Madison WI: State Historical Society of Wisconsin, 30, 1928.

Schurz, Carl. *Speeches, Correspondence and Political Papers of Carl Schurz*. Edited by Frederick Bancroft. 6 vols. New York: G. P. Putnam, 1913.

"The Seward-Johnson Reaction." *North America Review* 103:520-49.

Sherman, John. *Recollections of Forty Years in the House, Senate and Cabinet: An Autobiography*. 2 vols. Chicago: Werner Co., 1895.

_____. "The True Problem." *Atlantic Monthly* 19 (March 1867): 371-78.

The Sherman Letters: Correspondence Between General and Senator Sherman from 1837 to 1891. Edited by Rachel Sherman Thorndike. New York: Charles Scribner's Sons, 1894.

South Carolina House Journal, 1866, 1868.

South Carolina Senate Journal, 1866, 1868.

Sumner, Charles. *Works of Charles Sumner*. 15 vols. Boston: Lee and Shephard, 1870-1883.

Sumner, Charles. *Memoir and Letters of Charles Sumner*. Edited by Edward L. Pierce. 4 vols. Boston: Roberts Brothers, 1877-1893.

Swayne, General Wager to Salmon P. Chase, 10 December 1866, printed in Vol. 2 of *Annual Report of the American Historical Association*, 1902.

Taylor, Richard. *Destruction and Reconstruction, Personal Experiences of the Late War*. New York: Appleton Co., 1879.

Tennessee House Journal, 1866.

Tennessee Senate Journal, 1866.

Texas House Journal, 1866, 1870.

Texas Senate Journal, 1866, 1870.

Thorpe, Francis Newton, ed. *The Federal and State Constitutions: Colonial Charters and other Organic Laws of the States, Territories and Colonies Now or Heretofore Forming the United States of America*. 7 vols. Washington DC: Government Printing Office, 1909.

Toombs, Robert, Alexander H. Stephens, and Howell Cobb. *Correspondence of Robert Toombs, Alexander H. Stephens, and Howell Cobb*. Edited by Ulrich B. Phillips. Vol. 2 of *Annual Report of American Historical Association, 1911*. Washington DC: Government Printing Office, 1913.

United States Reports.

United States Senate Documents. 39th Cong. 1st sess.

United States Statutes at Large.

"The Usurpation." *Atlantic Monthly* 18:506-13.

Vermont House Journal, 1866.

Vermont Senate Journal, 1866.

Virginia House Journal, 1866, 1870.

Virginia Senate Journal, 1866, 1870.

Welles, Gideon. *Diary of Gideon Welles, Secretary of the Navy under Lincoln and Johnson*. Edited by John T. Morse, Jr. 3 vols. Boston: Houghton Mifflin Co., 1911.

West Virginia Senate Journal, 1867.

Wisconsin House Journal, 1867.

Wisconsin Senate Journal, 1867.

Worth, Jonathan. *Correspondence of Jonathan Worth*. Edited by J. G. de R. Hamilton. Raleigh: North Carolina Historical Commission, 1909.

SECONDARY BOOKS AND ARTICLES

Abbot, Martin. *The Freedmen's Bureau in South Carolina*. Chapel Hill: University of North Carolina Press, 1967.

Abraham, Henry J. *Justice and Presidents: A Political History of Appointments to the Supreme Court*. New York: Oxford University Press, 1974.

Amann, William Frayne. *Personnel of the Civil War*. 2 vols. New York: Thomas Yoseloff, 1961.

Ames, Herman V. "The Proposed Amendments to the Constitution of the United States During the First Century of its History." Vol. 2 of *Annual Report of the American Historical Association*, 1891. Washington DC, 1897.

Baker, Jean H. *The Politics of Continuity: Maryland Political Parties from 1865-1870*. Baltimore: Johns Hopkins University Press, 1973.

Beale, Howard K. *The Critical Year: A Study of Andrew Johnson and Reconstruction*. New York: Harcourt, Brace, 1930.

Benedict, Michael Les. *A Compromise of Principle: Congressional Republicans and Reconstruction 1863-1869*. New York: W. W. Norton and Co., 1974.

Bentley, George R. *A History of the Freedmen's Bureau.* Philadelphia: University of Pennsylvania Press, 1955.

Berrier, G. Galen. "The Negro Suffrage Issue in Iowa 1865-1868." *Annals of Iowa* 39 (Spring 1968): 241-61.

Biographical Dictionary of the American Congress, 1774-1949. Washington DC: Government Printing Office, 1950.

Brant, Irving. *The Bill of Rights.* Indianapolis: Bobbs Merrill Co., 1965.

Bridges, Roger D. "The Constitutional World of John Sherman, 1861-1869". Ph.D. diss., University of Illinois, 1970.

Brock, W. R. *An American Crisis: Congress and Reconstruction, 1865-1867.* New York: St. Martin's Press, 1963.

Caskey, Willie Malvin. *Secession and Restoration of Louisiana.* Baton Rouge: Louisiana State University Press, 1938.

Clemenceau, Georges. *American Reconstruction 1865-1870, and the Impeachment of President Johnson.* Translated by Margaret McVeagh. Edited by Fernand Baldensperger. New York: New York Dial Press, 1928.

Coleman, Charles H. *The Election of 1868: The Democratic Effort to Regain Control.* New York: Columbia University Press, 1933.

Collins, Charles Wallace. *The Fourteenth Amendment and the States.* Boston: Little, Brown Co., 1912.

Conway, Alan. *The Reconstruction of Georgia.* Minneapolis: University of Minnesota Press, 1966.

Cooley, Thomas M. *A Treatise on the Constitutional Limitation which Rest upon the Legislative Power of the States of the American Union.* Boston: Little, Brown Co., 1868.

Coulter, E. M. *Negro Legislators in Georgia During the Reconstruction Period.* Athens: Georgia Historical Society, 1968.

——————————. *The Civil War and Readjustment in Kentucky.* Chapel Hill: University of North Carolina Press, 1926.

——————————. *The South During Reconstruction, 1865-1877.* Vol. 8 of *A History of the South.* Edited by W. H. Stephenson and E. M. Coulter. Baton Rouge: Louisiana State University Press, 1947.

Cox, Lawanda, and John H. Cox. "Negro Suffrage and Republican Politics." *Journal of Southern History* 33 (1 August 1967): 303-30.

——————————. "Andrew Johnson and His Ghost Writers." *Mississippi Valley Historical Review* 48 (December 1961): 460-79.

Cox, Merlin L. "Military Reconstruction in Florida." *Florida Historical Quarterly* 46 (January 1968): 219-88.

Craven, Avery. *Reconstruction: The Ending of the Civil War.* New York: Holt, Rinehart and Winston, 1969.

Curry, Richard O., ed. *Radicalism, Racism, and Party Realignment: The Border States During Reconstruction.* Baltimore: Johns Hopkins University Press, 1969.

Donald, David. *The Politics of Reconstruction 1863-1867.* Baton Rouge: Louisiana State University Press, 1965.

_____. "Why They Impeached Andrew Johnson." *American Heritage* 8 (December 1956): 20-26.

_____. "The Scalawag in Mississippi Reconstruction." *Journal of Southern History* 10 (November 1944): 447-60.

Dorris, Jonathan T. *Pardon and Amnesty Under Lincoln and Johnson: The Restoration of the Confederates to their Rights and Privileges*. Chapel Hill: University of North Carolina Press, 1953.

DuBoise, W. E. B. *Black Reconstruction*. Philadelphia: Albert Saifer, 1935.

DuBose, John W. *Alabama's Tragic Decade; Ten Years of Alabama, 1865-1874*. Edited by James K. Greer. Birmingham AL: Webb Book Co., 1940.

Dunning, William A. *Reconstruction, Political and Economic, 1865-1877*. New York: Harper and Brothers, 1907.

Elliott, Ward E. Y. *The Rise of Guardian Democracy: The Supreme Court's Role in Voting Rights Disputes, 1845-1969*. Cambridge: Harvard University Press, 1974.

Fairman, Charles. *Reconstruction and Reunion, 1864-1888*. Part 1 in *History of the Supreme Court of the United States*. Edited by Paul A. Freund. New York: MacMillan, 1971.

_____. *Mr. Justice Miller and the Supreme Court*. Cambridge: Harvard University Press, 1939.

Fernandez, Ferdinand F. "The Constitutionality of the Fourteenth Amendment." *Southern California Law Review* 39 (1966): 378-407.

Fischer, Roger A. *The Segregation Struggle in Louisiana, 1862-1877*. Urbana: University of Illinois Press, 1974.

Flack, Horace E. *The Adoption of the Fourteenth Amendment*. Baltimore: Johns Hopkins University Press, 1908.

Fleming, Walter L. *Civil War and Reconstruction in Alabama*. New York: Columbia University Press, 1905.

Fortier, Alcie A. *History of Louisiana*. 4 vols. New York: Goupiland Co., 1904.

Franklin, John Hope. *Reconstruction: After the Civil War*. Chicago: University of Chicago Press, 1961.

Gambill, Edward L. "Northern Democrats and Reconstruction, 1865-1868". Ph.D. diss., University of Iowa, 1969.

Garner, J. W. *Reconstruction in Mississippi*. New York: MacMillan, 1901.

Gillette, William. *The Right to Vote: Politics and the Passage of the Fifteenth Amendment*. Baltimore: Johns Hopkins University Press, 1965.

Hale, Edward Everett, Jr. *The Life and Letters of Edward Everett Hale*. Boston: Little, Brown and Co., 1917.

Harris, William C. "The Reconstruction of the Commonwealth, 1865-1870." in *A History of Mississippi*. Edited by Richard Aubrey McLemore. 2 vols. Jackson MS: University and College Press of Mississippi (1973): 1:542-70.

Heard, Thomas B. *Political Reconstruction in Tennessee*. Nashville: Vanderbilt University Press, 1950.

Henry, Robert Selph. *The Story of Reconstruction*. Indianapolis: Bobbs-Merrill Co., 1938.

Hill, Adams Sherman. "The Chicago Convention." *North American Review* 108 (July 1868): 167-86.

Holtzman, Robert S. *Stormy Ben Butler*. New York: Macmillan Co., 1954.

Horn, Stanley F. *The Invisible Empire: The Story of the Ku Klux Klan, 1866-1871*. Cos Cob CT: J. E. Edwards, 1969.

Hume, Richard L. "Membership of the Florida Constitutional Convention of 1868." *Florida Historical Quarterly*, 1972.

Hyman, Harold M., ed. *The Radical Republicans and Reconstruction, 1861-1870*. Indianapolis: Bobbs-Merrill Co., 1967.

James, Joseph B. *The Framing of the Fourteenth Amendment*. Urbana: University of Illinois Press, 1956.

Johannsen, Robert W. "The Oregon Legislature of 1868 and the Fourteenth Amendment." *Oregon Historical Quarterly* 51 (March 1950): 3-12.

Johnson, Frank. "Suffrage and Reconstruction in Mississippi." *Mississippi Historical Society Publications* 6 (1902): 141-243.

Kelly, Alfred H., and Winfred A. Harbison. *The American Constitution*. 5th ed. New York: W. W. Norton and Co., 1976.

Kibler, Lillian Adele. *Benjamin F. Perry: South Carolina Unionist*. Durham: Duke University Press, 1946.

Lander, Ernest McPherson, Jr. *A History of South Carolina, 1865-1960*. Chapel Hill: University of North Carolina Press, 1960.

Lerche, Charles O., Jr. "Congressional Interpretation of the Guarantee of a Republican Form of Government During Reconstruction." *Journal of Southern History* 15 (May 1949): 192-211.

Lowe, Richard G. "Virginia's Reconstruction Convention." *Virginia Magazine of History and Biography* (1972): 341-60.

McKitrick, Eric L. *Andrew Johnson and Reconstruction*. Chicago: University of Chicago Press, 1960.

Mantell, Martin E. *Johnson, Grant and the Politics of Reconstruction*. New York: Columbia University Press, 1973.

Merrill, Horace Samuel. *Bourbon Democracy of the Middle West, 1865-1896*. Baton Rouge: University of Louisiana Press, 1953.

Moore, Albert Burton. *History of Alabama*. University AL: University Supply Store, 1934.

Morgan, Donald G. *Congress and the Constitution*. Cambridge: Belknap Press of Harvard University, 1966.

Morrow, Ralph E. "Northern Methodism in the South During Reconstruction." *Mississippi Valley Historical Review* 41 (September 1954): 197-218.

Nathans, Elizabeth Studley. *Losing the Peace: Georgia Republicans and Reconstruction, 1865-1871*. Baton Rouge: Louisiana State University Press, 1968.

Oberholtzer, Ellis P. *A History of the United States Since the Civil War*. 5 vols. New York: Macmillan and Co., 1917-1937.

Paludin, Phillip S. *A Covenant With Death: The Constitution, Law and Equality in the Civil War Era*. Urbana: University of Illinois Press, 1975.

Parish, William E. *Missouri Under Radical Rule, 1865-1870*. Columbia MO: University of Missouri Press, 1965.

Patrick, Rembert W. *The Reconstruction of the Nation*. New York: Oxford University Press, 1967.

Perman, Michael. *Reunion Without Compromise: The South and Reconstruction: 1865-1868*. London: Cambridge University Press, 1973.

Ramsdell, C. W. *Reconstruction in Texas*. New York: Columbia University Studies in History, Economics, and Public Law, vol. 36., no. 1, 1910.

Randall, J. G., and David Donald. *The Civil War and Reconstruction*. Lexington MA: D. C. Heath and Co., 1969.

Reynolds, John S. *Reconstruction in South Carolina*. Columbia SC: State Company, 1905.

Richardson, Joe M. *The Negro in Reconstruction of Florida, 1865-1877*. Tallahassee: Florida State University Studies, vol. 46, 1965.

Robinson, William M., Jr. *Justice in Grey*. Cambridge: Harvard University Press, 1941.

Roseboom, E. H., and F. P. Weisenburger. *A History of Ohio*. New York: Prentiss Hall Co., 1934.

Russell, James F. S. "The Railroads in the Conspiracy Theory of the Fourteenth Amendment." *Mississipi Valley Historical Review* 41 (March 1955): 601-22.

Saye, Albert B. *A Constitutional History of Georgia, 1732-1945*. Athens: University of Georgia Press, 1948.

Shofner, Jerrell H. *Nor Is It Over Yet: Florida in the Era of Reconstruction, 1863-1877*. Gainesville: University Presses of Florida, 1974.

—————————. "Political Reconstruction in Florida." *Florida Historical Quarterly* (1966): 145-94.

Simkins, Francis Butler, and Robert Hilliard Woody. *South Carolina During Reconstruction*. Chapel Hill: University of North Carolina Press, 1932.

Smith, William C. *The Francis Preston Blair Family in Politics*. 2 vols. New York: Macmillan Co., 1933.

Sproat, John C. "Blueprint for Radical Reconstruction." *Journal of Southern History* 23 (February 1957): 25-44.

Stampp, Kenneth M. *The Era of Reconstruction*. New York: Alfred A. Kropf, 1965.

Staples, Thomas S. *Reconstruction in Arkansas, 1862-1874*. New York: Columbia University Studies in History, Economics, and Public Law, vol. 109, 1923.

Stebbins, Homer Adolph. *A Political History of the State of New York, 1865-1869*. New York: Columbia University Studies in History, Economics, and Public Law, vol. 55, 1913.

Taylor, Joe Gray. *Louisiana Reconstructed, 1863-1877*. Baton Rouge: Louisiana State University Press, 1974.

Thompson, C. Mildred. *Reconstruction in Georgia*. New York: Columbia University Press, 1915.

Toombs, Robert. "Correspondence of Robert Toombs." Edited by Ulrich Bonnel Phillips. Vol 2 of *Annual Report of the American Historical Association*. (1911) Washington DC: Government Printing Office, 1913.

Toppin, Edgar A. "The Negro Suffrage Issue in Postbellum Ohio Politics." *Journal of Human Relations* 11 (Winter 1963): 232-44.

Voegeli, Jacque. "The Northwest and the 'Race Issue.'" *Mississippi Valley Historical Review* (September 1963): 235-51.

Ware, Ethel K. *A Constitutional History of Georgia*. New York: Columbia University Press, 1947.

White, Howard R. *The Freedmen's Bureau in Louisiana*. Baton Rouge: Louisiana State University Press, 1970.

Woodward, C. Vann. "Seeds of Failure in Radical Race Policy." *New Frontiers of the American Reconstruction*. Edited by Harold M. Hyman. Urbana: University of Illinois Press, 1966.

Wooley, Edwin C. *The Reconstruction of Georgia*. New York: Columbia University Studies in History, Economics and Public Law, vol. 13, no. 3, 1901.

BIOGRAPHIES

Abbot, Richard H. *Cobbler in Congress: Life of Henry Wilson, 1812-1875*. Lexington: University of Kentucky Press, 1972.

Adams, Charles Francis. *Richard Henry Dana*. 2 vols. Boston: Houghton Mifflin Co., 1890.

Ames, Blanche Ames. *Adelbert Ames: 1835-1933, General, Senator, Governor*. New York: Argosy Antiquarian Ltd., 1964.

Barnard, Henry. *Rutherford B. Hayes and His America*. Indianapolis: Bobbs-Merrill Co., 1954.

Brigance, William Norwood. *Jeremiah Sullivan Black: A Defender of the Constitution and the Ten Commandments*. Philadelphia: University of Pennsylvania Press, 1934.

Brodie, Fawn M. *Thaddeus Stevens: Scourge of the South*. New York: W. W. Norton and Co., 1959.

Cain, Marvin R. *Lincoln's Attorney General, Edward Bates of Missouri*. Columbia MO: University of Missouri Press, 1965.

Caldwell, Robert Granville. *James A. Garfield: Party Chieftan*. New York: Dodd, Mead & Co., 1931.

Carpenter, John A. *Sword and Olive Branch: Oliver Otis Howard*. Pittsburg CA: University of Pittsburg Press, 1964.

Clapp, Margaret. *Forgotten First Citizen: John Bigelow*. Boston: Little, Brown and Co., 1947.

Conkling, Alfred R. *Life and Letters of Roscoe Conkling: Orator, Statesman and Advocate.* New York: C. L. Webster, 1889.

Coulter, E. M. *William G. Brownlow: Fighting Parson of the Southern Highlands.* Chapel Hill: University of North Carolina Press, 1937.

Donald, David. *Charles Sumner and the Rights of Man.* New York: Alfred A. Knopf, 1970.

Durden, Robert Franklin. *James Shepherd Pike: Republicanism and the American Negro, 1850-1882.* Durham NC: Duke University Press, 1957.

Eckenrode, H. J. *Rutherford B. Hayes: Statesman of Reunion.* New York: Dodd, Mead & Co., 1930.

Egle, William H., ed. *Andrew Gregg Curtin: His Life and Services.* Philadelphia: Avil Printing Co., 1895.

Fairman, Charles. *Mr. Justice Miller.* Cambridge MA: Harvard University Press, 1939.

Fessenden, Francis. *Life and Public Service of William Pitt Fessenden.* 2 vols. Boston: Houghton Mifflin Co., 1907.

Flick, Alexander C., and Guster S. Lobrano. *Samuel J. Tilden: A Study in Political Sagacity.* New York: Dodd, Mead & Co., 1939.

Flippen, Percy Scott. *Herschel V. Johnson of Georgia: State Rights Unionist.* Richmond VA: Deite Printing Co., 1931.

Freeman, Douglas Southall. *R. E. Lee.* 4 vols. New York: Charles Scribner's Sons, 1935.

Gorham, George C. *Life and Public Services of Edwin M. Stanton.* 2 vols. Boston: Houghton Mifflin Co., 1899.

Harrington, Fred Harvey. *Fighting Politician, Major General N. P. Banks.* Philadelphia: University of Pennsylvania Press, 1948.

Harris, Wilmer C. *Public Life of Zachariah Chandler, 1851-1875.* Chicago: University of Chicago Press, 1917.

Hay, Thomas Robson. *James Longstreet: Politician, Officeholder, and Writer.* Baton Rouge: Louisiana State University Press, 1952.

Heseltine, William B. *U. S. Grant, Politician.* New York: Dodd, Mead & Co., 1935.

Hill, Louise Biles. *Joseph E. Brown and the Confederacy.* Chapel Hill: University of North Carolina Press, 1939.

Holtzman, Robert S. *Stormy Ben Butler.* New York: Macmillan Co., 1954.

Hunt, Gaillard. *Israel, Elihu and Cadwallader Washburne: A Chapter in American Biography.* New York: Macmillan Co., 1925.

Jarrell, Hampton M. *Wade Hampton and the Negro: The Road Not Taken.* Columbia SC: University of South Carolina Press, 1949.

Kibler, Lillian Adele. *Benjamin F. Perry: South Carolina Unionist.* Durham NC: Duke University Press, 1946.

Klein, Philip Shriver. *President James Buchanan.* University Park PA: Pennsylvania State University Press, 1962.

Krug, Mark M. *Lyman Trumbull, Conservative Radical*. New York: A. S. Barnes and Co., 1965.

Lamson, Peggy. *The Glorious Failure: Black Congressman Robert Brown Elliott and the Reconstruction of South Carolina*. New York: W. W. Norton and Co., 1973.

McDonough, James L. *Schofield: Union General in the Civil War and Reconstruction*. Tallahassee: Florida State University Press, 1972.

McFeely, William S. *Yankee Stepfather: General O. O. Howard and the Freedmen*. New Haven: Yale University Press, 1968.

McKay, Ernest. *Henry Wilson: Practical Radical. A Portrait of a Politician*. Port Washington NY: Kennikat Press, 1971.

Muzzy, David Saville. *James G. Blaine, A Political Idol of Other Days*. New York: Dodd, Mead & Co., 1935.

Nevins, Allen. *Hamilton Fish: The Inner History of the Grant Administration*. New York: Dodd, Mead & Co., 1936.

Parks, Joseph H. *Joseph E. Brown of Georgia*. Baton Rouge: Louisiana State University Press, 1977.

Pearson, Henry Greenleaf. *The Life of John A. Andrew, Governor of Massachusetts, 1861-1865*. 2 vols. Boston: Houghton Mifflin and Co., 1904.

Pereyra, Lillian A. *James Lusk Alcorn: Persistent Whig*. Baton Rouge: Louisiana State University Press, 1966.

Peterson, Norma L. *Freedom and Franchise: The Political Career of B. Gratz Brown*. Columbia MO: University of Missouri Press, 1965.

Poore, Benjamin P. *The Life of Ambrose E. Burnside*. Providence RI: J. A. and R. A. Reid, 1882.

Richardson, Leon Burr. *William E. Chandler, Republican*. New York: Dodd, Mead & Co., 1940.

Roberts, Derrell C. *Joseph E. Brown and the Politics of Reconstruction*. University AL: University of Alabama Press, 1973.

Salter, William. *The Life of James W. Grimes: Governor of Iowa, 1854-1858, Senator of the United States, 1859-1869*. New York: D. Appleton Co., 1876.

Smith, Theodore Clarke. *The Life and Letters of James Abram Garfield*. 2 vols. New Haven: Yale University Press, 1925.

Smith, W. E., and D. D. Smith. *A Buckeye Titan*. Cincinnati: Historical and Philosophical Society of Ohio, 1953.

Smith, Willard H. *Schuyler Colfax: The Changing Fortunes of a Political Idol*. Vol. 23 of Indiana Historical Collections. Indianapolis: Indiana Historical Bureau, 1952.

Smith, William Ernest. *The Francis Preston Blair Family in Politics*. 2 vols. New York: Macmillan Co., 1969.

Swisher, Carl Brent. *Roger B. Taney*. New York: Macmillan Co., 1935.

Tankersley, Allen P. *John B. Gordon: A Study in Gallantry*. Atlanta: Whitehall Press, 1955.

Thomas, Benjamin P., and Harold M. Hyman. *Stanton: Life and Times of Lincoln's Secretary of War*. New York: Alfred A. Knopf, 1962.

Thompson, E. Bruce. *Mathew Hale Carpenter: Webster of the West*. Madison WI: State Historical Society of Wisconsin, 1954.

Thompson, William Y. *Robert Toombs of Georgia*. Baton Rouge: Louisiana State University Press, 1966.

Tinkcom, Harry Martin. *John White Geary, Soldier Statesman*. Philadelphia: University of Pennsylvania Press, 1940.

Van Deusen, Glyndon G. *Horace Greeley: Nineteenth Century Crusader*. Philadelphia: University of Pennsylvania Press, 1953.

——————————. *Thurlow Weed: Wizard of the Lobby*. Boston: Little, Brown Co., 1947.

——————————. *William Henry Seward*. New York: Oxford University Press, 1967.

Wellman, Manly Wade. *Giant in Gray: A Biography of Wade Hampton of South Carolina*. New York: Charles Scribner's Sons, 1949.

West, Richard S., Jr. *Lincoln's Scapegoat General: A Life of Benjamin F. Butler, 1818-1893*. Boston: Houghton Mifflin, 1965.

White, Horace. *The Life of Lyman Trumbull*. Boston: Houghton Mifflin, 1913.

Wilson, James Harrison. *The Life of John A. Rawlins: Lawyer, Assistant Adjutant—General, Chief of Staff, Major General of Volunteers, and Secretary of War*. New York: Neal Publishing Co., 1916.

Winston, Robert. *Andrew Johnson: Politician and Patriot*. New York: Henry Holt, 1928.

Index

Adams, John Quincy, 120
Alabama, 125-28, 133-34, 143, 144-45, 146, 239, 242, 256-60, 272; rejection of amendment, 130-31; ratification of amendment, 259
Alcorn, James L., 148, 152, 154, 212, 254
alliance, political, 42, 68, 85, 139, 143-44, 146, 193, 199, 266
Allee, R. P., 70
Ames, Adelbert, 150
Ames, Herman T., 301
amnesty, 28, 55, 118, 128-29, 182, 205, 227. 249-50
Andrew, Gov. John A., 52, 182, 221
Arizona, 31, 53, 243
Arkansas, 106, 113, 153, 233, 235-36; rejection of amendment, 97-99; ratification of amendment, 238; readmitted, 238-39
Ashley, Rep. James M., 129, 229

Baber, Richard P. L., 134-37
Bailey, Joseph, 71
Bank, James M., 223
Bates, Edward D., 84, 165
Beale, Howard K., 35

Beauregard, Gen. P. G. T., 253, 263
Beecher, Henry Ward, 86, 159
Benneson, Maj. H. H., 74
Bingham, Rep. John, 5, 25, 32, 45-47, 243, 278, 279, 281
Bird, F. W., 185-86
Black, Jeremiah S., 55, 210, 267
Blaine, James G., 109-10, 123, 208
Blair, Francis P., Jr., 290
Blair, Montgomery, 83, 85, 174
"bloody shirt" campaign, 63, 190, 193
bondholders, 18, 45, 50, 69, 192, 196, 222, 224, 232, 280-81
bonds, Confederate, 69, 87
Borman, Arthur T., 177
Boutwell, George S., 8, 25-26, 39-40, 183
Boyden, Nathaniel, 138, 144
Bradley, Aaron A., 267
Bramlette, Gov. Thomas E., 168
Brooks, Rep. James, 210
Broomall, Rep. John M., 7, 35
Brown, Gov. Joseph E., 80-81, 152, 212, 219, 254, 256, 261-62, 265-68, 272, 275
Browning, Orville H., 31, 75, 77, 137

Brownlow, Gov. William G., 19, 22-23, 89, 182, 267, 273
Bryan, Guy M., 58
Buchanan, Pres. James, 212, 226
Buckalew, Sen. Charles F., 280
Buckingham, Gov. William A., 12
Bulloch, Gov. Alex H., 184
Bulloch, Gov. Rufus B., 272-73, 299
Burnside, Gov. Ambrose E., 195
Butler, Rep. Benjamin F., 54-55, 170, 182, 218, 222
Butler, Gov. David, 218

California, 112, 227, 277
Campbell, Justice John A., 254
Canby, Gen. Edward R. S., 244, 248, 251, 253
caucus, Republican, 2, 184
Chamberlain, Gov. Joshua L., 196
Chandler, Sen. Zachariah, 120, 194, 222
Chase, Chief Justice Salmon P., 14, 40, 119, 127, 205, 211, 215, 256, 289-90
civil rights, as election issues, 12, 164, 220, 226; according to framers of amendment, 8, 43, 223, 292; in states, 99, 104-105, 117, 126, 131-32, 162, 166, 168, 174, 176, 234, 255; press discussion of, 101, 109
Clemenceau, George E. B., 292, 296
Coleman v. Miller (1939), 302
Colfax, Schuyler, 26, 190, 210, 218, 228, 281, 286
Colorado, 14, 201, 203
Committee of Fifteen, Report of, 2, 4. See Joint Committee on Reconstruction
compromise, 3, 8, 30, 39-40, 49, 64, 86, 108, 119, 128-29, 131, 133-46, 159-60
confiscation of Southern land, 102, 213, 219, 225, 262
Connecticut, ratification of amendment, 11-13, 65; representation of, 38, 264
contracts, corporate charters as, 172
conventions, state constitutional, 235, 240, 244, 250-51, 254, 257, 268; legislative acts of, 235, 255, 270; loyalists, Southern, 30; soldiers and sailors, 54. See National Union Convention

corporations, not included under amendment, 172
counterproposal for amendment, 132-37, 157, 202-203, 261, 275; published, 143-44; in Alabama legislature, 144, 256; in Congress, 144; in North Carolina legislature, 144-46
coup d'etat, feared, 15-16; rumors of, 174, 229
courts, 75, 105-106, 121, 126, 151, 166, 172, 186, 215, 220, 248, 275; military influence in, 54-55, 234-40, 248, 264. See Supreme Court
Cowan, Sen. Edgar A., 31, 74
Cox, Gov. Jacob D., 161-62
Coyle v. Smith (1911), 243
Crawford, Gov. S. J., 173, 179
Curtin, Gov. Andrew G., 164, 225
Dana, Richard Henry, 182
Davis, Justice David, 121, 205
Davis, Sen. Garrett, 16, 222
Davis, Jefferson, 63, 163
debt, national, 18, 45, 47, 69, 179, 189, 192, 224-25, 232, 280-81, 288, 291-92; Confederate, 80-81, 192
Delano, Rep. Columbus, 34
Delaware, 14, 83, 90, 103-104, 120, 149, 175, 178, 223, 277; rejection of amendment, 157-58
Dennison, Postmaster-general William, 30, 32, 82
disqualification of ex-Confederates, reaction to, in North, 12, 18, 47, 136-37, 162, 176, 209, 213, 228-29; in South, 61, 65, 81, 99, 100-101, 105-106, 111, 125, 129, 149, 151, 213, 236, 264, 272, 299
District of Columbia, 228
Dix, John A., 52
Dixon, Sen. James, 31, 53, 144
Doolittle, Sen. James R., 30-31, 52-53, 86, 122, 134, 137, 187
Douglass, Frederick, 53, 87
Drake, Sen. Charles D., 242
economic recovery, 50, 97-98, 102, 108, 127, 220, 226, 234, 237, 264-67, 273, 275
Edmunds, Sen. George F., 73, 293-94

Egan, in re, (1866), 55
elections, of 1866, 4-5, 43-50, 61-65, 74-76; of 1867, 219-28, 231-32, 282; of 1868, 243, 289-92, 300
Emancipation Proclamation, 253
emigration, to Brazil, 239-40; to Honduras, 248
equality of states, 243, 292
Este, Gen. George, 137
Ewing, Thomas, 31, 109, 205, 224

Fairchild, Gov. Lucius, 188
Fenton, Gov. Reuben E., 160
Fessenden, Sen. William P., 4, 67-68, 123, 197, 219, 227, 242
Fifteenth Amendment, 8, 100, 274
Fish, Hamilton, 159-60
Fletcher, Gov. Thomas C., 165-66
Florida, 117, 137-38, 241, 245, 295; rejection of amendment, 109-12; ratification of amendment, 239-41
Forney, John W., 89, 206
Fourteenth Amendment, resolution certifying adoption, 278; status of, 206-208, 215, 230, 242-43, 281, 287; text of, 305-306; variations, 242-43
Fowler, Samuel, 31
Freedmen's Bureau, 81-82, 168, 244, 249, 254
Frelinghuysen, Frederick T., 243
Fullerton, Gen. J. H., 81

Garfield, James A., 55, 227
Geary, Gov. John W., 164
Georgia, 116, 131, 257, 262-70, 272-73, 275; rejection of amendment, 79-95, 104-105, 112; ratification of amendment, 273-74, 277, 288, 290; readmitted to Union, 261; ratification of amendment, second time, 288, 297-98; readmitted to Union, second time, 300
Georgia v. Stanton (1867), 270-71, 275
Gillem, Gen. A. C., 237
Gordon, Gen. John B., 80, 85, 264
Graham, W. A., 108
Grant, Gen. Ulysses S., 40, 84, 214, 217, 225, 234, 267, 272-73, 291
Greeley, Horace, 205, 219
greenbacks, 220, 224-25, 280
Grimes, Sen. James G., 209, 232

habeas corpus, 204, 271
Haight, Rep. Charles, 286
Hamilton, Jack, 87
Hampton, Gen. Wade, 115, 212, 248, 250
Hanes, Lewis, 100, 103, 138
Harlan, Secretary of Interior James, 84
Harris, Rep. Benjamin G., 40
Hawley, Gov. Joseph H., 11-13
Hayes, Rep. and Gov. Rutherford B., 63, 226, 282-83
Hendricks, Sen. Thomas A., 31, 44, 190
Hill, Andrew Sherman, 291
Hill, Benjamin H., 263
Hill, Joshua, 273
Hilyer, Giles, 149
Hoffman, John T., 70, 159
Holden, Gov. William W., 100, 103, 244-45
Hood, Gen. John B., 253
Howard, Sen. Jacob M., 193, 202, 207, 242, 293
Howe, Sen. Timothy, 187
Humphreys, David C., 127
Humphreys, Gov. Benjamin G., 103, 144, 148, 150

Illinois, 14, 48, 169, 291; ratification of amendment, 170-71; sectional attitudes, 179
Impeachment of President, 68, 217, 219, 223, 229, 239, 242, 248
Indiana, 42, 68, 90, 134, 190, 203; representation of, 48; ratification of amendment, 14, 191-93
injunction, writ of, 263-64, 267
integration of public facilities, 254
Iowa, 209, 277; ratification of amendment, 231-32

Jenkins, Gov. Charles J., 90-91, 116, 263, 265, 270-71, 275.
Johnson, Pres. Andrew, 5-6, 14, 24, 26-27, 29, 36, 41, 67-68, 74, 76-77, 79, 81, 83-84, 86, 88, 100-102, 104, 118-19, 131, 214, 219, 287, 290, 292; counterproposal by, 135-45, proclamations, amnesty, 149-50, 261; reports on ratifications, 293-94, 297
Johnson, Herschel V., 52, 84, 87, 89, 212, 266, 269

Johnson, Sen. Reverdy, 4, 10, 174, 206
Joint Committee on Reconstruction, 2, 4, 7, 81-82, 218
Jones, Isaac D., 175
Jones, John, 270
Julian, George W., 121

Kansas, 14, 173; ratified by, 173, 179
Kelley, Rep. William B., 266
Kentucky, 14, 83, 103, 167, 175, 179, 198, 222, 277; rejection of amendment, 168-69
Kerr, Rep. Michael C., 281
Knapp, Rep. Charles, 31
Ku Klux Klan, 244, 264, 275

Lee, Gen. Robert E., 119
Longstreet, Gen. James, 153, 155, 219, 253, 263
Loring, George B., 184
Louisiana, 147, 152-53, 253, 256, 295; rejection of amendment, 154, ratification of amendment, 255-56
Low, Gov. F. F., 112
Lumpkin, Judge, Joseph Henry, 262

McCardle, ex parte, 122, 131, 204, 234, 267, 271, 279
McCulloch, Hugh, 30, 67, 137, 177
McPherson, Edward, 210
Maine, 14, 123, 196-97, 230, 278; ratification of amendment, 198
Medill, Joseph, 26, 33-34
Memphis, riots, 40
Michigan, 14, 21, 193-94, 222; ratification of amendment, 194
Miller, Justice Samuel F., 205, 257
Milligan, ex parte, 54-55, 121-22, 131-32, 203-205, 215, 271
Minnesota, 14, 194-95, 222; ratification of amendment, 195
minority report, of Reconstruction Committee, 2-5, 9-10; of New Hampshire, 17-18; of Massachusetts, 186
Mississippi, 52, 147-51, 154, 233, 267, 274; rejection of amendment, 151-52, 298; ratification of amendment, 274, 298
Missouri, 14, 165-66, 290; ratification of amendment, 167, 179, 278
Montana, 53

Moore, Col. W. G., 140, 144
Morrill, Sen. Justin, 45, 73
Morton, Gov. Oliver P., 42, 72, 190-91, 228, 292
Murphy, Gov. Isaac, 97-98, 153, 238

National Union Convention, 29-33, 36-37, 51-53, 65, 83, 85-86, 115, 125, 149, 165
National Union Party, 9, 36, 184
Nebraska, 199, 201-203, 295; ratification of amendment, 218-19
Nelson, Justice Samuel, 55
Nesmith, Rep. James W., 31
Nevada, 14, 187, 201; ratification of amendment, 187
New England, 192, 259
New Hampshire, 14, 63, 220, 281; ratification of amendment, 16-18
New Jersey, 14, 28, 48, 53, 221; ratification of amendment, 55-56; rescinding of amendment, 284-86
New Orleans, riots, 51, 85
New York, 14, 158-60, 178, 223-25; ratification of amendment, 160-61
North Carolina, 10, 100-105, 112-13, 138, 243-45, 295; counterproposal in, 139, 194-96; rejection of amendment, 105-107; ratification of amendment, 245
North Carolina Proclamation, 100
Norton, David S., 31

Oberholzer, Ellis P., on Tennessee ratification, 23
Oglesby, Gov. Richard, 170-71
Ohio, 14, 48, 179, 256, 259, 282, 295-97; ratification of amendment, 161-63
"Ohio Idea", 225
Ord, Gen. Edward O. C., 233, 235
Oregon, 14, 65, 198; ratification of amendment, 56-58; rescinding of amendment, 300
Orr, Gov. James L., 52, 116-17, 137, 144, 251-52

pardons, 28, 42, 80, 94, 111, 118-19, 128, 249, 262, 279
Parsons, Gov. Lewis E., 125, 130, 134, 138, 143
parties, realignment of, 42, 50, 68, 84-

85, 199, 201-202, 219, 264-65
patronage, 26, 100, 223, 225, 230
Patton, Gov. R. M., 126-27, 144, 213, 256-57, 279
Pendleton, George H., 69, 290
Pennsylvania, 14, 48, 163-64, 225-26; ratification of amendment, 164-65
perpetual suffrage guarantee, 8, 192, 202, 239, 242-43, 259, 292.
Perry, Gov. B. F., 165, 116-17, 266
Phillips, Wendell, 122, 184
Pierpoint, Gov. Francis H., 123, 213
Pike, Rep. Frederick A., 197
Pike, James Shepherd, 198
platform, Republican, in 1868, 290
Poland, Sen. Luke, 73
Pope, Gen. John, 237, 241, 263, 270
population, minimum necessary for statehood, 202
President. *See* Johnson, Pres. Andrew
proclamation, of adoption, 283-84; second proclamation, 297; of emancipation, 253, on North Carolina, 100
purposes, Southern, 80, 303-304; Northern, 303

quorum, problem in Tennessee legislature, 21-22, 26

Randall, Postmaster-general A. W., 31, 137
ratification, tabulation of states in prediction, 14
Ray, C. H., 291
Raymond, Rep. Henry J., 6, 30, 52
Readmission of states to Union, pledge of on ratifying, 33, 74, 185; lack of pledge, 3, 34, 40, 71, 92, 104, 109-10, 113-23, 128, 181; implied, 3, 33-34, 40, 49, 150
reconstruction acts (1867), passage of, 197, 206-209, 277; effect of, 210-12, 215-16; Southern reaction to, 212-13, 249, 267-68; court appeals concerning, 212, 215, 243, 264-65, 270-72, 275
Reconstruction Committee. *See* Joint Committee on Reconstruction
Reed, Gov. Harrison, 241
regionalism in North, 134-35, 179

Reid, Whitelaw, 41
reparations, 225
representation, 7-8, 18, 48-49, 68, 89, 120, 135-36, 138, 162-63, 187, 189, 191, 274, 278, 292
requirements for ratification, 7, 277, 287
rescinding ratifications, in New Jersey, 271, 284-86; in Ohio, 226, 282-83; in Oregon, 300; problem of, 287-288, 301-302
resolution, to amend Fourteenth Amendment, 145; to instruct congressmen, 145; to proclaim adoption of amendment, 294, 297
restoration of states, changes needed in state constitutions for, 180, 202, 239, 242-43, 259-60; minimum conditions, 2-3
Rhode Island, 14; ratification of amendment, 185-96
Robinson, John W., 214
Rockwell, Capt. Charles F., 270
Ruger, Gen. Thomas H., 270

Saulsbury, Gov. Gove, 157
Saulsbury, Sen. Willard, 64-65
Schenck, Rep. Robert C., 7, 44
Schofield, Rep. George W., 278
Schofield, Gen. John M., 125
schools, public, 230, 234, 236
Schurz, Carl, 61-63, 76
Segar, Joseph, 125
Seward, Secretary of State William H., 30, 83, 242, 278, 294; proclamation by, on adoption of amendment, 295; second proclamation by, on adoption, 297
Seymour, Gov. Horatio, 290
Seymour, Gov. O. S., 12
Sharkey, Gov. William L., 52, 74, 103, 126, 144-45, 149
Shellabarger, Rep. Samuel, 209
Sherman, Sen. John, 15, 64, 68, 126, 208, 227, 246, 280, 283, 295
Sherman, Gen. William T., 15, 226
Sickles, Gen. Daniel E., 137, 243
Slaughter House Cases (1873), 205
Soldiers and Sailors Convention, 53, 65, 86, 149

South Carolina, 53, 115-19, 123, 212, 247-51; rejection of amendment, 118-19; ratification of amendment, 247-52, 295; readmitted to Union, 252-53

Southern Loyalists Convention, 30, 53, 87. Also called Southern Unionist Convention

Speed, Attorney-Gen. James, 89, 127, 137

Sprague, Col. John, 240-41

Stanbery, Attorney-Gen. Henry, 211, 233, 267

Stanton, Secretary of War Edwin M., 32, 71, 84, 127, 217, 267

statehood, eligibility for, 202; Nebraska admitted to, 203

Steedman, Gen. James, 81, 137

Stephens, Alexander H., 9, 52, 81, 83, 85, 268, 293

Stephens, Judge Linton, 83-84

Stevens, Rep. Thaddeus, compromise approved by, 2, 9; states counted for ratification by, 7; on readmitting Tennessee, 25; influence of, 77, 82, 178; on status of amendment, 281; campaign speeches of, 62-63, 164, 292

Stewart, Sen. William M., 128, 182

Stone, Gov. William M., 232

suffrage, opinion on, in North, 12, 15, 18, 42-43, 48, 65, 68, 77, 135, 145, 160, 176, 178-85, 190-92, 194, 199, 208, 219, 221, 224, 228-29, 231-32, 257, 280, 282, 290-91; in South, 9, 81, 85, 92, 94, 102-104, 107, 115, 154, 174, 197, 210, 212, 215, 230, 234-35, 237, 250, 254, 264, 275; women's, 229

Sullivan, Major H. V., 74

Sumner, Sen. Charles, counting of states in ratification, 6, 129, 191, 278, 284; influence of, 64, 77, 188, 199; demands of guarantees, 70-71, 183-84; opposition to statehood for Nebraska, 202

Supreme Court, 1, 220, 248, 267, 275, 279; on equality of states, 243; on limits of military power, 54, 121-22, 131, 204, 269, 271; on regulation of corporations, 172; on rescinding ratifications, 288, 302

Swain, David L., 105

Swann, Gov. Thomas, 174

Swayne, Gen. Wager, 126-27, 130

Tammany Hall, 159

Taney, Chief Justice Roger B., 172

Taylor, Gen. Richard, 52

Tennessee, ratification of amendment, 19-23, 63, 82, 295; readmitted to Union, 25-27; implication of readmission, 108, 150-51, 166, 242, 277

Tenure of Office Act, 217

test oaths, 127, 166, 224, 274

Texas, 103, 134, 214, 216, 274-75; rejection of amendment, 58-61, 65-66, 79, 112; ratification of amendment, 298

Texas v. White (1869), 270-271

Thirteenth Amendment, 80, 111-12, 125-26, 151; ratification of, 7; effect of, 68, 76

Three-fifths Compromise, 12, 68

Throckmorton, Gov. J. W., 44

Toombs, Robert, 273

tribunals, military, 54, 121-22, 131, 203, 215, 240, 271

Trumbull, Sen. Lyman, 4, 26, 43-44, 170, 242, 248

Turner, Henry M., 267

Union League, 264

Utah, 53

Vallandigham, Clement L., 52

Vermont, 220; ratification of amendment, 72-74

Virginia, 119, 216; ratification of amendment recommended, 123; rejection of amendment, 124, 178; restoration postponed, 274, 298

Wade, Sen. Benjamin F., 123, 202, 218, 226

Wade-Davis Bill, 253

Walker, Gov. David S., 109

Ward, Rep. Hamilton, 279

Ward, Gov. Marcus, 55, 285

Washburne, Rep. Elihu, 21, 34, 54, 80, 112, 205, 286

Washington, D. C. *See* District of Columbia

Weatherly, Col. T. C., 118

Weed, Thurlow, 159

Welles, Secretary of the Navy Gideon, 30, 137-39
Wells, Gov. Madison, 153, 155
West Virginia, 14, 123, 131, 198, 278, 295; ratification of amendment, 177
Whigs, 266
White, Horace, 26, 291
Wilson, Sen. Henry, 64-65, 182-83, 219, 254, 266

Wilson, Rep. James F., 209
Wisconsin, 14, 187, 199, 222; ratification of amendment, 188
Wood, Fernando, 52
Woodbridge, Rep. Frederick E., 73
Woods, Gov. George L., 57
Worth, Gov. Jonathan, 10, 100, 102, 245

MUP THE RATIFICATION OF THE FOURTEENTH AMENDMENT

Designed by Margaret Jordan Brown

Composition by MUP Composition Department

Production Specifications:
    text paper—60-pound Warren's Olde Style
    endpapers—Multicolor Textured Black
    cover—(on .088 boards) Holliston Roxite B 51575
        Vellum finish
    dust jacket—100-pound enamel, printed four colors
        (PMS 165 orange, PMS 116 yellow, PMS 312 blue, and black),
        and varnished

Printing (offset lithography) by Omnipress of Macon, Inc.,
    Macon, Georgia

Binding by John H. Dekker and Sons, Inc.,
    Grand Rapids, Michigan